Views To Take Y

DESIGN:
www.mortonward.co.uk

PHOTOGRAPHY:
Scottish Viewpoint, Paul Tomkins, Chris Close
Britainonview: Pawel Libera, Natalie Pecht, Rod Edwards, Dennis Hardley
Edinburgh Inspiring Capital:
www.edinburgh-inspiringcapital.com

SCOTLAND: PURE INDULGENCE, NATURAL RELAXATION

Castle Stalker, Loch Laich, Argyll & Bute

Views to take your breath away

CONTRASTING SPACES

You'd expect to find wonderful scenery in Scotland, though you might be surprised at the sheer variety in so compact a country. City skylines give way to rolling hills and rugged coastlines in less than an hour. There are castles on lochs set against impressive mountain ridges. It's also just a short hop from the Scottish mainland to the islands, home to vibrant communities and natural wildlife habitats. Discover it all from the comfort of a traditional country house, a boutique city hotel or an historic castle.

RELAXING PACES

Everyone finds different ways to relax. The diversity of Scotland's countryside is easily matched by the assortment of ways to enjoy it. Play a round on championship links in the Home of Golf. Try fishing on a river trout beat. Take to the hills or woodland trails for a bracing hike. Get sand between your toes as you stroll along golden coastal beaches. Walk in regal steps at castles and palaces or trace your own Scottish roots. Or to really unwind, escape to the pampering environment of a spa resort.

WELCOMING PLACES

There's always something going on in Scotland. Whenever you come, there's sure to be a festival or cultural event. Join in at Hogmanay to give your year a rousing start. If you're here in summer, look out for Highland Games across the country. Take some Scottish specialities home with you from year-round farmers' markets and food festivals. You'll also discover the freshest and finest local flavours on the menus of restaurants, bistros and cafés throughout Scotland. And it's so easy to get here, you can make Scotland your regular indulgent treat.

Discover your very own Scotland

THE GREAT OUTDOORS
Actively enjoy Scotland's scenery. Hike in the hills, mountain bike along woodland trails, sail Scotland's coast or soar over the countryside in a hot air balloon. Or try them all!

WILDLIFE
From dolphins in the Moray Firth to red deer in the Highlands and seals and puffins on the coastline, you never know what you might spot.

BEACHES
Breathe in the fresh sea air on a romantic stroll along the golden sands of Scotland's beaches. Discover Fife's Blue Flag beaches or the breathtaking stretches of sand in the Outer Hebrides.

GOLF
The country that gave the world the game of golf is still the best place to play it. With more than 500 courses in Scotland, take advantage of the many regional golf passes on offer.

CASTLES
Wherever you are in Scotland you are never far from a great Scottish icon, whether it's an impressive ruin or an imposing fortress, a fairytale castle or country estate.

HIGHLAND GAMES
From the famous Braemar Gathering in Aberdeenshire to the spectacular Cowal Highland Gathering in Argyll, hot foot it to some Highland Games action for pipe bands, dancers, and tossing the caber.

EVENTS & FESTIVALS
In Scotland there's so much going on with fabulous events and festivals throughout the year, from the biggest names to the quirky and traditional.

CULTURE & HERITAGE
From the mysterious standing stones in Orkney and the Outer Hebrides to Burns Cottage and Rosslyn Chapel, Scotland's fascinating history can be found everywhere.

FOOD AND DRINK
Holidays let you try new flavours or sample local specialities. From freshly-caught seafood to estate-reared beef, Scotch malt whiskies to island ales, you'll find quality produce right across Scotland.

SPAS AND RESORTS
Spas offering a range of treatments are a welcome feature of many of Scotland's top hotels. The beauty and tranquillity of Scotland's countryside are also the perfect setting for rural spa resorts.

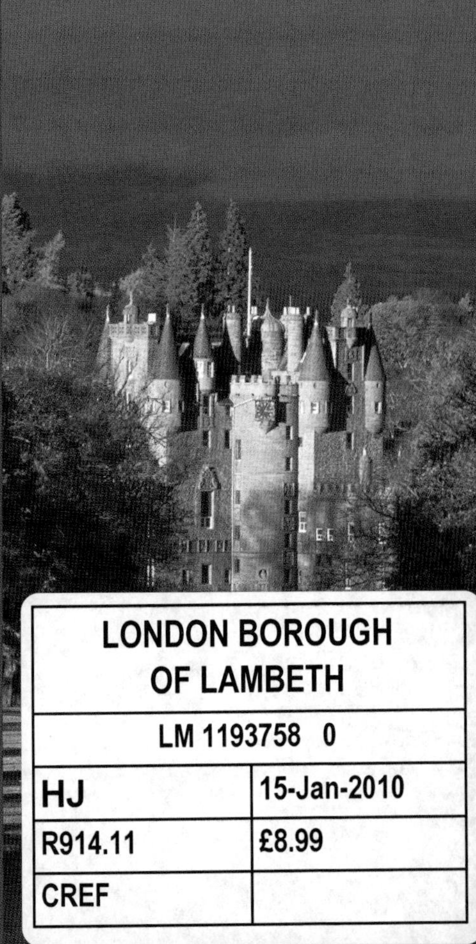

01 Glamis Castle; Angus

02 Rodin's "The Thinker", Burrell Collection, Glasgow

03 Al fresco dining – a leisurely lunch

04 Sword dancing at Ballater Highland Games

05 Turnberry Links hosted the 2009 Open Championships

06 Cycling around Newton Stewart, Dumfries & Galloway

07 The Scottish Traditional Boat Festival, Portsoy, Aberdeenshire

08 Turnberry Resort Spa

09 Traigh An Ior, Isle of Harris

10 Red deer stag, Glen Coe

02

03

04

05

06

07

08

10

EATING & DRINKING

If you love food, get a taste of Scotland. Scotland's natural larder offers some of the best produce in the world. Scotland's coastal waters are home to an abundance of lobster, prawns, oysters and more, whilst the land produces world-famous beef, lamb and game.

There's high quality food and drink on menus all over the country, often cooked up by award-winning chefs in restaurants where the view is second to none. You'll find home cooking, fine dining, takeaways and tearooms. Whether you're looking for a family-friendly pub or a romantic Highland restaurant, there's the perfect place to dine. And there's no better time to indulge than when you're on holiday!

EATSCOTLAND QUALITY ASSURANCE SCHEME

EatScotland is a nationwide Quality Assurance Scheme from VisitScotland. The scheme includes all sectors of the catering industry from chip shops, pubs and takeaways to restaurants.

A trained team of assessors carry out an incognito visit to assess quality, standards and ambience. Only those operators who meet the EatScotland quality standards are accredited to the scheme so look out for the logo to ensure you visit Scotland's best quality establishments.

The newly launched EatScotland Silver and Gold Award Scheme recognises outstanding standards, reflecting that an establishment offers an excellent eating out experience in Scotland.

To find great EatScotland places to dine throughout the country visit eatscotland.com

TRADITIONAL FARE

Haggis and whisky are probably the best known but not the only traditional Scottish fare. Discover the rich tastes behind such ancient names as Cullen Skink, Cranachan, clapshot and clootie dumpling. Sample some local hospitality along with regional specialities such as the Selkirk Bannock or Arbroath Smokies. Or experience the freedom of eating fish and chips straight from the wrapper while breathing in the clear evening air. Visit eatscotland.com and see our 'Food & Drink' section to find out more.

FARMERS' MARKETS

Scotland is a land renowned for producing ingredients of the highest quality. You can handpick fresh local produce at farmers' markets in towns and cities across the country. Create your own culinary delights or learn from the masters at the world-famous Nick Nairn Cook School in Stirling. Savour the aroma, excite your taste buds and experience the buzz of a farmers' market. To find out more visit the Farmers' Market information on the eatscotland.com website that can be found in the 'Food & Drink' section.

EVENTS

Scotland serves up a full calendar of food and drink festivals. Events like Taste of Edinburgh and Highland Feast are a must for foodies. Whisky fans can share their passion at the Islay Malt Whisky Festival, the Highland Whisky Festival, or the Spirit of Speyside Whisky Festival. Visit eatscotland.com to find out more about the events and festivals that are on in the 'What's on' section.

TOURS AND TRAILS

If you're a lover of seafood, spend some time exploring the rugged, unspoilt coastline of mid-Argyll following The Seafood Trail. Or if you fancy a wee dram, visit the eight distilleries and cooperage on the world's only Malt Whisky Trail in Speyside.

GREEN TOURISM

Scotland is a stunning destination and we want to make sure it stays that way. That's why we encourage all tourism operators including accommodation providers to take part in our Green Tourism Business Scheme. It means you're assured of a great quality stay at an establishment that's trying to minimise its impact on the environment.

VisitScotland rigorously assesses accommodation providers against measures as diverse as energy use, using local produce on menus, or promoting local wildlife walks or cycle hire. Environmentally responsible businesses can achieve Bronze, Silver or Gold awards, to acknowledge how much they are doing to help conserve the quality of Scotland's beautiful environment.

Look out for the Bronze, Silver and Gold Green Tourism logos throughout this guide to help you decide where to stay and do your bit to help protect our environment.

For a quick reference, see our directory at the back of the guide. This highlights all quality-assured accommodation that has been awarded with the Gold, Silver or Bronze award.

green-business.co.uk

BRONZE
GREEN TOURISM AWARD

SILVER
GREEN TOURISM AWARD

GOLD
GREEN TOURISM AWARD

QUALITY ASSURANCE

It's written in the stars.....
A simple, impartial, consistent approach to quality

VisitScotland, under the Scottish Tourist Board brand, administers the star grading schemes which assess the quality standards of all types of accommodation and visitor attractions from castles and historic houses to garden centres and arts venues. We quality assure over 70 per cent of the accommodation in Scotland and 90 per cent of the visitor attractions – so wherever you want to stay or visit, we've got it covered. Schemes are monitored all year round – each establishment is reviewed once a year. We do the hard work so you can relax and enjoy your holiday.

HOW DOES THE SYSTEM WORK?
Our advisors visit and assess establishments on up to 50 areas, from quality, comfort and cleanliness to welcome, ambience and service. The same star scheme runs in England and Wales, so you can follow the stars wherever you go.

GRADED VISITOR ATTRACTIONS
From tourist shops and museums to leisure centres and tours, visitor attractions are graded with one to five stars, depending on their level of customer care. The focus is on the standard of hospitality and service as well as presentation, quality of shop or café (if there is one) and toilet facilities.

THE PROMISE OF THE STARS:

★ it is clean, tidy and an acceptable, if basic, standard

★★ it is a good, all round standard

★★★ it is a very good standard, with attention to detail in every area

★★★★ it is excellent – using high quality materials, good food where provided and friendly, professional service

★★★★★ an exceptional standard where presentation, ambience, food where provided and service are hard to fault.

Establishments awarded gold stars have consistently achieved the highest levels of excellence within their star grading.

ACCESS ALL AREAS
The following symbols will help visitors with physical disabilities to decide whether accommodation is suitable:

- Unassisted wheelchair access
- Assisted wheelchair access
- Access for visitors with mobility difficulties.

We grade businesses that try to work in a sustainable, environmentally friendly way: Bronze, Silver or Gold

WE WANT YOU TO FEEL WELCOME
VisitScotland has developed Welcome Schemes to complement the Star Quality Assurance grades. These schemes tell you about establishments who pay particular attention to the specific needs of these visitors. As well as the established Walkers Welcome and Cyclists Welcome schemes, there are similar schemes for Anglers, Bikers, Classic Cars, Golfers, Children, Field sports, Film crews, Groups and Ancestral Tourism.

This means that a bothy or bod has been inspected.

The Thistle symbol recognises a high standard of caravan holiday home.

This means individual caravan holiday homes have been inspected.

THE VERY BEST OF FOOD AND DRINK

We assess the presentation, quality and service of food in every kind of eating establishment in Scotland.

The EatScotland logo tells you that the eating place has reached the standard for this accolade. Those with extra special standards of food are awarded EatScotland Silver or Gold. EatScotland gives a reliable, authoritative and comprehensive guide to eating out in Scotland.

FURTHER INFORMATION

For more information on Quality Assurance at VisitScotland, please contact us:

Tel. 01463 244 111 **Fax.** 01463 244 181
qainfo@visitscotland.com

We welcome your comments on star-awarded properties:

VisitScotland – Quality & Standards
Cowan House
Inverness Retail & Business Park, Inverness IV2 7GF

Tel. 01463 244 111 **Fax.** 01463 244 181
qa@visitscotland.com

Call into any VisitScotland Information Centre for further information:

www.visitscotland.com/wheretofindus

The Atholl Palace Hotel above the River Tummel, Pitlochry, Perthshire

Your guide to luxury 4 & 5 Star accommodation and dining in Scotland

- Establishments are listed **by location** in alphabetical order.
- For more **4 & 5 star accommodation** throughout Scotland go to VisitScotland.com.
- You will also find an **Index by location** which will tell you where to look if you already know where you want to go.
- Inside the back cover flap you will find a **key to the symbols**.

SOUTH OF SCOTLAND

The spa overlooking Ailsa Craig, Turnberry Resort, Ayrshire

Welcome to the South of Scotland

From St Abb's Head in the east to the Isle of Arran in the west, the South of Scotland encapsulates everything from whisky distilleries to ancient standing stones. Historically the scene of many a cross-border skirmish, the region is now a peaceful haven of lush countryside.

A long history of romantic gestures continues at Gretna Green's blacksmith's shop. Castles and stately homes populate the area, among them ancient royal residences and decadent Edwardian country retreats. Botanic Gardens nurture native and exotic species in beautiful surroundings.

Golfers are spoilt for choice with a range of championship links like Turnberry and challenging courses like Eyemouth to play. The South of Scotland is equally well-known for its salmon and trout fishing on rivers like the Tweed.

Choose an indulgent treat at one of the region's luxurious spa resorts. Wrap yourself in the luxury of locally-produced cashmere knitwear or dine out on the best of the region's seafood and Scotch beef.

AYRSHIRE & ARRAN

01 Glenrosa Water, Cir Mhor, Isle of Arran

02 Lochranza, Isle of Arran

03 Ailsa Course, Turnberry, Ayrshire

04 Culzean Castle, South Ayrshire

05 The Graffiti Project, Kelburn Castle

If you like a mixture of coastline, countryside and islands, then Ayrshire & Arran in South West Scotland is for you. The proximity of mainland to islands lets you enjoy so much more, even on a shorter stay.

You can easily get to the isles of Cumbrae and Arran by ferry. The crossing is only 10 minutes to Cumbrae and 55 minutes to Arran. You might be surprised to find palm trees there, thanks to the warm wash of the Gulf Stream.

It's an area rich in castles and stately homes, from Culzean Castle to Dumfries House, with luxurious historic rooms and elegant manicured gardens to explore. Golf is also strong here, with championship links at Turnberry and Royal Troon joining rising stars Dundonald Links and Western Gailes.

However and wherever you choose to spend your time here, you'll feel the benefit of the quieter pace in no time.

04

Inspired ideas for you to indulge

CULZEAN CASTLE
Now cared for by the National Trust for Scotland, Culzean Castle at Maybole is an outstanding example of the work of architect Robert Adam. Its setting atop a cliff is pure romance and the period furnishings and interior detail are simply breathtaking. You can even stay in one of six bedrooms in the Eisenhower Apartment.
culzeanexperience.org

ISLAND LIFE
The ferry from Ardrossan takes less than an hour to reach the delightful island of Arran. There are easy, scenic walks to enjoy, as well as a distillery and historic sites. You can see Arran from the neighbouring island of Great Cumbrae, itself only a 10-minute ferry from Largs. Its capital, Millport, is a model Victorian resort.
ayrshire-arran.com

GOLF
South West Scotland is home to some of the world's finest links golf courses. Royal Troon and Turnberry are the most famous but there are plenty more to play in the Great Scottish Links Collection. Local golf passes are an easy and cost effective way to play a variety of courses during your stay.
ayrshire-arran.com/golf

WHISKY
The Isle of Arran Distillery began production in 1995. Based at Lochranza, you can follow the journey from grain to glass on a fully-guided tour at the visitor centre. You can also pour your own bottle of what the distillers proudly call 'the true spirit of nature'.
arranwhisky.com

CRAFT TOWN
The picturesque town of West Kilbride is also known as Craft Town Scotland. This haven for local fine crafts allows you to view and buy a wide range of quality items in one location from established and new talents. There are eight craft studio workshops, where work is produced by a single maker.
westkilbride.org.uk

Savour the real taste of Scotland

BRAEHEAD COOK SCHOOL
Whether you're a novice or an expert in the kitchen, you're sure to pick up some tips, techniques and trade secrets at the recently-opened five-star Braehead Cook School. There are more than 21 masterclasses to choose from, giving you the chance to work with eminent chefs and the finest local ingredients.
braeheadfoods.co.uk

01 Sunset on the Firth of Clyde, North Ayrshire

02 Afternoon tea with a view at Turnberry Resort, Ayrshire

03 A cool head in the kitchen! Learn the skills of the experts

04 The finest wines to accompany your meal

FINS RESTAURANT AT FENCEBAY
Not only does this renowned Ayrshire restaurant know the exact provenance of all its fish, much of it is caught by their own boatman. Custom seafood platters, where you select your favourites, are a speciality. Fencebay also hosts a monthly Farmers' Market, including Scotch meat and game, local fish and fresh home-baking.
EatScotland Silver Award
fencebay.co.uk

THE GRAND TEA LOUNGE
The relaxed refinement of the luxurious Turnberry Resort is just the place to enjoy that age-old tradition of Scottish afternoon tea. Choose from a menu of thirty or so teas, all brewed to order using a traditional samovar. Add some sparkle with a glass of champagne.
turnberryresort.co.uk

CORNEY & BARROW
Whigham's of Ayr was established back in 1766. From its start, the company supplied fine wines and spirits to many of Southern Scotland's great houses. Now joined with Corney & Barrow, they regularly hold tastings in the original underground cellars. Cellar wine tastings can be either informal or tutored.
corneyandbarrow.com

Something a little bit different

03

DUMFRIES HOUSE
The former home of the Marquises of Bute was saved by a consortium led by Prince Charles. Now this Georgian masterpiece is opening its doors again for the first time in 250 years. Discover the house for yourself on a series of Connoisseur Tours, ending with a glass of champagne in sumptuous surroundings.
dumfries-house.org.uk

BURNS COUNTRY TOURS
The land and people of Ayrshire were the inspiration for much of the work of Robert Burns. You can visit places from his life and his poetry on bespoke tours. Your guide is Robert McKinnon, who personally tailors each tour to your own specific interests and budget.
burnscountrytours.com

BEGG FOR CASHMERE
Some of the finest cashmere seen on the world's catwalks and in its leading boutiques is created in Ayr. From humble handcrafted beginnings in 1869, Begg Scotland now creates endless colourways of pure cashmere scarves, shawls, stoles and throws. You can arrange an exclusive behind-the-scenes tour.
beggscotland.com

CATIMA SAILING
You can tour Scotland's rugged west coastline and see its wildlife in close-up by chartering a luxury private yacht from Catima Sailing. Set sail for Arran to tour the island and sample its whisky. Or pack a picnic, anchor in a secluded bay and just enjoy the spectacular views.
catimasailing.co.uk

01 The Burns Monument, Kilmarnock

02 Scottish Grand National, Ayr Racecourse

03 Sailing in Brodick Bay, Isle of Arran

04 Seals, Kildonan, Isle of Arran

05 Begg cashmere – direct from the catwalk!

Time to plan your perfect day

SCOTLAND'S SCOTTISH GRAND NATIONAL

April 2010

Ayr Racecourse hosts National Hunt and Flat fixtures throughout the year. This dual-purpose track is also the venue for the Scottish Grand National every April. Make a day of it with lunch before the race in the Champagne and Seafood Bar next to the Parade Ring.

ayr-racecourse.co.uk

BURNS AN' A' THAT! FESTIVAL

May 2010

As the birthplace of Scotland's national poet, Robert Burns, Ayr celebrates his legacy every year with the best in contemporary Scottish music and arts. The programme covers everything from well-known comedians, bands and musicians to food and drink events. And of course, there are poetry and cultural events dedicated to Burns himself.

burns.visitscotland.com/festival

ISLE OF ARRAN WILDLIFE FESTIVAL

12 – 19 May 2010

The local wildlife and sea-life are the stars of this festival started in 2006. Golden eagles, otters and porpoises are all likely to make an appearance. There are deer walks, boat trips, minibus safaris and beach strolls to enjoy as part of this fascinating eight-day event.

arranwildlife.co.uk

AYR FLOWER SHOW

6 – 8 August 2010

Scotland's answer to the Chelsea Flower Show has been delighting visitors to Ayr since 1960. It's held in the beautiful setting of Rozelle Estate where the cream of British horticulture creates stunning gardens especially for the show. Expect a bumper year in 2010 as the show marks its 50th anniversary.

ayrflowershow.org

DUMFRIES & GALLOWAY

Over the centuries, poets and artists have been inspired by this south-western region of Scotland. Robert Burns has strong associations here and the area continues to capture the artistic imagination with flourishing creative communities like the Artists' Town of Kirkcudbright.

Choose some local culture from the regular programme of events and festivals held throughout the year in towns and villages. Some towns have special designated titles to highlight their attractions. There's the Food Town of Castle Douglas or Wigtown, Scotland's Book Town. And Gretna remains a draw for the romantics at heart.

A rich variety and abundance of wildlife calls this area home. Keep a look out as you travel around for red deer, red kites, wild goats, ospreys and red squirrels. You can develop a taste for the region, too, with freshly-caught lobster and Galloway beef featuring on many local menus.

Inspired ideas for you to indulge

GOLF
Dumfries & Galloway is as popular with the holiday golfer as the serious one. Choose from a range of highly-rated courses participating in the region's Golf Pass or try one of three golfing trails to help you get the most from a few days of golf.
visitdumfriesandgalloway.co.uk/golf

SWEETHEART ABBEY
You'll find the origin of 'sweetheart' at a Cistercian abbey in the delightful village of New Abbey. Sweetheart Abbey was established by Lady Devorgilla in memory of her husband, whose embalmed heart she carried around with her in an ivory box. The lady and the heart are now buried together at the high altar.
historic-scotland.gov.uk

COASTAL CHARM
Dumfries & Galloway gives you a great big breath of fresh sea air. More than 200 miles of coastline provides beaches, bays, coves and inlets that are great for relaxing strolls or picnics with stunning panoramas. Discover Kippford and other attractive seaside villages before a spot of lunch in a harbour-side café.

RED SQUIRRELS
20% of Scotland's population of red squirrels have made their home in Dumfries & Galloway so your chances of seeing one or more are good. Red squirrels have settled in well to their woodland habitat here. Follow the signs on the Red Squirrel Walk within Dalbeattie Forest and see if you can spot one.
www.red-squirrels.org.uk

'THE SPIRIT OF THE LOWLANDS'
Bladnoch Distillery is the most southerly distillery in Scotland and has produced the 'Spirit of the Lowlands' since 1817. You can see barrels full of whisky resting in warehouses, the steam and noise of the Mash House and the heady smell of the Tun Room before trying a dram of Bladnoch Single Malt for yourself.
bladnoch.co.uk

01 The ruins of Sweetheart Abbey, New Abbey, Dumfries & Galloway

02 Dunskey Golf Course, Portpatrick, Dumfries & Galloway

03 The elusive red squirrel

04 The sandy beach at Killantringan Bay, Dumfries & Galloway

Savour the real taste of Scotland

01 Knockinaam Lodge Hotel, near Portpatrick

02 Drumlanrig Castle, Dumfries & Galloway

03 Al fresco dining at Campbell's Restaurant, Portpatrick

CAMPBELL'S RESTAURANT

Campbell's Restaurant makes the most of its seafront location in the quaint harbour village of Portpatrick. Seafood, particularly lobster, is a speciality, with platters and grills especially popular. Galloway beef and Wigtownshire lamb feature among meat dishes, with locally-sourced produce used as much as possible.
campbellsrestaurant.co.uk

KNOCKINAAM LODGE

With a Michelin star to its name, Knockinaam Lodge is a country house close to Portpatrick with an excellent reputation for fine dining. Look out over the sea to Ireland as you enjoy Sunday lunch or witness stunning sunsets over dinner. Then retire to one of the nine elegant bedrooms, each with its own individual style.
knockinaamlodge.com

DRUMLANRIG CASTLE

Drumlanrig Castle houses one of the UK's finest private art collections. Once a month it also acts as a beautiful backdrop to a farmers' market for local growers and producers. You can also enjoy local produce and the fruits of the Buccleuch estate with a combined Castle Tour and Afternoon Tea ticket.
drumlanrig.com

BLACKADDIE COOKERY SCHOOL

Blackaddie Country House Hotel in Sanquhar holds cookery school classes on one day every month. You can arrive the night before for a drinks reception followed by a wonderful four-course dinner. Next day you work with a top chef, learn how to cook like a professional then taste what you've prepared.
EatScotland Silver Award
blackaddiehotel.co.uk

Something a little bit different

ENVIRONMENTAL ARTWORKS

There's more to Dumfries & Galloway's scenery than meets the eye. As you travel around, look out for some intriguing environmental artworks set in different landscapes. Discover head carvings in a sheep pen at Galloway Forest Park and watch out for Andy Goldsworthy's Striding Arches near Moniaive. stridingarches.com

LOGAN BOTANIC GARDEN

Logan Botanic Garden is known as 'Scotland's most exotic garden'. Its outstanding collection of southern hemisphere plants thrives and flourishes outdoors thanks to the passing Gulf Stream. Logan is home to weird and wonderful species that aren't grown anywhere else in Scotland in this plantsman's paradise. rbge.org.uk/logan

TIBETAN BUDDHIST MONASTERY

It's a wonderful surprise to discover a traditional Tibetan Buddhist temple in the tranquil setting of the south of Scotland. The Kagyu Samye Ling Tibetan Buddhist Monastery at Eskdalemuir was the first to be established in the West. You are welcome to visit, enjoy the Peace Garden or take tea in the Tibetan Tea Room. samyeling.org

02

Time to plan your perfect day

KIRKCUDBRIGHT SUMMER FESTIVITIES

May – August 2010

The 'Artists' Town' of Kirkcudbright runs a full programme of summer events from early May to the August Bank Holiday. Highlights include a four-day jazz festival in June, while 'Scottish Nights' of traditional music and dancing fill Thursday evenings in July and August. The four-month programme comes to a spectacular close with a floodlit Tattoo.

summerfestivities.com

SPRING FLING

29 – 31 May 2010

Spring Fling is Scotland's foremost open studios event for arts and crafts. Over 80 artists across Dumfries & Galloway open their studio doors to the public over the weekend. It's an ideal opportunity to buy direct from the artist, join a workshop or just get to know the wealth of local talent.

spring-fling.co.uk

FOOD TOWN DAY

29 May 2010

Castle Douglas is home to more than 50 local food-related businesses. It is little surprise then to learn it's been designated a Food Town. The annual Food Town Day fills the whole town with foodie activities. Look out for cooking demonstrations, a farmers' market and those all-important local speciality tastings.

cd-foodtown.org

WIGTOWN BOOK FESTIVAL

24 September – 3 October 2010

For ten days each year, this charming town becomes a mecca for leading authors and passionate readers alike. The festival regularly attracts over 10,000 visitors to Scotland's National Book Town to soak up the literary atmosphere and browse through an estimated quarter of a million books!

wigtownbookfestival.com

LOCKERBIE JAZZ FESTIVAL

22 – 24 October 2010

Lockerbie's Jazz Festival brings a foot-tapping mixture of mainstream and contemporary jazz and blues to venues around the town. Local musicians join with Scottish and international artists for more than a dozen concerts in the town's hall, hotels and theatre over the festival weekend.

lockerbiejazz.com

03

04

01 Logan Botanic Garden, Dumfries & Galloway

02 Andy Goldsworthy's Striding Arches near Moniaive

03 Greengate Close, Kirkcudbright

04 Caerlaverock Castle, Dumfries & Galloway

SCOTTISH BORDERS

The rivers and hills that shape and define the Scottish Borders also provide some of the best ways to enjoy them.

The River Tweed is well known in fishing circles for its first-class beats for salmon and trout. Golfers have 21 different courses from which to choose. 1500 miles of dedicated walking routes let you discover the Scottish Borders at your own pace. You can walk in steps inspired by local authors and history or try a series of themed strolls. 1200 miles of quiet country roads put the pleasure back into your driving as you discover interesting towns and historic villages.

While away a relaxing day or longer at luxury spa resorts and facilities in the area. Towns like Peebles are full of independent boutique shops just perfect for browsing. Fine locally-produced woollens and cashmere make a great memento. So, too, do sweet Scottish Borders confections like Selkirk Bannock and Hawick Balls.

Inspired ideas for you to indulge

FREEDOM OF THE FAIRWAYS

Playing golf in the Scottish Borders is made easier and even more affordable with the 'Freedom of the Fairways' golf passport scheme. 21 courses throughout the region are included. Try to fit in Eyemouth Golf Course, whose sixth hole was voted Britain's Most Extraordinary Golf Hole – it certainly is that!
visitscottishborders.com/golf

01 Roxburghe Golf Club, near Kelso

02 Contemporary Craft at Real Wood Studios

03 Floors Castle and the River Tweed, Scottish Borders

04 Manderston House, near Duns, Scottish Borders

THE ROXBURGHE ESTATE

The Roxburghe Estate is an agricultural and sporting estate owned by the Duke and Duchess of Roxburghe and spans more than 54,000 acres. You can visit their home at Floors Castle, the largest inhabited castle in Scotland, tour the gardens and buy some home-made produce from the Castle Kitchen Produce Shop.
roxburghe.net

MANDERSTON HOUSE

Manderston House near Duns is an Edwardian masterpiece, often described as the 'swansong of the great classical houses'. No expense was spared on its opulent staterooms and it has the only silver staircase in the world. Beyond the house, you can explore the impressive stables, amazing marble dairy and 56 acres of formal gardens.
manderston.co.uk

REAL WOOD STUDIOS

Just outside Jedburgh, you'll find a co-operative of furniture designer-makers specialising in wood. From their woodland base at Monteviot Nurseries, they use their creativity to transform sustainable native Scottish hardwoods into bespoke, hand-crafted furniture like coffee tables, chairs and kist boxes.
realwoodstudios.com

HAWICK CASHMERE

The Hawick Cashmere Company has over a century's experience of working with this softest of wools. Founded in 1874, Hawick Cashmere is still based in its original 19th-century mill. You'll find a kaleidoscope of the finest knitwear and scarves in pure Scottish cashmere at the Hawick Factory Visitor Centre shop.
hawickcashmere.com

TWIST GLASS STUDIO

Glass-blowing and glass-making have a long heritage and you can see these ancient arts for yourself at Twist Glass Studio in Selkirk. The studio creates a range of 18th century-style drinking glasses as well as individual contemporary works of art in 24% lead crystal. Each piece is hand-signed and dated.
visitscottishborders.com

Savour the real taste of Scotland

01 The Wheatsheaf at Swinton, Scottish Borders

02 Chef applies the finishing touches at The Wheatsheaf, Scottish Borders

03 Dining in style at The Roxburghe Hotel, Scottish Borders

04 Mouthwatering high tea at The Black Bull, Lauder, Scottish Borders

TWEED RESTAURANT

The Tweed Restaurant within St Boswells' Dryburgh Abbey Hotel has a brand-new look. This warm and contemporary restaurant, overlooking the River Tweed, specialises in fine Scottish cuisine. The eight-course dinner menu allows you to fully enjoy the creative flair of the Head Chef and his team.
dryburgh.co.uk

THE HORSESHOE INN

Just north of Peebles, you'll find the charming Horseshoe Inn in the village of Eddleston. You can choose to dine in either the relaxed Bistro or the elegant Bardoulet's Restaurant of this former blacksmith's shop. After your meal, an overnight stay in one of the Inn's eight individually-decorated bedrooms is highly recommended.
EatScotland Gold Award
horseshoeinn.co.uk

THE WHEATSHEAF AT SWINTON

The Wheatsheaf is a cosy, comfortable inn which has received many plaudits and awards for its food. Eyemouth Harbour is only 12 miles away so the fish and seafood are fresh from the sea. Meat and other produce are also all locally sourced where possible. Ten adjoining rooms mean you can stay for breakfast, too.
wheatsheaf-swinton.co.uk

TEVIOT GAME FARE SMOKERY

The Scottish Borders are known for the quality of their salmon, trout, eels and wild game. Using home-grown herbs, Teviot Smokery in Kelso brines and slowly smokes such local produce over a bed of oak chips. They'll even smoke your own fishing successes. Alternatively you can choose from a wide selection in the Smokery Food Hall.
teviotgamefaresmokery.co.uk

Something a little bit different

DUNS CASTLE

Spending a night or two in a Scottish castle is high on many wish lists. Duns Castle, on the edge of the market town of Duns, has been home to the Hay family since 1696. Now you can stay in one of the castle's 25 bedrooms and enjoy the grand period setting and furnishings.
dunscastle.co.uk

TRAQUAIR HOUSE AND BREWERY

Traquair is well-known as the oldest inhabited house in Scotland. Originally owned by Scotland's kings, the house is open to the public in the summer. You can stay in one of three spacious antique-filled double bedrooms, each with private bathrooms and central heating. There's also a brewery at Traquair, which makes its own beers and ales.
traquair.co.uk

LOCHCARRON OF SCOTLAND

Lochcarron is the world's leading tartan manufacturer, weaving and stocking over 700 tartans. Lochcarron combines 60 years of tradition and craftsmanship with the latest technology to supply high quality innovative textiles.

Time to plan your perfect day

KELSO RACES

Kelso is the home of National Hunt racing in the Scottish Borders. Known as 'Britain's Friendliest Racecourse', the challenging course attracts top-grade jumpers prior to the Cheltenham Festival and Aintree. You can make a real day of it at the races with various dining and ticket combinations or cheer home the winner from a private box. kelso-races.co.uk

BORDERS BANQUET

November 2010

The Scottish Borders region is known for having some of Scotland's finest fish, game, beef and lamb. The Borders Banquet is a ten-day celebration of this rich larder of locally-produced food and drink. It's a wonderful opportunity to savour the best local dishes created by inventive chefs, from gourmet dining to an informal bistro lunch. bordersfoodnetwork.co.uk

Go behind-the-scenes in Selkirk on a factory tour to follow the route from original design to finished garment. lochcarron.com

COCOA BLACK CHOCOLATE SCHOOL

If you're a lover of fine chocolate, you can now learn how to work with it at the Chocolate and Patisserie School in Peebles. Chef Ruth Hinks brings fun, enthusiasm and more than 20 years' experience of working with chocolate to each class, from tasting sessions to making your own truffles to take home. cocoablack.co.uk

01 Traquair House, Innerleithen, Scottish Borders

02 Kelso, home of national hunt racing in the Scottish Borders

03 Cocoa Black Chocolate School

04 Tartan tradition, craftsmanship and contemporary designs

SOUTH OF SCOTLAND

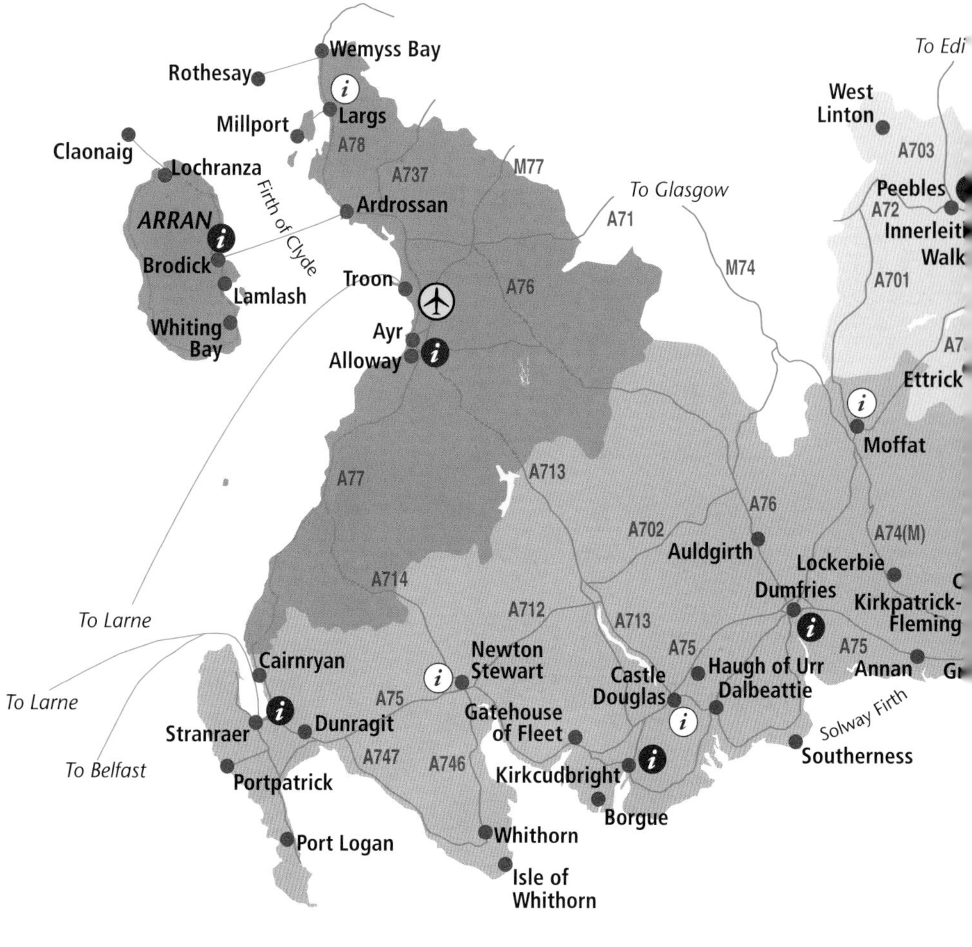

Wemyss Bay
Rothesay
Largs
Millport
A78
Claonaig
Lochranza
Firth of Clyde
A737
M77
ARRAN
Ardrossan
Brodick
Lamlash
Whiting Bay
Troon
Ayr
Alloway
A76
A71
To Glasgow
M74
West Linton
A703
Peebles
A72
A701
Ettrick
Moffat
A77
A713
A76
A702
Auldgirth
A74(M)
Lockerbie
Dumfries
Kirkpatrick-Fleming
A714
A712
A713
To Larne
Cairnryan
Newton Stewart
A75
Castle Douglas
Haugh of Urr
Dalbeattie
A75
Annan
To Larne
A75
Stranraer
Dunragit
Gatehouse of Fleet
Solway Firth
Southerness
To Belfast
A747
A746
Kirkcudbright
Portpatrick
Borgue
Port Logan
Whithorn
Isle of Whithorn

Eyemouth
A1
Berwick-upon-Tweed
A68
Duns
Swinton
A7
Lauder
A6112
A697
Coldstream
Galashiels
To Newcastle
Melrose
Kelso
St Boswells
Selkirk
A698
A7
Jedburgh
Campdown
Hawick
A68
A6088
To Hexham
M6
To Carlisle
Southwaite Services

VisitScotland Information Centres

To help you plan and book your trip to Scotland email our travel experts at info@visitscotland.com. When you arrive call into one of our Information Centres where our friendly experts can offer advice on all things local as well as sharing their wider knowledge of Scotland. We don't just advise either. We can sort out your accommodation and all your travel needs, as well as tickets for events across Scotland. So if you're looking to get the most from your visit, there really is only one place to go.

AYRSHIRE & ARRAN	
Ayr	22 Sandgate, Ayr, KA7 1BW
Brodick	The Pier, Brodick, Isle of Arran, KA27 8AU
DUMFRIES & GALLOWAY	
Dumfries	64 Whitesands, Dumfries DG1 2RS
Gretna	Unit 38, Gretna Gateway Outlet Village, Glasgow Road, Gretna, DG16 5GG
Kirkcudbright	Harbour Square, Kirkcudbright DG6 4HY
Southwaite	M6 Service Area, Southwaite, CA4 0NS
Stranraer	28 Harbour Street, Stranraer, DG9 7RA
THE SCOTTISH BORDERS	
Hawick	Tower Mill, Heart of Hawick Campus, Kirkstile, Hawick, TD9 0AE
Jedburgh	Murray's Green, Jedburgh, TD8 6BE
Melrose	Abbey House, Abbey Street, Melrose TD6 9LG
Peebles	23 High Street, Peebles, EH45 8AG

- LOCAL KNOWLEDGE
- WHERE TO STAY
- ACCOMMODATION BOOKING
- PLACES TO VISIT
- THINGS TO DO
- MAPS AND GUIDES
- TRAVEL ADVICE
- ROUTE PLANNING
- WHERE TO SHOP AND EAT
- LOCAL CRAFTS AND PRODUCE
- EVENT INFORMATION
- TICKETS

SouthernScotland
Luxury Accommodation
live it. love it.
Enjoy the Wolsey Lodge personalised service in unique places to stay:
• All quality 4* and 5* accommodation.
• Explore this wonderful area with suggested activity linked itineraries.
• A directory of all the best places to stay, eat and drink.
• Fascinating insights into local history and heritage.
• A comprehensive range of Scottish produce, arts and crafts.
• Find the best gardens and golf courses; castles and abbeys; walks, fishing & racing
Southern Scotland is made up of Ayrshire, the Borders, Dumfries & Galloway, East Lothian and South Lanarkshire
www.holidaysouthernscotland.co.uk
www.blogsouthernscotland.com
info@holidaysouthernscotland.co.uk

Ayrshire & Arran: Guest Houses and B&Bs

le of Arran, Lochranza

pple Lodge

Open: All year excl Xmas & New Year **Map Ref: 1E6**

★★★★
GUEST HOUSE

Lochranza, Isle of Arran, KA27 8HJ
T: 01770 830229

Indicated Prices:

Single	from £54.00	Twin	from £38.00 per person
Double	from £38.00 per person	Suite	from £44.00 per person

12337

y Ayr, Alloway

unnyside Bed and Breakfast

Open: All year **Map Ref: 1G7**

★★★★
BED AND BREAKFAST

26 Dunure Road, Alloway, Ayr, Ayrshire, KA7 4HR
T: 01292 441234 E: ayrbandb@hotmail.com W: ayrbandb.co.uk

Indicated Prices:

Single	from £39.50 per room	Twin	from £59.00 per room
Double	from £59.00 per room	Family	from £70.00 per room

57253

Ayrshire & Arran: EatScotland Gold and Silver establishments

Brodick

Eighteen69

SILVER

Auchrannie Country House Hotel, Brodick, KA27 8BZ
T: 01770 302 234

Eighteen69 is Auchrannie resort's flagship award-winning restaurant. In the glasshouse enjoy an individually priced menu exquisitely prepared with vibrant, contemporary Scottish flair.

Nr Largs

Fins Seafood Restaurant

Fencefoot Farm,
Nr Largs, Ayrshire,
KA29 0EG
T: 01475 568 918

Fresh from the sea off their own and local boats, the fish and shellfish is prepared and cooked by a skilled team of chefs. You can also buy their own smoked Fairlie Kippers and smoked salmon.

Ballantrae

Glenapp Castle

Ballantrae,
Girvan,
KA26 0NZ
T: 01465 831 212

A member of the prestigious Relais & Chateau Association, the castle offers internationally renowned standards of quality and service including superb fine dining in its AA Three Rosette restaurant.

Turnberry

The Turnberry Restaurant

The Westin Turnberry Resort,
Turnberry,
KA26 9LT
T: 01655 331 000

The restaurant at the Turnberry Hotel is an excellent example of the grand hotel dining room style, but brought into the 21st Century and has stunning views to Ailsa Craig. The Chef blends classical French influences with seasonal Scottish ingredients.

Whisky barrels at the Isle of Arran Distillery

Machrie Moor Stone Circle, Isle of Arran

Dumfries & Galloway: Guest Houses and B&Bs

Dalbeattie

Heritage Guest House and Holistics

Open: All year **Map Ref: 2A1**

Superior guest house for the more discerning visitor. Quiet location with easy access to rural facilities. Double en-suite rooms. Spacious lounge with open fire and 42" Sky TV. Ground floor suite with private lounge. Evening meals, wireless broadband, massage therapist. Ample off-road parking. Secure storage for equipment/bikes. Open all year.

★★★★
BED AND BREAKFAST

273 High Street, Dalbeattie, Galloway, DG5 4DW
T: 01556 610817 E: reception@heritage-house.info W: heritage-house.info

Indicated Prices:

Double	from £35.00 per person	Suite	from £45.00 per person

803

 PRICES STATED ARE ESTIMATES AND MAY BE SUBJECT TO CHANGE. PRICES ARE PER PERSON PER NIGHT UNLESS OTHERWISE STATED. AWARDS CORRECT AS OF BEGINNING OF OCTOBER 2009

irkcudbright

ludha Guest House

Open: All year

Map Ref: 2A10

ınding in two acres of mature ɔunds and gardens, Fludha erlooks the River Dee from unrivalled position, enjoying noramic views over Kirkcudbright d Galloway Hills. Adjacent riverside lks make Fludha feel like a very ecial place. Dine while watching e sun set with a glass of wine... rfect.

★★★★★
GUEST HOUSE

Tongland Road, Kirkcudbright, Dumfries and Galloway, DG6 4UU
T: 01557 331443 E: stay@fludha.com W: fludha.com

Indicated Prices:

Single	from £70.00 per room	Twin	from £80.00 per room
Double	from £80.00 per room	Suite	from £85.00 per room

28210

irkcudbright

umber One Bed and Breakfast

Open: All year excl Xmas & New Year

Map Ref: 2A10

★★★★ GOLD
BED AND BREAKFAST

1 Castle Gardens, Kirkcudbright, DG6 4JE
T: 01557 330540 E: annenisbet1@btinternet.com W: number1bedandbreakfast.co.uk

Indicated Prices:

Double from £70.00 per room

70404

loffat

artfell House

Open: All year excl Xmas

Map Ref: 2B8

★★★★
GUEST HOUSE

Hartfell Crescent, Moffat, DG10 9AL
T: 01683 220153 E: enquiries@hartfellhouse.co.uk W: hartfellhouse.co.uk

Indicated Prices:

Single	from £40.00 per room	Twin	from £70.00 per room
Double	from £70.00 per room	Family	from £85.00 per room

29655

Moffat

Woodhead Farm

Open: All year **Map Ref: 2B**

Woodhead, Old Carlisle Road, Moffat, DG10 9LU
T: 01683 220225 E: sylvia@woodhead4.freeserve.co.uk

Indicated Prices:

Single	from £40.00 per room	Twin	from £75.00 per room
Double	from £70.00 per room		

645

Dumfries & Galloway: Self Catering

Borgue, Kirkcudbright

Brighouse Holiday Cottages

Open: All year **Map Ref: 1H1**

★★★★
SELF CATERING

Borgue, Kirkcudbright, DG6 4TS
T: 01557 870606 E: margaret@brighouse.wanadoo.co.uk W: brighousebayholidaycottages.cor

1 House 3 Bedrooms Sleeps 1-6

Prices – House:
£300.00-£595.00 Per Week

Short breaks available

813

 PRICES STATED ARE ESTIMATES AND MAY BE SUBJECT TO CHANGE. PRICES ARE PER PERSON PER NIGHT UNLESS OTHERWISE STATED. AWARDS CORRECT AS OF BEGINNING OF OCTOBER 2009

y Castle Douglas

he Old Sunday School

Open: All year **Map Ref: 2A10**

ilt in 1793 this detached property s been tastefully converted. Set jacent to the owners' home, its ound floor formerly housed cattle d the upper was the village Sunday hool. This area of the Solway s beautiful beaches, especially ndyhills and the close by 'Galloway rest' has been awarded the untry's first 'Dark Sky Park'.

★★★★ SELF CATERING

Buittle, Castle Douglas, DG7 1NP
T: 01556 610811/07717 853465 E: jamietat08@btinternet.com W: oldsundayschool.com

1 Cottage 2 Bedrooms Sleeps 4

Prices – Lodge:
£330.00-£746.00 Per Week

Short breaks available

77017

y Gretna Green, Kirkpatrick Fleming

ove House

Open: All year **Map Ref: 2C9**

★★★★ SELF CATERING

Cove Estate, Kirkpatrick Fleming, by Gretna Green, Dumfriesshire, DG11 3AT
T: 01461 800285/07779 138694 E: info@coveestate.co.uk W: coveestate.co.uk

2 Apartments 2 Bedrooms Sleeps 4-6

Prices – Apartments:
£450.00-£600.00 Per Week
£70.00-£90.00 Per Night

Short breaks available

83629

View across Loch Ken

Kirkcowan

Dirnow Schoolhouse

Open: All year **Map Ref: 1G1**

★★★★ SELF CATERING

Kirkcowan, DG8 0ET
T: 01671 830297 E: dirnow-schoolhouse@supanet.com

1 Wing of house 1 Bedroom Sleeps 1-2

Prices – Wing of house:
£170.00-£300.00 Per Week

Short breaks available

227

Port Logan

Aileen & Matthew Caughie

Open: All year **Map Ref: 1F1**

Kirkbride Farm Cottages offers a unique self catering holiday experience for all the family, whether you prefer a cosy traditional Galloway cottage or a contemporary new property. All have magnificent sea views, cosy log burners and the peace and tranquillity of this very special part of south west Scotland.

★★★★★ SELF CATERING

Kirkbride Farm Holiday Cottages, Kirkbride Farm, Port Logan, DG9 9NP
T: 07769 806259/07766 257771 E: stay@kirkbridecottages.co.uk W: kirkbridecottages.co.u

2 Cottages 6 Bedrooms Sleeps 2-12
1 House 4 Bedrooms Sleeps 2-8

Prices – Cottage: £360.00-£1650.00 Per Week
Prices – House: £750.00-£1850.00 Per Week

Short breaks available

799

 PRICES STATED ARE ESTIMATES AND MAY BE SUBJECT TO CHANGE. PRICES ARE PER UNIT PER WEEK UNLESS OTHERWISE STATED. AWARDS CORRECT AS OF BEGINNING OF OCTOBER 2009

Dumfries & Galloway: EatScotland Gold and Silver establishments

Sanquhar

Blackaddie Country House Hotel

Blackaddie Road, Sanquhar,
DG4 6JJ
T: 01659 50270

A superb Hotel set in its own gardens on the banks of the River Nith, one of Scotland's great yet little known salmon rivers; there's extensive views across Scotland's Southern Upland Way.

Dumfries

Casa Mia

53 Nunholm Road,
Nunholm, Dumfries,
DG1 1JW
T: 01387 267 835

This authentic Italian restaurant has freshly prepared and flavoursome food with a range of options to cater for all tastes. The atmosphere is buzzing but relaxed.

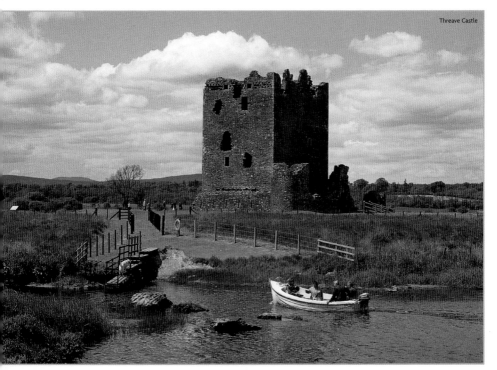

Threave Castle

Scottish Borders: Hotels

Chirnside, by Duns

Chirnside Hall Hotel

Open: All year excl Mar **Map Ref: 2F**

★★★★
COUNTRY HOUSE HOTEL

Chirnside, nr Duns, Berwickshire, TD11 3LD
T: 01890 818219 E: reception@chirnsidehallhotel.com W: chirnsidehallhotel.com

Indicated Prices:

Single	from £85.00 per room	Twin	from £130.00 per room
Double	from £130.00 per room	Family	from £180.00 per room
		Suite	from £150.00 per room

191

Walkerburn

Windlestraw Lodge

Open: All year excl Xmas & New Year **Map Ref: 2C**

A stunning house in the country with spectacular views of the Tweed Valley. This luxurious hideaway, owned by chef Alan Reid and his wife Julie offers the warmest of welcomes. Sublime food and ultimate relaxation – the perfect location for exploring the Borders, Edinburgh and Northumberland.

★★★★
COUNTRY HOUSE HOTEL

Galashiels Road, Walkerburn, Peeblesshire, EH43 6AA
T: 01896 870636 E: reception@windlestraw.co.uk W: windlestraw.co.uk

Indicated Prices:

Single	from £85.00 per room	Twin	from £150.00 per room
Double	from £130.00 per room	Family	on request

623

PRICES STATED ARE ESTIMATES AND MAY BE SUBJECT TO CHANGE. PRICES ARE PER PERSON PER NIGHT UNLESS OTHERWISE STATED. AWARDS CORRECT AS OF BEGINNING OF OCTOBER 2009

Scottish Borders: Guest Houses and B&Bs

nnerleithen

raquair House

Open: All year excl 24-26 Dec 2009

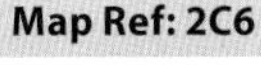
Map Ref: 2C6

u are welcome to stay at aquair. There are three spacious uble bedrooms, furnished with tique furniture, canopied beds d private bathrooms. Traquair as originally owned by the Kings Scotland. It later became home the Earls of Traquair and is still ed in by descendents of the axwell-Stuart family.

★★★★
BED AND BREAKFAST

Innerleithen, Peeblesshire, EH44 6PW
T: 01896 830323 E: enquiries@traquair.co.uk W: traquair.co.uk

Indicated Prices:

Single	from £100.00 per room	Twin	please contact
Double	from £180.00 per room	Family	please contact

61882

y Jedburgh, Camptown

he School House Bed and Breakfast

Open: Mar-Dec

Map Ref: 2E7

★★★★★ GOLD
BED AND BREAKFAST

Edgerston School House, Camptown, Jedburgh, TD8 6PW
T: 01835 840267 E: a-robinson@supanet.com W: theschoolhousebedandbreakfast.com

Indicated Prices:

Single	from £50.00	Twin	from £36.00 per person
Double	from £36.00 per person		

60297

St Boswells
Whitehouse
Open: All year **Map Ref: 2E**

★★★★★
BED AND BREAKFAST

St Boswells, TD6 0ED
T: 01573 460343/07877 800582
E: staying@whitehousecountryhouse.com W: whitehousecountryhouse.com

Indicated Prices:

Single	from £75.00	Twin	from £50.00 per person
Double	from £50.00 per person	D,B&B	from £79.00

640

Scottish Borders: Self Catering

by Melrose, Darnick
Old Dairy
Open: All year **Map Ref: 2D**

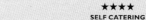

★★★★
SELF CATERING

Darnick, Melrose
T: 01507 606757 E: canham.paul@gmail.com W: olddairymelrose.co.uk

1 Cottage 2 Bedrooms Sleeps 2-4

Prices – Cottage:
£325.00-£475.00 Per Week

Short breaks available

732

Peebles
Kerfield Coach House
Open: All year **Map Ref: 2C**

★★★★
SELF CATERING

Innerleithen Road, Peebles, EH45 8BG
T: 01721 720264 E: ph.kerfield@tiscali.co.uk W: kerfieldcoachhouse.co.uk

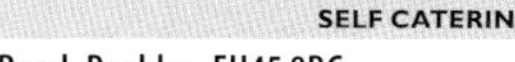

1 House 2 Bedrooms Sleeps 2-4

Prices – House:
£350.00-£500.00 Per Week

Short breaks available

336

PRICES STATED ARE ESTIMATES AND MAY BE SUBJECT TO CHANGE. PRICES ARE PER PERSON PER NIGHT UNLESS OTHERWISE STATED. AWARDS CORRECT AS OF BEGINNING OF OCTOBER 2009

Scottish Borders: EatScotland Gold and Silver establishments

Peebles

Cringletie House Hotel

SILVER

Edinburgh Road,
Peebles,
EH45 8PL
T: 01721 725 750

You are always assured of a warm welcome at Cringletie House. The culinary delights from the skilled kitchen team are enjoyed in the stunning dining room with its hand painted ceiling.

By Biggar

Skirling House

Skirling,
by Biggar,
ML12 6HD
T: 01899 860 274

Specially designed as a country retreat, the sense of style remains at this luxury 5 star Bed & Breakfast Inn, recognised as one of the best places to eat in the South of Scotland.

Eddleston

The Horseshoe Inn

Eddleston,
Peebles,
EH45 8QP
T: 01721 730 225

The growing reputation of the Horseshoe Inn is built around the quality of the food served in both Bardoulet's Restaurant and the Bistro.

Melrose Abbey

EDINBURGH & LOTHIANS

Malmaison Hotel, The Shore, Edinburgh

Welcome to Edinburgh & Lothians

Readers of luxury Condé Nast Traveller magazine have voted Edinburgh their favourite UK city on three occasions. It's an easy city to get around, though with so much on offer, it may take you several visits to fit everything in.

Edinburgh Castle, with its uninterrupted views over the city, is a great place to start. It sits at the top of the Royal Mile, which extends to the Palace of Holyroodhouse and the new Scottish Parliament. You can easily spend a day discovering the Mile's vibrant and quirky mix of shops, visitor attractions, museums, cafés and bistros, many tucked away down narrow closes.

The city fills its year with an impressive diary of events, beginning and ending with Edinburgh's Hogmanay. August is the main festival season when every available space is transformed into a gallery, stage or concert hall.

There's much to enjoy beyond the many charms of Edinburgh's city centre. The historic port of Leith has been transformed in recent years with the arrival of Michelin-starred restaurants, stylish bars and cafés. The area around the city is popular with golfers for its combination of championship courses and less challenging local ones, while a drive along East Lothian's coastline takes in picturesque villages like Aberlady and Gullane as the road leads towards North Berwick and beyond.

01 Linlithgow Palace

02 Museum of Scotland, Edinburgh

03 Whisky tasting at The Scotch Malt Whisky Society, Edinburgh

04 The famous Jenners department store, Princes Street, Edinburgh

05 Tantallon Castle, East Lothian

06 Statue of Robert the Bruce, Edinburgh Castle (Courtesy of Historic Scotland)

Inspired ideas for you to indulge

HISTORIC EDINBURGH
Edinburgh hosts two World Heritage sites: the medieval Old Town and the Georgian New Town. A new House Histories Trail focuses on six buildings, from the early 16th to late 19th centuries, highlighting the stories of those who lived in them. The trail leads you from the Old Town through to the New Town and Dean Village.
ewht.org.uk

GALLERY WALKS
The Scottish National Gallery of Modern Art and the neighbouring Dean Gallery connect with the Water of Leith walkway. It's an ideal and easy stroll from the Dean Gallery past Dean Village and St Bernard's Well towards bohemian Stockbridge with its cafés, craft shops and galleries.
edinburgh.org

INDEPENDENT SHOPPING
Edinburgh excels in small specialist shops in village-like areas around the city. You'll find unusual boutiques and individual retailers in Stafford Street and William Street at the west end of Princes Street. Venture further to Victoria Street (Old Town), Stockbridge and Bruntsfield for even more.
edinburghshopper.com

A NOSE FOR WHISKY
Edinburgh has its own whisky, Glenkinchie, distilled just outside the city at Pencaitland. Tours introduce you to how it is made and how it tastes. The world's largest collection of whiskies is one of the brand-new features at Edinburgh's Scotch Whisky Experience. The new Collection Tour takes you into its vaults to sample two malts from the vast collection.
visiteastlothian.org
scotchwhiskyexperience.co.uk

MARY, QUEEN OF SCOTS
Much of the tragic history of Mary, Queen of Scots took place in the Lothians. A detailed trail lets you trace her story from her birthplace at Linlithgow Palace, to Dunbar, Craigmillar and Tantallon Castles and Newbattle Abbey. The Palace of Holyroodhouse also features in her tale of love, betrayal and murder.
edinburgh.org/queenofscots

ROYAL AND STATELY
Edinburgh has many royal connections: the Royal Yacht *Britannia*, Edinburgh Castle and the Palace of Holyroodhouse among them. The Royal Botanic Garden provides a haven of calm to the north of the city centre. Beyond the city, discover impressive stately homes such as Hopetoun House, a splendid example of Georgian architecture.
visitwestlothian.co.uk
edinburgh.org

01 Valvona & Crolla's VinCaffè, Edinburgh

02 Sparkling wine – just right for any occasion!

03 Stunning city view from The Tower Restaurant, Edinburgh

04 IJ Mellis Cheese Shop, Victoria Street, Edinburgh

05 The Kitchin, Leith, Edinburgh

Savour the real taste of Scotland

DINE WITH A VIEW

The Tower Restaurant not only has a chic interior and a sublime menu but makes the most of its open views of Edinburgh Castle and the Old Town. Floodlit at night, the scene is magical. The Forth Floor Brasserie and Restaurant within Harvey Nichols sees the castle from a different angle.

EatScotland Award

tower-restaurant.com
harveynichols.com

EDINBURGH BRUNCH

Brunch is how Edinburgh likes to begin its weekend. Grab the papers or the day's first coffee before choosing from a stylish selection of sweet and savoury starts to the day. Local favourites include Montpelier's (Bruntsfield), Heller's Kitchen (Newington) and Olive Branch bistros on George IV Bridge and Broughton Street.

montpeliersedinburgh.co.uk
hellerskitchen.co.uk
theolivebranchscotland.co.uk

MARKETS

Edinburgh's Farmers' Market brings the freshest local produce from source to city. It is held every Saturday morning from 9am to 2pm on Castle Terrace against the backdrop of Edinburgh Castle. As well as the best Scotch beef and lamb, you may also find Scottish cheeses, heather honey and whisky-based liqueurs.

edinburghfarmersmarket.com

LEITH STARS

The port of Leith has become a centre for culinary excellence in recent years. First Martin Wishart opened his eponymous restaurant on The Shore and gained a Michelin star. Then Tom Kitchin achieved a star at The Kitchin on Commercial Quay. And most recently a star was awarded to The Plumed Horse on Henderson Street.

plumedhorse.co.uk
martin-wishart.co.uk

EatScotland Gold Award

thekitchin.com

FOODIE SHOPPING

It's always nice to take new or evocative flavours home from a holiday. IJ Mellis specialises in cheeses while Crombie's creates gourmet sausages and haggis. Enjoy a glass of fizz with Old Town views before exploring Valvona and Crolla's specialities in Jenners Food Hall. And for some Scottish preserves or pickles, head to Baxter's at Ocean Terminal.

eatscotland.com

TEA TIME

Tea is becoming the new coffee in Edinburgh as specialist tea-houses open around the city. Eteaket (Hanover Street) serves the best leaf teas with freshly-baked scones. A world of teas is poured from silver teapots into antique cups at Anteaques (Clerk Street). While at Loopy Lorna's (Morningside Road), tea is accompanied by irresistibly fabulous cakes.

eteaket.co.uk
anteaques.co.uk
loopylornas.com

01 Torch-lit Castle esplanade, Edinburgh Military Tattoo

02 The Witchery by the Castle, Edinburgh

03 A Winter Wonderland, Princes Street, Edinburgh

04 The Forth Bridge and Firth of Forth

Something a little bit different

MAID OF THE FORTH

Take a seasonal evening cruise on the Maid of the Forth to see the sun set behind the Forth Bridges. The boat's resident band brings some Dixieland jazz onboard. On calm nights the boat can sail near the Seal Colony where these inquisitive creatures come so close, you can almost touch them.
maidoftheforth.co.uk

BALLOONING OVER EDINBURGH

You see Edinburgh and its surrounding countryside from an amazing angle on a hot air balloon ride. Edinburgh-based Alba Ballooning organises balloon trips near the city, as well as other scenic regions nearby. Baskets are roomy and comfortable so relax and enjoy the wonderful panoramic views.
albaballooning.co.uk

THE WITCHERY BY THE CASTLE

The plain stone exterior cleverly hides the theatrical and decadent interior of The Witchery. Dinner in The Secret Garden, lit only by candles, is rounded off perfectly with an overnight stay in one of the seven lavishly-decorated private suites. Evocative names like The Old Rectory and The Inner Sanctum set the scene even before you check in.
EatScotland Silver Award
thewitchery.com

Time to plan your perfect day

FESTIVAL EDINBURGH

The word 'festival' is synonymous with Edinburgh. Each year brings celebrations of science, cinema, books, jazz, art, music, dance, comedy, theatre, opera and politics. The Castle Esplanade also gets involved as host to the spectacular Edinburgh Military Tattoo. This festival atmosphere extends to Christmas, New Year and even the annual Six Nations rugby matches at Murrayfield.
edinburghfestivals.co.uk

WINTER IN EDINBURGH

Edinburgh really brightens up winter months with its famous Hogmanay celebrations. In the run-up to the festive season, Princes Street Gardens become an open-air ice rink and Christmas street market. Christmas over and the city instantly gears itself up to bring in the New Year. Hotels and restaurants across the city host a relaxing and enjoyable start to your year.
edinburgh.org

EDINBURGH & LOTHIANS

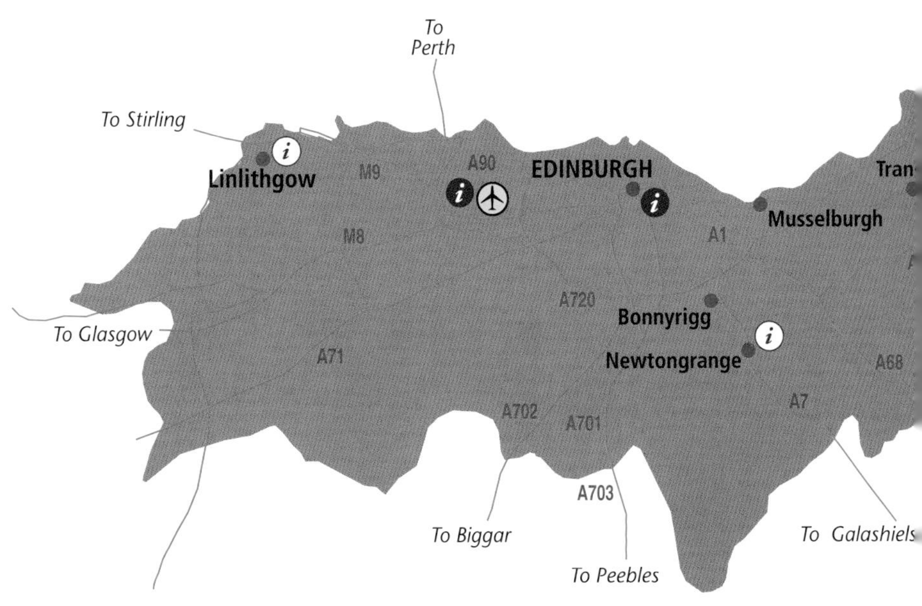

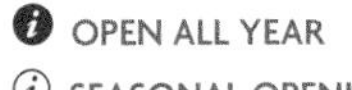

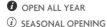

North Berwick
East Linton
A198
Dunbar
A1
Haddington
A1
To Berwick-upon-Tweed

VisitScotland Information Centres

To help you plan and book your trip to Scotland email our travel experts at info@visitscotland.com. When you arrive call into one of our Information Centres where our friendly experts can offer advice on all things local as well as sharing their wider knowledge of Scotland. We don't just advise either. We can sort out your accommodation and all your travel needs, as well as tickets for events across Scotland. So if you're looking to get the most from your visit, there really is only one place to go.

EDINBURGH

Edinburgh	Princes Mall, 3 Princes Street, Edinburgh, EH2 2QP
Edinburgh Airport	Main Concourse, Edinburgh International Airport, EH12 9DN
North Berwick	1 Quality Street, North Berwick, EH39 4HJ

- LOCAL KNOWLEDGE
- WHERE TO STAY
- ACCOMMODATION BOOKING
- PLACES TO VISIT
- THINGS TO DO
- MAPS AND GUIDES
- TRAVEL ADVICE
- ROUTE PLANNING
- WHERE TO SHOP AND EAT
- LOCAL CRAFTS AND PRODUCE
- EVENT INFORMATION
- TICKETS

Edinburgh & Lothians: Hotels

Bonnyrigg

Dalhousie Castle & Spa

Open: All year

Map Ref: 2C

★★★★ HOTEL

Bonnyrigg, Midlothian, EH19 3JB
T: 01875 820183 E: info@dalhousiecastle.co.uk W: dalhousiecastle.co.uk

Indicated Prices:

Single	from £85.00 per room	Twin	from £125.00 per room
Double	from £125.00 per room	Family	from £160.00 per room
		Suite	from £230.00 per room

C V

220

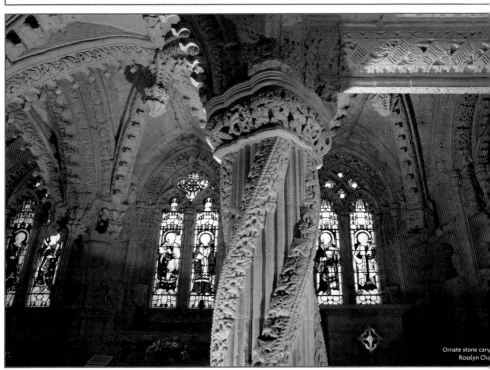

Ornate stone carv
Rosslyn Ch

 PRICES STATED ARE ESTIMATES AND MAY BE SUBJECT TO CHANGE. PRICES ARE PER PERSON PER NIGHT UNLESS OTHERWISE STATED. AWARDS CORRECT AS OF BEGINNING OF OCTOBER 2009

dinburgh

pex Hotels

Open: All year* **Map Ref: 2C5**

★★★ UP TO ★★★★ HOTEL

Apex Waterloo Place
23-27 Waterloo Place, Edinburgh EH1 3BH

Apex International
31-35 Grassmarket, Edinburgh EH1 2HS

Apex City
61 Grassmarket, Edinburgh EH1 2JF

Apex European
90 Haymarket Terrace, Edinburgh EH12 5LQ

T: 0845 365 0000
E: reservations@apexhotels.co.uk
W: apexhotels.co.uk

Features:

- 543 bedrooms across the city
- Yu Spa and Yu Time Leisure
- Award winning restaurants
- Free wi-fi and local calls

*Apex Waterloo & International open all year
Apex City & European closed for Christmas

Indicated Prices:

Double	from £95.00 per room
Twin	from £95.00 per room
Family	from £95.00 per room
Suite	from £195.00 per room

C £ V

65838

:h four Edinburgh hotels ı're spoilt for choice of how to ɔerience the capital of Scotland. ɔose Apex Waterloo Place ɨ be moments from Waverley n station and the shops of ıces Street and George Street. ɔose the central Apex City or ex International and you'll be awarded with views of Edinburgh Castle. Choose the Apex European to be just minutes from the city venues of Lothian Road and a short walk from the roar of Murrayfield.

Edinburgh

Apex International Hotel

Open: All year **Map Ref: 2C**

Located in Edinburgh's historic Grassmarket with stunning views of Edinburgh Castle, the Apex International is a hotel with real contemporary style. All 171 bedrooms are stylish and chic in decor. Heights restaurant with two AA rosettes offers fine dining with classic views. Relax and unwind in Yu Time pool, gym and tropicarium.

★★★★
HOTEL

31-35 Grassmarket, Edinburgh, EH1 2HS
T: 0845 365 0000 E: reservations@apexhotels.co.uk W: apexhotels.co.uk

Indicated Prices:

Double	from £115.00 per room	Twin	from £115.00 per room
		Family	from £115.00 per room

123

Edinburgh

Apex Waterloo Place Hotel

Open: All year **Map Ref: 2C**

The Apex Waterloo Place Hotel offers style, comfort and exceptional service combining contemporary design with innovative amenities. The hotel features 187 luxury bedrooms and suites. Elliot's Bar and Restaurant offers modern Scottish cuisine. Yu Spa is a calm retreat including pool, sauna, steam room and fully equipped gym.

★★★★
HOTEL

23-27 Waterloo Place, Edinburgh, EH1 3BH
T: 0845 365 0000 E: reservations@apexhotels.co.uk W: apexhotels.co.uk

Indicated Prices:

Double	from £125.00 per room	Twin	from £125.00 per room
		Family	from £125.00 per room
		Suite	from £244.00 per room

844

dinburgh

he Balmoral Hotel

Open: All year **Map Ref: 2C5**

★★★★★ GOLD
HOTEL

1 Princes Street, Edinburgh, EH2 2EQ
T: 0131 556 2414 E: reservations.balmoral@roccofortecollection.com W: roccofortecollection.com

Indicated Prices:

Single	from £160.00 per room	Twin	from £175.00 per room
Double	from £175.00 per room	Suite	from £535.00 per room

C £ V

58132

dinburgh

unstane City Hotel

Open: All year **Map Ref: 2C5**

ontemporary, luxury boutique tel situated in Edinburgh's West d. Minutes from Edinburgh siness Centre and city attractions. e 17 bedrooms are stylish and ntemporary offering a choice of ndard and superior rooms. Hotel ers free wi-fi and car parking. Our endly staff are here to help and sure a truly memorable break.

★★★★
TOWN HOUSE HOTEL

5 Hampton Terrace, Haymarket, Edinburgh, EH12 5JD
T: 0131 337 6169 E: reservations@dunstanehotels.co.uk W: dunstanehotels.co.uk

Indicated Prices:

Single	from £95.00 per room	Twin	from £119.00 per room
Double	from £99.00 per room	Suite	from £149.00 per room

C £ V

79350

Edinburgh
Dunstane House Hotel
Open: All year **Map Ref: 2C**

The friendliest hotel in Edinburgh, where you will enjoy country style tranquility of a small castle in a city setting. Located only a 10 minute walk to the city centre with free private parking. Hotel offers free wi-fi and a unique lounge bar and restaurant themed on the Scottish Isles.

★★★★
SMALL HOTEL

4 West Coates, Haymarket, Edinburgh, EH12 5JQ
T: 0131 337 6169 E: reservations@dunstanehotels.co.uk W: dunstanehotels.co.uk

Indicated Prices:

Single	from £85.00 per room	Twin	from £98.00 per room
Double	from £98.00 per room		

C £ V

238

Edinburgh
Fraser Suites Edinburgh
Open: All year **Map Ref: 2C**

AWAITING GRADING

12-26 St Giles Street, Edinburgh, EH1 1PT
T: 0131 221 7200 E: sales.edinburgh@frasershospitality.com W: frasershospitality.com

75 Bedrooms — Sleeps 1-3

Classic Room from £110.00 per room per night
Junior Suites from £140.00 per room per night
One bedroom apartments from £210.00 per room per night
Bespoke Suites from £240.00 per suite per night

Short breaks available

847

Edinburgh
The Glasshouse
Open: All year **Map Ref: 2C**

★★★★★
METRO HOTEL

2 Greenside Place, Edinburgh, EH1 3AA
T: 0131 525 8200 E: resglasshouse@theetoncollection.com W: theetoncollection.com/glasshouse

Indicated Prices:

Double	from £150.00 per room	Family	from £195.00 per room
Twin	from £150.00 per room	Suite	from £195.00 per room

C £ V

590

 PRICES STATED ARE ESTIMATES AND MAY BE SUBJECT TO CHANGE. PRICES ARE PER PERSON PER NIGHT UNLESS OTHERWISE STATED. AWARDS CORRECT AS OF BEGINNING OF OCTOBER 2009

dinburgh

ildonan Lodge Hotel

Open: All year **Map Ref: 2C5**

★★★★
SMALL HOTEL

27 Craigmillar Park, Edinburgh, EH16 5PE
T: 0131 667 2793 E: info@kildonanlodgehotel.co.uk W: kildonanlodgehotel.co.uk

Indicated Prices:

Single	from £69.00 per room	Twin	from £89.00 per room
Double	from £89.00 per room	Family	from £108.00 per room
		Suite	from £138.00 per room

33763

dinburgh

he Scotsman

Open: All year **Map Ref: 2C5**

★★★★★
HOTEL

20 North Bridge, Edinburgh, EH1 1YT
T: 0131 556 5565 E: resscotsman@theetoncollection.com W: theetoncollection.com/scotsman

Indicated Prices:

Single	from £150.00 per room	Twin	from £150.00 per room
Double	from £150.00 per room	Family	from £250.00 per room
		Suite	from £250.00 per room

60321

dinburgh

heraton Grand Hotel and Spa

Open: All year **Map Ref: 2C5**

the Sheraton Grand Hotel & ›a, you know you've arrived mewhere special. From the nuine warmth of the welcome the soothing sanctuary of our oms, we look to relax and reward equal measure. With restaurants r every occasion, lounges for inks and conversation and an spirational spa, the Sheraton and is a place to feel connected.

★★★★★
HOTEL

1 Festival Square, Edinburgh, EH3 9SR
T: 0131 229 9131 E: grandedinburgh.sheraton@sheraton.com W: sheratonedinburgh.co.uk

Indicated Prices:

Single	from £109.00 per room	Twin	from £119.00 per room
Double	from £119.00 per room	Suite	from £224.00 per room

54420

Edinburgh
Tigerlily

Open: All year excl 24-25 Dec **Map Ref: 2C**

★★★★
HOTEL

125 George Street, Edinburgh, EH2 4JN
T: 0131 225 5005 E: info@tigerlilyedinburgh.co.uk W: tigerlilyedinburgh.co.uk

Indicated Prices:

Double	from £120.00 per room	Mini Suite	from £150.00 per room
Twin	from £120.00 per room	Suite	from £225.00 per room

TV C £ V

714

Edinburgh & Lothians: Guest Houses and B&Bs

East Linton
Crauchie Farmhouse

Open: All year excl Xmas & New Year **Map Ref: 2D**

★★★★
BED AND BREAKFAST

Crauchie, East Linton, East Lothian, EH40 3EB
T: 01620 860124 E: crauchiefarmhouse@supanet.com W: crauchiefarmhouse.co.uk

Indicated Prices:

Single	from £45.00 per room	Twin	from £65.00 per room
Double	from £65.00 per room		

TV P C V

687

 PRICES STATED ARE ESTIMATES AND MAY BE SUBJECT TO CHANGE. PRICES ARE PER PERSON PER NIGHT UNLESS OTHERWISE STATED. AWARDS CORRECT AS OF BEGINNING OF OCTOBER 2009

dinburgh

aron Lodge

Open: All year **Map Ref: 2C5**

★★★★
GUEST HOUSE

**128 Old Dalkeith Road,
Edinburgh, EH16 4SD
T: 0131 664 2755
E: dot@baigan.freeserve.co.uk
W: aaronlodgeedinburgh.co.uk**

Features:

- All rooms decorated to very high standard
- Rooms have LCD TV's with Sky Sports 1, 2 and 3
- Dine in our new conservatory restaurant
- Wi-fi access available
- Closest guest house to new Royal Infirmary

'on Lodge is a luxurious 4 r guest house situated on the ıth side of Edinburgh, ideally ated to make the most of the /'s many attractions. Aaron dge neighbours world famous ractions such as Rosslyn apel and the Museum of Flight. ı minutes from the centre of Edinburgh, guests are on the doorstep of an eclectic mix of historic, beautiful and entertaining attractions such as Edinburgh Castle and the Royal Yacht *Britannia*. At Aaron Lodge, what you see is what you get!

Indicated Prices:

Single	from £40.00 per room
Double	from £30.00 per person
Twin	from £30.00 per person
Family	from £30.00 per person

34321

Edinburgh

Bield Bed and Breakfast

Open: All year **Map Ref: 2C**

BED AND BREAKFAST

3 Orchard Brae West, Edinburgh, EH4 2EW
E: bieldltd@hotmail.com W: bieldbedandbreakfast.com

Indicated Prices:

Single	from £50.00 per person	Twin	from £30.00 per person
Double	from £30.00 per person		

150

Edinburgh

Doris Crook Bed and Breakfast

Open: All year **Map Ref: 2C**

★★★★
BED AND BREAKFAST

2 Seton Place, Edinburgh, EH9 2JT
T: 0131 667 6430 E: mail@dcrook.co.uk W: dcrook.co.uk

Indicated Prices:

Double	from £56.00 per room	Twin	from £56.00 per room

429

Edinburgh

Gifford House

Open: All year excl Xmas & New Year **Map Ref: 2C**

Gifford House is an elegant Victorian house with a warm and friendly atmosphere. It is a leisurely 20 minute walk to the Royal Mile and many tourist attractions. Also close to Edinburgh University. Uniquely stylish bedrooms and bathrooms individually designed. An ideal base for business or pleasure. Delicious breakfast choice.

★★★★
GUEST HOUSE

103 Dalkeith Road, Edinburgh, EH16 5AJ
T: 0131 667 4688 E: giffordhouse@btinternet.com W: giffordhouseedinburgh.com

Indicated Prices:

Single	from £55.00	Twin	from £35.00 per person
Double	from £35.00 per person	Family	from £30.00 per person

276

 PRICES STATED ARE ESTIMATES AND MAY BE SUBJECT TO CHANGE. PRICES ARE PER PERSON PER NIGHT UNLESS OTHERWISE STATED. AWARDS CORRECT AS OF BEGINNING OF OCTOBER 2009

linburgh

ldun Guest House

Open: All year **Map Ref: 2C5**

GUEST HOUSE

9 Spence Street, Edinburgh, EH16 5AG
T: 0131 667 1368 E: gildun.edin@btinternet.com W: gildun.co.uk

Indicated Prices:

Single	from £35.00 per room	Twin	from £70.00 per room
Double	from £70.00 per room	Family	from £97.50 per room

27612

linburgh

enalmond House

Open: All year excl 24-25 Dec **Map Ref: 2C5**

:urious accommodation in
ached Victorian house just over
ile from the main tourist
ractions and centre of Edinburgh.
e private car parking and wi-fi.
und floor rooms available.
uxe rooms with Queen Anne
r-poster and Rococco beds.
ensive breakfast menu with
litional Scottish and vegetarian
ions. Outdoor patio area.

★★★★
GUEST HOUSE

25 Mayfield Gardens, Edinburgh, EH9 2BX
T: 0131 668 2392 E: enquiries@glenalmondhouse.com W: www.glenalmondhouse.com

Indicated Prices:

Single	from £50.00 per room	Twin	from £65.00 per room
Double	from £65.00 per room	Family	from £80.00 per room

80429

linburgh

ingsburgh House

Open: All year **Map Ref: 2C5**

★★★★★ GOLD
GUEST HOUSE

2 Corstorphine Road, Edinburgh, EH12 6HN
T: 0131 313 1679 E: sales@thekingsburgh.co.uk W: thekingsburgh.co.uk

Indicated Prices:

Double	from £120.00 per room	Twin	from £120.00 per room
		Suite	from £150.00 per room

79234

Edinburgh

The Town House

Open: All year

Map Ref: 2C

The Town House is located in central Edinburgh just a few minutes walk from Edinburgh's International Conference Centre (EICC). All city centre historical attractions are easily accessible on foot with Edinburgh Castle a pleasant fifteen minute walk through the Old Town. The house is fully wi-fi enabled.

★★★★ GOLD
GUEST HOUSE

65 Gilmore Place, Edinburgh, EH3 9NU
T: 0131 229 1985 E: susan@thetownhouse.com W: thetownhouse.com

Indicated Prices:

Single	from £45.00 per person	Twin	from £45.00 per person
Double	from £45.00 per person		

606

Edinburgh C

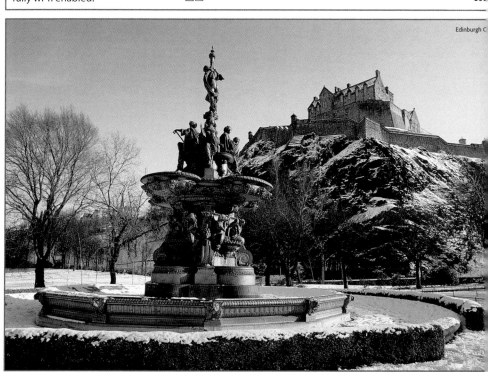

 PRICES STATED ARE ESTIMATES AND MAY BE SUBJECT TO CHANGE. PRICES ARE PER PERSON PER NIGHT UNLESS OTHERWISE STATED. AWARDS CORRECT AS OF BEGINNING OF OCTOBER 2009

Edinburgh & Lothians: Self Catering

dinburgh
andlemaker Row

Open: All year **Map Ref: 2C5**

★★★★
SELF CATERING

48/1 Candlemaker Row, Edinburgh, EH1 2QE
T: 0131 538 0352 E: juliewatt630@gmail.com W: edinburghselfcatering.webeden.co.uk

1 Apartment 1 Bedroom Sleeps 2

Prices – Apartment:
£290.00-£370.00 Per Week

Short breaks available

17886

dinburgh
5 Cumberland Street

Open: All year **Map Ref: 2C4**

★★★★★
SELF CATERING

Margaret Kingan, Blairshinnoch, Kirkgunzean, Dumfries, DG2 8JJ
T: 01387 760230 E: info@45cumberlandstreet.co.uk W: 45cumberlandstreet.co.uk

1 Apartment 2 Bedrooms Sleeps 1-3

Prices – Apartment:
£70.00-£140.00 Per Night

Short breaks available

15425

Edinburgh

EdinburghFlats

Open: All year **Map Ref: 2C**

Beautifully renovated superbly furnished apartments in Georgian townhouses only metres from central Princes Street. Period elegance with hi-tech specifications (plasma TVs, integrated sound systems, wireless internet). Combining hotel facilities with home comforts. 24 hour on-call service.

★★★ UP TO ★★★★★
SELF CATERING

27 Queen Street, Edinburgh, EH2 1JX
T: 07973 345559 E: info@edinburghflats.co.uk W: edinburghflats.co.uk

3 Apartments 1-2 Bedrooms Sleeps 1-

Prices – Apartment:
£300.00-£1250.00 Per Week

Short breaks available

10

Edinburgh

Fairnington Premier Properties

Open: All year **Map Ref: 2C**

Superb apartments viewing Holyrood Park with access to pool and leisure centre. Five minutes Royal Mile. Plus luxury villa in exclusive area with panoramic views of city and castle. Double garage, electronic doors.

★★★ UP TO ★★★★
SELF CATERING

Office 152, Dalkeith Road, Edinburgh, EH16 5DX
T: 01890 820590/0131 667 7161 E: muriel@fairnington.com W: www.fairnington.com

1 House 4 Bedrooms Sleeps 10-1
3 Apartments 6 Bedrooms Sleeps 1

Prices – House: £800.00-£2100.00 Per Week
Prices – Apartment: £320.00-£900.00 Per Week

Short breaks available

255

ıinburgh

ıradise Penthouse

Open: All year **Map Ref: 2C5**

ıtastic architect designed five
r penthouse in heart of historic
ı Town, near the Castle, Princes
eet and all major attractions.
ıoramic views of Arthur's Seat.
nished and equipped to the
hest standards. Free wi-fi.
cure entryphone and lift access.
xury welcome hamper on arrival.
ctly no smoking or pets.
ekly discounts available.

★★★★★
SELF CATERING

Paradise Penthouse, 19/10 Old Fishmarket Close, Royal Mile, Edinburgh, EH1 1RW
T: 0191 384 3904 E: info@heavenlyholidayhomes.co.uk W: heavenlyholidayhomes.co.uk

1 Apartment | 2 Bedrooms | Sleeps 4+2

Prices – Apartment:
£135.00-£270.00 Per Night

73772

orth Berwick

shermen's Hall

Open: All year **Map Ref: 2D4**

★★★★
SELF CATERING

32 Victoria Road, North Berwick, EH39 4JL
T: 0131 331 3878 E: boggon@lineone.net W: fishermenshall.com

1 House | 4 Bedrooms | Sleeps 6-8

Prices – House:
£550.00-£850.00 Per Week

Short breaks available

58142

ranent

ı'side Castle

Open: All year **Map Ref: 2D5**

★★★★
SELF CATERING

Tranent, EH33 2LE
T: 0131 665 7654 E: enquiry@faside-estate.com W: faside-estate.com

2 Units | 2 Bedrooms | Sleeps 4

Prices – Unit:
£525.00-£945.00 Per Week

81153

Edinburgh & Lothians: Food & Drink

Edinburgh

Stac Polly Restaurant

Open: All year

Map Ref: 2(

Exciting interpretations of modern and traditional Scottish cuisine sourcing quality local produce. Tastefully and beautifully decorated restaurants with friendly and professional service to match. Aberdeen Angus beef, fish and game. Private dining spaces, outdoor dining area. Open seven days. Now in its 21st year.

Culinary Type:
SCOTTISH

29 Dublin Street, Edinburgh
Also at Grindlay Street (0131 229 5405) and St Mary's Street (0131 557 5754)

T: 0131 556 2231
E: bookings@stacpolly.com
W: stacpolly.com

Best For:
- Kids and Families • Romantic Meals
- Special Occasion • Outdoor dining
- Group dining

Prices:

Starter from:	£6.
Main Course from:	£16.
Dessert from:	£6.

Opening Times:
Lunch from 1200-1400
Dinner from 1800-2130

56

 PRICES STATED ARE ESTIMATES AND MAY BE SUBJECT TO CHANGE. PRICES ARE PER PERSON PER NIGHT UNLESS OTHERWISE STATED. AWARDS CORRECT AS OF BEGINNING OF OCTOBER 2009

Edinburgh & Lothians: EatScotland Gold and Silver establishments

Edinburgh
21212 (Restaurant)

3 Royal Terrace,
Edinburgh,
EH7 5AB
T: 0845 22 21212

21212 is a luxury fine dining restaurant with Michelin Starred chef Paul Kitching at the helm of the adventurous menu. The grand public rooms of this restaurant have been transferred into a stylish modern venue.

Edinburgh
Atrium

10 Cambridge Street,
Edinburgh,
EH1 2ED
T: 0131 228 8882

The Atrium is a well established landmark on the gourmet dining circuit in Edinburgh. Their philosophy is simple: quality produce handled lightly, cooked precisely and presented with minimum fuss.

Edinburgh
Forth Floor Brasserie & Bar, Harvey Nichols

Forth Floor Brasserie & Bar,
30-34 St Andrews Square,
Edinburgh, EH2 2AD
T: 0131 524 8350

The Forth Floor Brasserie & Bar offer the best in contemporary eating & drinking in Edinburgh's most stunning modern dining room. Fine Scottish produce is used to create dishes that match modern flavours with classical techniques.

Edinburgh
Forth Floor Restaurant, Harvey Nichols

30-34 St Andrew Square,
Edinburgh,
EH2 2AD
T: 0131 524 8350

As well as delicious food this restaurant offers truly spectacular views of the Castle, Edinburgh rooftops and the Firth of Forth, through the floor to ceiling windows. The best in Scottish produce is sourced to offer innovative modern Scottish food.

Edinburgh
Hadrian's

Balmoral Hotel,
1 Princes Street,
Edinburgh, EH2 2EQ
T: 0131 557 6727

Hadrian's is The Balmoral's chic and buzzy brasserie. The restaurant is a real favourite with Edinburgh locals who enjoy the informal ambience and delicious cuisine, with consistent service.

Edinburgh
La Garrigue

31 Jeffrey Street,
Edinburgh,
EH1 1DH
T: 0131 557 3032

La Garrigue is a family run restaurant specialising in Languedoc cuisine from South West France, and has 2 AA Rosettes. Chef/Patron Jean-Michel Gauffre presents classic Provencal dishes with loving care.

Edinburgh
Mussel Inn

61-65 Rose Street,
Edinburgh,
EH2 2NH
T: 0131 225 5979

Situated on Rose Street in the centre of Edinburgh, Mussel Inn is one of the city's premier destinations for fresh seafood. And for good reason!

Edinburgh
Mya Restaurant

SILVER

92 Commercial Street,
Edinburgh,
EH6 6LX
T: 0131 554 4000

This is the first restaurant of its kind in Scotland. An eating house that brings together the exciting flavours of two countries, Thailand and India, under one roof.

Edinburgh
Number One Restaurant, Balmoral Hotel

GOLD

1 Princes Street,
Edinburgh,
EH2 2EQ
T: 0131 557 6727

For a memorable culinary experience visit Number One Restaurant where Jeff Bland, Executive Chef, is dedicated to promoting the best of Scotland's natural larder.

Edinburgh
Restaurant at the Rutland Hotel

SILVER

1-3 Rutland Street,
Edinburgh,
EH1 2AE
T: 0131 229 3402

Sumptuous yet contemporary surroundings, accompanied by ambient music, complements the menu created by head chef David Haetzman and his team.

Edinburgh
Restaurant Martin Wishart

GOLD

54 The Shore,
Edinburgh,
EH6 6RA
T: 0131 553 3557

Combining a calm and welcoming ambience with superb modern French cuisine, and using the freshest ingredients sourced throughout Scotland, this restaurant epitomises excellence in modern Scottish cooking.

Edinburgh
Rhubarb at Prestonfield House

SILVER

Prestonfield House,
Prestonfield Road,
Edinburgh, EH16 5UT
T: 0131 225 0976

Rhubarb is decorated and furnished in a rich, sumptuous style, with a profusion of candles. It serves only high quality, fresh ingredients, handled with skill and delicacy

Bonnyrigg
The Dungeon Restaurant

SILVER

Dalhousie Castle & Spa,
Cockpen Road,
Bonnyrigg, EH19 3JB
T: 01875 820 153

The ancient barrel-vaulted dungeons at Dalhousie Castle provide an unusual setting to enjoy the fine, traditional Scottish and classical French castle cuisine, from fresh local produce.

Edinburgh
The Kitchin

78 Commercial Quay,
Edinburgh,
EH6 6LX
T: 0131 555 1755

Awarded a Michelin star in January 2007, just six months after opening, The Kitchin consistently offers seasonal menus using local produce.

Edinburgh

The Stockbridge Restaurant

54 St Stephen Street,
Edinburgh,
EH3 5AL
T: 0131 226 6766

This restaurant serves excellent food in opulent and comfortable surroundings. The service is friendly and attentive yet relaxed, allowing diners to spend time enjoying the cuisine.

Edinburgh

The Witchery by the Castle

Castlehill, The Royal Mile,
Edinburgh,
EH1 2NF
T: 0131 225 5613

At the Witchery the cuisine is consistently good and served with skill, using high quality fresh ingredients. The ambience and location are unique and lend much to the eating experience.

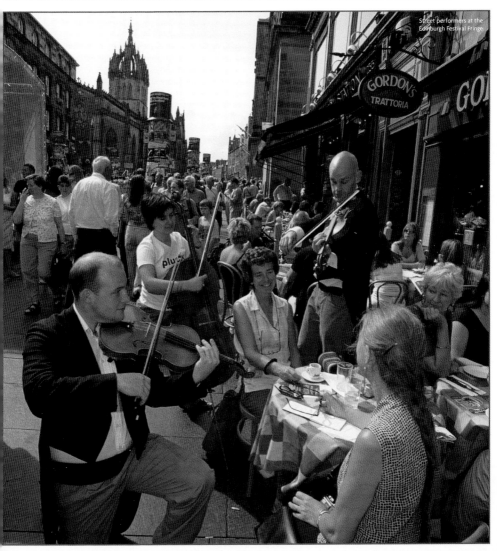

Street performers at the Edinburgh Festival Fringe

GREATER GLASGOW, CLYDE VALLEY & LOCH LOMOND

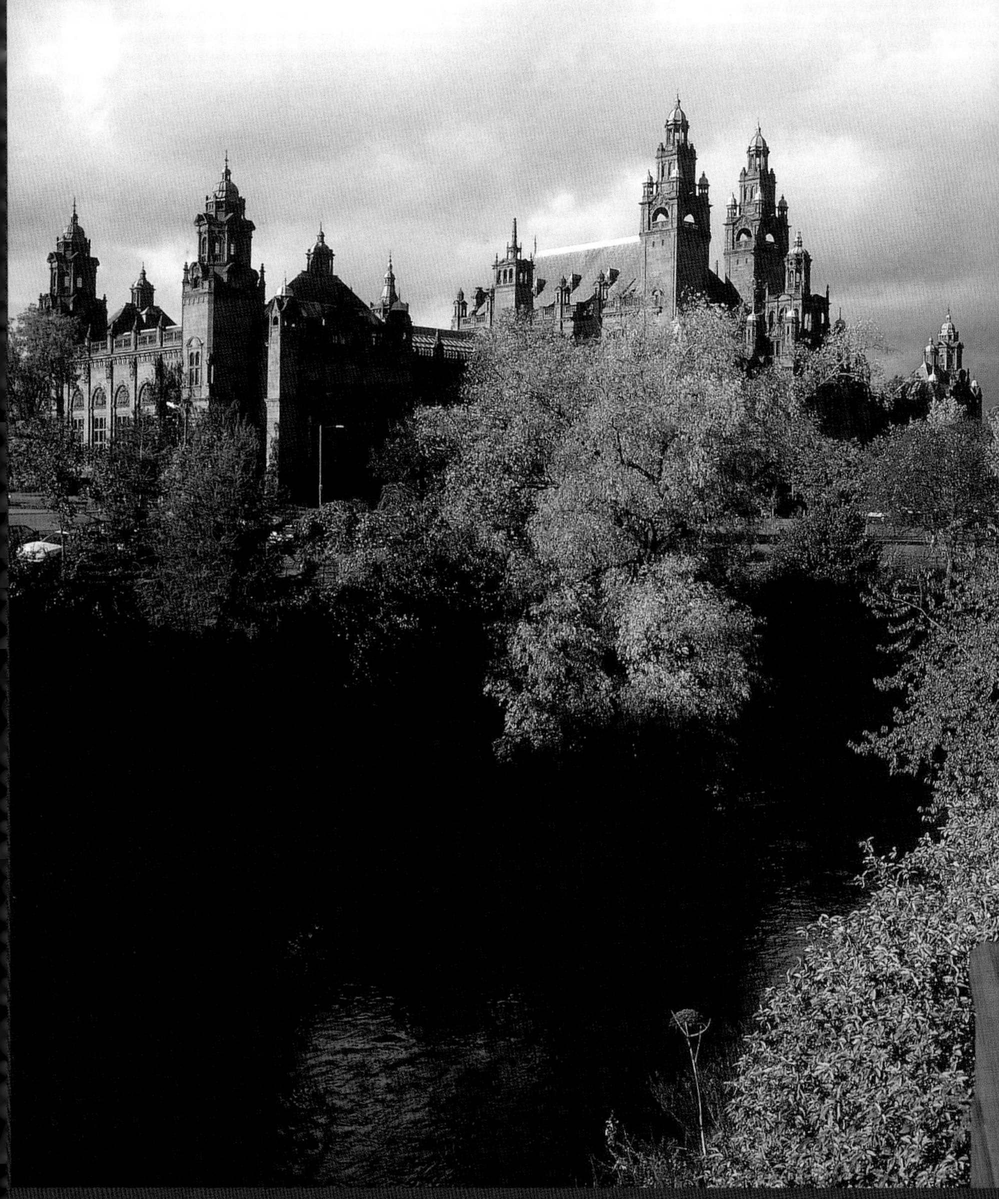

Kelvingrove Art Gallery and Museum, Glasgow

Welcome to Greater Glasgow, Clyde Valley & Loch Lomond

Glasgow is a city which proudly displays its heritage and embraces its future. Dubbed 'Scotland with style', Scotland's largest city offers a winning combination of exclusive shopping, top hotels, stylish bars and restaurants and lush open green spaces.

The River Clyde brought Glasgow much of its wealth through shipbuilding and trading routes around the world. Nowadays culture and arts draw visitors from far and near. The unmistakeable influence of Glasgow-born architect and designer, Charles Rennie Mackintosh, is evident throughout the city.

Art lovers should also head to Kelvingrove Art Gallery and Museum, home to Europe's largest civic collection, and the central Gallery of Modern Art. The Burrell Collection within Pollok Country Park houses more than 9,000 works of world art amassed by merchant collector, Sir William Burrell.

Just outside the city you'll find a wildlife reserve at the Falls of Clyde and a distillery at Glengoyne. The beautifully-restored cotton mill village at New Lanark World Heritage Site offers an insight to a bygone era. Within an hour you can reach the bonnie banks of stunning Loch Lomond, the UK's largest expanse of water, set within Scotland's first-ever National Park.

01 House for an Art Lover, Bellahouston Park, Glasgow

02 The Merchant City, Glasgow

03 Retail therapy – Glasgow style!

04 Sunset at Loch Lomond

Inspired ideas for you to indulge

THE MERCHANT CITY

This former playground of Glasgow's wealthy 18th century tobacco lairds now houses designer names like Mulberry, Armani and Versace. The area's cool credentials are further enhanced with stylish bars and restaurants. Join Glasgow's café culture for a spot of people-watching over lunch at terrace tables.

merchantcityglasgow.com

HOUSE FOR AN ART LOVER

House for an Art Lover took its inspiration from a 1901 portfolio of Mackintosh drawings. It's a timeless masterpiece, testament to the vision and skill of Glasgow's most influential architect. The pure white music room or the iconic high-back chairs may even inspire you to take some ideas home.

houseforanartlover.co.uk

GREENBANK GARDEN, CLARKSON

The garden at Greenbank House inspires and educates visitors on what and how to grow a wide range of more unusual plants. Look out for the huge collection of Narcissus, currently 447 different named forms, and the national collection of 108 named Bergenia.

nts.org.uk

THIS NEW LANARK WORLD HERITAGE SITE

This beautifully restored 18th century cotton mill village is an oasis of tranquillity in a breathtaking setting. Discover the award-winning visitor centre which brings this village's fascinating history back to life. Afterwards take a walk along the river and witness the mighty Falls of Clyde, the largest of which is the Corra Linn at 28 metres.

newlanark.org

LOCH LOMOND

Loch Lomond is the largest body of freshwater in Britain so where do you begin? Loch Lomond Shores at Balloch is a great starting point to find your bearings and admire the loch view over lunch. You can then follow one of the woodland trails or take a loch cruise.

lochlomondshores.com

GLASGOW NECROPOLIS

This Victorian garden cemetery overlooking the city was built when Glasgow was the second city of the empire. Perched on a hill near Glasgow Cathedral, the Necropolis features monuments designed by world-renowned Glasgow architects Alexander 'Greek' Thomson and Charles Rennie Mackintosh.

glasgownecropolis.org

01 Ashton Lane, West End, Glasgow

02 Drinks at The Corinthian, Merchant City, Glasgow

03 Princes Square, Glasgow

04 Ubiquitous Chip, Ashton Lane, Glasgow

01

03

Savour the real taste of Scotland

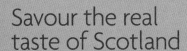

UBIQUITOUS CHIP
Tucked down Ashton Lane, the Ubiquitous Chip is a Glasgow favourite with its cobblestones, greenery and fresh Scottish produce. Book the restaurant for dishes such as Orkney salmon, west coast langoustines and The Chip's own venison haggis. Or tuck into Loch Etive mussels in the brasserie or stovies in the bar.
ubiquitouschip.co.uk

MICHAEL CAINES @ ABODE
Striking design and historic features are the perfect backdrop for Michael Caines Restaurant at Abode Glasgow on Bath Street. The cuisine is modern and the service relaxed and efficient. The team of chefs makes full use of Scotland's seasonal larder. The 'Amazing Grazing' lunch menu is particularly popular.
michaelcaines.com

AFTERNOON TEA IN PRINCES SQUARE
Take the glass elevator to the second level of Princes Square for a Scottish tradition with a designer twist. Cranachan and neighbour Fifi and Ally both offer stylish afternoon teas for two, with or without a glass of fizz. Cranachan adds some extra Scottish notes with macaroons and clootie dumpling.
cranachancafe.co.uk
fifiandally.com

BRIAN MAULE AT CHARDON D'OR
There are several ways to enjoy Brian Maule's clever take on classic dishes. As well as lunch and dinner menus, you can book one of his year-round dinner and show packages. You can also enjoy one of Brian's regular morning cookery demonstrations followed by lunch in his West Regent Street restaurant.
brianmaule.com

COLQUHOUN'S ON LOCH LOMOND
Located within the Lodge on Loch Lomond in the village of Luss, Colquhoun's Restaurant serves up breathtaking views of the loch with a blend of traditional and contemporary cuisine. In summer you can dine on the balconied terrace as the waters of the loch lap the shoreline below.
loch-lomond.co.uk

04

02

Something a little bit different

LOCH LOMOND SEAPLANES

Enjoy spectacular views of Glasgow and the west coast from the lofty perspective of a seaplane. The 45-minute flight takes off along the River Clyde in the heart of the city then soars above castles, islands, mountains and lochs below. The UK's only commercial seaplane tour service is a 'must do' in any luxury itinerary.
lochlomondseaplanes.com

GLENGOYNE DISTILLERY

Different areas of Scotland produce different types of whisky: some sweet, some salty, some peaty. Near Glasgow at Dumgoyne you'll discover the subtle malt produced at Glengoyne Distillery, one of the most beautiful in Scotland. You can blend your own whisky on a Master Blender session or enjoy a cask tasting tour.
glengoyne.com

THE COOKERY SCHOOL AT PECKHAM'S

Whether you're a beginner or an experienced cook, there's always something new to learn. The Cookery School on Glassford Street lets you work with top chefs. One-day courses range from seafood to classic Scottish dishes. Alternatively you can brush up your culinary skills for dinner parties or even Christmas.
thecookeryschool.org

LOCH LOMOND CHAMPAGNE CRUISE

You really appreciate the sheer expanse of Loch Lomond when you're right in the middle of it. Take in the scene over a glass of champagne aboard Cameron House's luxury private motor yacht. After your 90-minute cruise you can indulge in a spa treatment at the five-star hotel or play its impressive Carrick golf course.
devere.co.uk

01 The Still Room, Glengoyne Distillery

02 Scottish Country dancing – perfectly synchronised!

03 Sea plane, River Clyde, Glasgow

04 Aerial view of Loch Lomond

05 The art of fine cuisine

Time to plan your perfect day

GLASGOW FILM FESTIVAL
18 – 28 February 2010

The Glasgow Film Festival seeks out the best in world cinema for its enthusiastic audiences. It is also committed to supporting Scottish talent. From features to shorts and work in all genres, the festival gives you an opportunity to see outstanding films you won't find at your local multiplex.
glasgowfilmfestival.org.uk

GLASGOW ART FAIR
25 – 28 March 2010

Artists from across Scotland, the UK and overseas descend annually on George Square for Scotland's national art fair. The Glasgow Art Fair features a huge selection of galleries showing their work, from well-known international names to emerging talent. Just the place to pick up a local masterpiece.
glasgowartfair.com

LOCH LOMOND HIGHLAND GAMES
17 July 2010

It doesn't really get more Scottish than Highland Games next to a loch. Head for Balloch Park at the southern end of Loch Lomond to see traditional events like tossing the caber and throwing the hammer. Loch Lomond Highland Games are ranked amongst Scotland's top three and are the only Highland Games to host a triathlon.
llhgb.com

PIPING LIVE! AND WORLD PIPE BAND CHAMPIONSHIPS
9 – 15 August 2010

Glasgow becomes the centre of the piping world for one week every August. Venues across the city, from Glasgow Royal Concert Hall to the Renfrew Ferry, provide the stage for piping concerts, street performances, masterclasses and ceilidhs. On Saturday 14 August, Glasgow Green is host to more than 200 bands for the highly-competitive World Pipe Band Championships.
pipingfestival.co.uk
theworlds.co.uk

02

GREATER GLASGOW, CLYDE VALLEY & LOCH LOMOND

To Fort William
A82
Arrochar
Tarbet
Loch Lomond
A814
Luss
A82
Loch Lomond and The Trossachs National Park
Drymen
Gartocharn
A814
Arden
A811
Helensburgh
A818
Balloch
Cove
Alexandria
Gourock
Cardross
Dunoon
Dumbarton
A809
A803
Firth of Clyde
A78
A8
M8
A82
M80
Wemyss Bay
A761
GLASGOW
M73
M8
Rothesay
A78
A737
Paisley
A749
M74
Lochwinnoch
A726
A725
M77
A723
A726
To Ardrossan
To Kilmarnock
A71
To Kilmarnock

OPEN ALL YEAR
SEASONAL OPENING

VisitScotland Information Centres

To help you plan and book your trip to Scotland email our travel experts at info@visitscotland.com. When you arrive call into one of our Information Centres where our friendly experts can offer advice on all things local as well as sharing their wider knowledge of Scotland. We don't just advise either. We can sort out your accommodation and all your travel needs, as well as tickets for events across Scotland. So if you're looking to get the most from your visit, there really is only one place to go.

GLASGOW	
Abington	Welcome Breaks Services, Junction 13, M74 Abington, ML12 6RG
Glasgow	11 George Square, Glasgow, G2 1DY
Glasgow Airport	International Arrivals Hall, Glasgow International Airport, PA3 2ST
Lanark	Horsemarket, Ladyacre Road, Lanark, ML11 7Ql
Paisley	9A Gilmour Street, Paisley, PA1 1DD
LOCH LOMOND	
Balloch	The Old Station Building, Balloch, G83 8LQ

- LOCAL KNOWLEDGE
- WHERE TO STAY
- ACCOMMODATION BOOKING
- PLACES TO VISIT
- THINGS TO DO
- MAPS AND GUIDES
- TRAVEL ADVICE
- ROUTE PLANNING
- WHERE TO SHOP AND EAT
- LOCAL CRAFTS AND PRODUCE
- EVENT INFORMATION
- TICKETS

Greater Glasgow, Clyde Valley & Loch Lomond: Hotels

Cove

Knockderry House Hotel

Open: All year excl 21-26 Dec **Map Ref: 1F**

★★★★
COUNTRY HOUSE HOTEL

Shore Road, Cove, G84 0NX
T: 01436 842283 E: info@knockderryhouse.co.uk W: knockderryhouse.co.uk

Indicated Prices:

Single	from £85.00 per room	Family	from £165.00 per room
Double	from £120.00 per room	Suite	from £155.00 per room

344

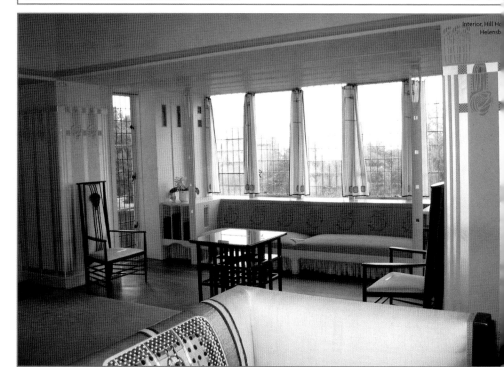

Interior, Hill House, Helensburgh

 PRICES STATED ARE ESTIMATES AND MAY BE SUBJECT TO CHANGE. PRICES ARE PER PERSON PER NIGHT UNLESS OTHERWISE STATED. AWARDS CORRECT AS OF BEGINNING OF OCTOBER 2009

lasgow

ilton Glasgow

Open: All year **Map Ref: 1H5**

★★★★★ HOTEL

1 William Street,
Glasgow, G3 8HT
T: 0141 204 5555
E: reservations.glasgow@hilton.com
W: hilton.co.uk/glasgow

Features:

- Convenient location for shopping and museums
- Executive suites and lounge
- Fine dining at Cameron's restaurant
- Lounge bar and Champagne Bar
- Leisure facilities including 15 metre pool
- Ample secure parking

Indicated Prices:

Single	from £69.00 per room
Double	from £69.00 per room
Twin	from £69.00 per room
Family	from £89.00 per room
Executive	from £119.00 per room
Suite	from £269.00 per room

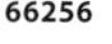

66256

:on Glasgow is within easy reach ;lasgow's shopping district, galleries and museums. The :el offers Hilton Rooms, Hilton ·cutive Rooms and Suites. ests in Executive Rooms and tes have access to the Executive ınge. Dine in style at Camerons taurant, serving quality produce with a Scottish flavour or enjoy international cuisine from our carvery in Minsky's Brasserie. Get fit in the 15-metre pool and fitness centre or indulge yourself with a treatment from The Ocean Rooms Spa.

Glasgow
Thistle Glasgow
Open: All year **Map Ref: 1H**

Situated in the heart of the city, Thistle Glasgow is a prime destination for both business and leisure guests. Our Otium Health and Leisure Club has all you need to relax and unwind after a busy day. Then enjoy dinner in our restaurant, Annlann and a drink in our bar.

★★★★ HOTEL

36 Cambridge Street, Glasgow, G2 3HN
T: 0871 376 9043 E: reservations.glasgow@thistle.co.uk W: thistle.com/glasgow

Indicated Prices:

Single	from £60.00 per room	Twin	from £70.00 per room
Double	from £70.00 per room	Family	from £90.00 per room
		Suite	from £170.00 per room

Upgrades available from £20.00 per room

 278

Luss
The Inn at Inverbeg
Open: All year **Map Ref: 1G**

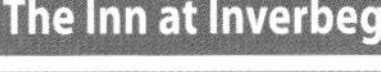

★★★★ INN

Luss, Loch Lomond, G83 8PD
T: 01436 860678 E: inverbeg.reception@loch-lomond.co.uk W: innatinverbeg.co.uk

Indicated Prices:

Single	from £69.00 per room	Family	from £119.00 per room
Double	from £79.00 per room		

794

Luss
Lodge on Loch Lomond Hotel
Open: All year **Map Ref: 1G**

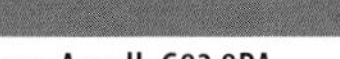

★★★★ HOTEL

Luss, Argyll, G83 8PA
T: 01436 860201 E: res@loch-lomond.co.uk W: loch-lomond.co.uk

Indicated Prices:

Single	from £89.00 per room	Family	from £129.00 per room
Double	from £99.00 per room	Suite	from £169.00 per room

 362

Greater Glasgow, Clyde Valley & Loch Lomond: Guest Houses and B&Bs

rrochar

urnbrae B&B

Open: All year excl Xmas **Map Ref: 1G3**

★★★★
BED AND BREAKFAST

Shore Road, Arrochar, G83 7AG
T: 01301 702988 E: janice.mathieson1@btopenworld.com W: www.scotland2000.com/burnbrae

Indicated Prices:

Single	from £65.00 per room	Twin	from £70.00 per room
Double	from £70.00 per room		

16902

ardross

en Rhydding

Open: All year **Map Ref: 1G4**

BED AND BREAKFAST

3 Ritchie Avenue, Cardross, Argyll & Bute, G82 5LL
T: 01389 841659 E: benrhydding@hotmail.co.uk W: benrhyddingbandb.co.uk

Indicated Prices:

Single	from £35.00 per person	Family	from £27.00 per person
Double	from £32.00 per person		

69928

artocharn

he Old School House

Open: All year **Map Ref: 1G4**

★★★★
BED AND BREAKFAST

Gartocharn, G83 8SB
T: 01389 830373/07739 463014 E: reservations@the-old-school-house.co.uk W: the-old-school-house.co.uk

Indicated Prices:

Single	from £37.00 per person	Twin	from £37.00 per person
Double	from £37.00 per person		

59909

Greater Glasgow, Clyde Valley & Loch Lomond: Self Catering

Arden

The Gardeners Cottages

Open: All year **Map Ref: 1G**

★★★★ SELF CATERING

Arden House Estate, Arden, Argyll & Bute, G83 8RD

T: 01389 850601 E: amacleod@gardeners-cottages.com W: gardeners-cottages.com

3 Cottages 1-2 Bedrooms Sleeps 2-5

Prices – Cottage:

£278.00-£609.00 Per Week

Short breaks available

272

Balfron Station

Ballat Smithy Cottage

Open: All year **Map Ref: 1H**

★★★★ SELF CATERING

Balfron Station, by Loch Lomond, G63 0SE

T: 01360 440269 E: a.h.currie@btopenworld.com W: ballatsmithycottage.com

1 Cottage 2 Bedrooms Sleeps 1-4

Prices – Cottage:

£295.00-£465.00 Per Week

Short breaks available

139

almaha

he Old Schoolhouse

Open: All year **Map Ref: 1G4**

'o luxury contemporary five star
'f catering holiday cottages in
ch Lomond. Furnished to an
ceptionally high standard with
ree luxurious bedrooms, dining
:chen, living area with sofa bed
d two bathrooms. Expansive
rdens with covered hot tub and
:cked bbq area. One mile from
e loch.

★★★★★
SELF CATERING

Milton of Buchanan, Loch Lomond, G63 0JE
T: 07815 810897 E: g8dixon@aol.com W: lochlomondluxuryselfcatering.co.uk

2 Cottages | 3 Bedrooms | Sleeps 1-8

Prices – Cottage:
£770.00-£1120.00 Per Week

Short breaks available

84743

y Drymen

omond Luxury Lodges

Open: All year **Map Ref: 1G4**

ixurious lodges offering you
e chance to experience holiday
commodation second to none.
:lax in your own covered luxury
ɔt tub, sauna or spa bath. Free
/imming pool and leisure club.
ivate gardens and parking.
ɔmplimentary wine, chocolates,
iffy bathrobes and much more –
y TV and free wi-fi. We look
rward to welcoming you!

★★★★ UP TO ★★★★★
SELF CATERING

Loch Lomond & Trossachs National Park, Croftamie, Glasgow, G63 0EX
T: 01360 660054 E: info@lochlomond-holidays.co.uk W: lochlomond-holidays.co.uk

5 Luxury Lodges | 2-4 Bedrooms | Sleeps 2-9

Prices – Luxury Lodge:
£490.00-£1490.00 Per Week

Short breaks available all year round

48042

Glasgow

My Place in Glasgow

Open: All year **Map Ref: 1H**

Our luxury apartments, within the impressive former Sheriff Court building, at the heart of the Merchant City, are ideally located to explore the city. Each apartment consists of a fully fitted kitchen, living and dining area, double bedroom with king-size bed, shower room and cloakroom. Free w-fi access is provided.

★★★★
SELF CATERING

The Old Sheriff Court, 149 Ingram Street, Glasgow, G1 1DW
T: 07858 381583 E: info@myplaceinglasgow.co.uk W: myplaceinglasgow.co.uk

3 Apartments | 1 Bedroom | Sleeps 2

Prices – Apartment:

£450.00-£510.00	Per Week
£85.00	Per Night

Short breaks available

749

Luss

Shegarton Farm Cottages

Open: All year **Map Ref: 1G**

★★★★
SELF CATERING

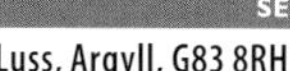

Shegarton Farm, Luss, Argyll, G83 8RH
T: 01389 850269 E: enquiries@shegartonfarmcottages.co.uk W: shegartonfarmcottages.co.uk

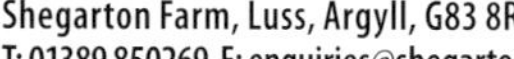

2 Cottages | 1-2 Bedrooms | Sleeps 2-4

Prices – Cottage:

£200.00-£450.00	Per Week

Short breaks available

5442

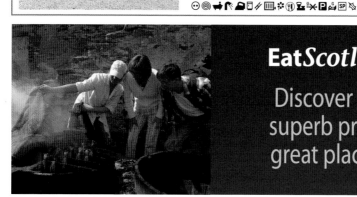

Greater Glasgow, Clyde Valley & Loch Lomond: EatScotland Gold and Silver establishments

Glasgow

Art Lovers' Café

House for an Art Lover,
Bellahouston Park, 10 Drumbreck Road,
Glasgow, G41 5BW
T: 0141 353 4779

The Art Lovers' Café is set in a contemporary space with an innovative menu of the highest quality. Visitors can admire the surrounding artworks, or relax on the café terrace.

Luss, Loch Lomond

Coach House Coffee Shop

Luss,
Loch Lomond,
G83 8NN
T: 01436 860 341

A popular establishment, serving a wide range of soups and snacks, incorporating many local and other Scottish produce, all of which is home made.

Glasgow

Dakhin

1st Floor, 89 Candelriggs,
Merchant City,
Glasgow, G1 1NP
T: 0141 553 2585

Dakhin is located in the heart of Glasgow and is the first authentic South Indian Kitchen in Scotland. It has recently been awarded a Cultural Cuisine Excellence award by VisitScotland (EatScotland).

Glasgow

Guy's Restaurant and Bar

24 Candleriggs,
Merchant City,
Glasgow, G1 1LD
T: 0141 552 1114

After more than twenty years feeding the film industry's A list with his Location Catering business, Guy decided to head home to Glasgow to set up this unique venue.

Glasgow

Mussel Inn

157 Hope Street,
Glasgow,
G2 2UG
T: 0141 572 1405

Enjoy delicious seafood at this stylish restaurant in the heart of Glasgow city centre, with direct access to the best shellfish available from Mull of Kintyre to Shetland.

Glasgow

Red Onion

257 West Campbell Street,
Glasgow,
G2 4TT
T: 0141 221 6000

Red Onion is a contemporary, smart, city centre brasserie offering a casual dining experience with a menu aimed to please every diner. Owner/chef John Quigley believes in using the finest natural, local produce

Glasgow
Stravaigin

SILVER

28-30 Gibson Street,
Glasgow,
G12 8NX
T: 01413 342 665

Stravaigin is a long-established restaurant with many Eastern influences. The daily changing menu incorporates seasonal produce with house specialties including award-winning haggis.

Glasgow
The Dhabba

44 Candleriggs,
Merchant City,
Glasgow, G1 1LE
T: 0141 553 1249

This award-winning restaurant has built up a reputation of providing excellent quality authentic North Indian food with chefs of the highest calibre imported from India.

Glasgow
The Grill Room at The Square

29 Royal Exchange Square,
Glasgow,
G1 3AJ
T: 0141 225 5615

The Grill Room at The Square is the ultimate dining experience for clients and guests to Glasgow, specialising in Scottish beef and local seafood.

Glasgow
The Sisters Restaurant

1a Ashwood Gardens,
Glasgow,
G13 1NU
T: 0141 434 1179

Stone walls, cosy atmosphere and a warm modern nod to tartan approach. Around the corner and up a wee staircase, it's worth seeking out this hidden gem!

Glasgow
The Sisters, Kelvingrove

36 Kelvingrove Street,
Glasgow,
G3 7RZ
T: 0141 564 1157

An extremely polished establishment hosted by extremely polished staff. The food is prepared to the highest standards using the finest fresh and seasonal ingredients available.

The Ben Nevis Bar, Argyle Street in the city centre of Glasgow

Sophy Grave's Expressions,
Kelvingrove Art Gallery & Museum

WEST HIGHLANDS & ISLANDS

The Sound of Iona,
Isle of Mull

Welcome to West Highlands & Islands

Set your compass for the west for a rugged mix of isles and peninsulas. Here the slower pace of life is instantly seductive and relaxing. Even the mainland around Kintyre feels more like an island with its watery views. Each island, from Gigha to Jura, holds its own particular charm.

Stop off in Oban with its bustling harbour and architectural folly on the hill. Oban is also the gateway to the isles, with frequent ferries to and from the likes of Mull, Coll, Tiree and Colonsay.

The Isle of Iona is known for its historic abbey and spiritual connections. The Isle of Islay produces some of Scotland's best known whiskies in its eight distilleries, while the row of brightly-coloured houses in Tobermory is a favourite with visitors to Mull.

Mainland or island, the passion for local life, culture, food and drink ensures a quality stay at any time of year.

01 The Drawing Room, Mount Stuart, Isle of Bute

02 Crarae. Glen Gardens, Cumlodden Estate

03 The first tee at Machrihanish Golf Club

04 Rothesay Castle, Isle of Bute

Inspired ideas for you to indulge

ISLE OF BUTE

Mount Stuart, home to descendants of the Royal House of Stuart, is a flamboyant discovery on the Isle of Bute. Tour the theatrical rooms of this Victorian Gothic mansion inspired by history, astrology, art and mythology. Also on Bute in the town of its name is Rothesay Castle, a largely circular castle dating from the 1200s.
mountstuart.com

MACHRIHANISH GOLF COURSE

Machrihanish Golf Club is just a few miles from the centre of Campeltown on the Kintyre Peninsula. It's a quiet course set amidst dunes with outstanding views of the islands of Jura and Islay. Your opening shot off the first tee needs to carry the Atlantic – no mean feat if it's windy!
machgolf.com

GLORIOUS GARDENS

If you've got green fingers, you'll have a field day touring The Glorious Gardens of Argyll and Bute. Twenty individual gardens of varying size, style and maturity make up the group. You'll find informal woodland versions as well as classic 18th century designs on both the mainland and islands.
gardens-of-argyll.co.uk

MCCAIG'S TOWER

A Roman-style colosseum is probably the last thing you'd expect to find in the Western Highlands. It was built above the town of Oban by a local banker as a family memorial. It's worth the climb to this Victorian folly for the rewarding views you get of Oban Bay and the isles of Kerrera and Mull.

ISLAND HOPPING

The islands of the West Highlands have so much diversity in such a compact area, it's a good idea to use the frequent ferries to island hop. You can trace Scotland's origins of Christianity to Iona. You can also seek out Fingal's Cave on Staffa and the peaty whiskies of Islay.
calmac.co.uk

01 Locally caught langoustine – simply delicious!

02 View from Loch Melfort Hotel, Argyll

03 Shellfish platter and a view from the Loch Fyne Oyster Bar, Cairndow

04 Isle of Jura Distillery

Savour the real taste of Scotland

WHISKY COAST

Whisky connoisseurs will find top quality names at the 16 distilleries on Scotland's Whisky Coast. The Isle of Islay is home to eight distilleries, producing the strongest flavoured Scotch malt whiskies with a peaty, salty 'nose'. Meanwhile, the Isle of Jura creates a sweeter whisky, still with a hint of island saltiness.

whiskycoast.co.uk

LOCH FYNE OYSTER BAR

From a roadside stall on the banks of the loch in the 1980s, the original Loch Fyne Oyster Bar and Shop opened in Cairndow in 1988. It has been listed in the Good Food Guide ever since. The emphasis has always been on good food, sustainably sourced and simply presented in a beautiful lochside location.

lochfyne.com

COAST RESTAURANT

A former bank building houses Coast, a stylish restaurant in Oban renowned for its modern approach to food. You'll find the fresh shellfish and seafood synonymous with the area feature highly on the menu, as well as fish and Scottish meat dishes. There's also a list of fine wines and local beers supplied by Fyne Ales.

EatScotland Silver Award

coastoban.com

ARGYLL SEAFOOD TRAIL

If you love seafood and shellfish, the Argyll Seafood Trail lets you sample the best of both against a backdrop of outstanding coastal scenery. Chefs at 11 different establishments, from the Seafood Cabin at Skipness to Creggans Inn at Strachar, share a passion for creating the freshest of dishes with flair.

theseafoodtrail.com

Something a little bit different

COASTAL CHARTERS

You can charter a skippered sailing boat for the day at many of the small ports you'll find along the extensive West Highland coast. Charter for You provides yachts from the sheltered Holy Loch, just north of Dunoon. Northern Light Charters specialises in wildlife trips and runs three vessels from Tobermory on Mull.
charterforyou.co.uk
northernlight-uk.com

SEA TRIP SAFARIS

Sea trip safaris around Oban and Mull give you the best chance of spotting native wildlife species in their spectacular natural habitat. Look up for seabirds, sea eagles and even golden eagles. Watch the water for seals, dolphins, porpoises and the occasional minke whale.

CORRYVRECKAN WHIRLPOOL

Between the islands of Jura and Scarba is The Corryvreckan, the world's third largest whirlpool. Flood tides and inflow can drive the Corryvreckan to high waves and the roar of the maelstrom can be heard for miles around. You can join a boat cruise to learn what makes The Corryvreckan so special.
whirlpool-scotland.co.uk

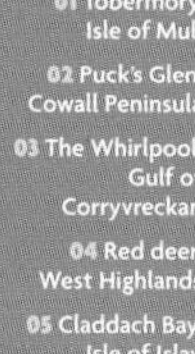

01 Tobermory, Isle of Mull

02 Puck's Glen, Cowall Peninsula

03 The Whirlpool, Gulf of Corryvreckan

04 Red deer, West Highlands

05 Claddach Bay, Isle of Islay

Time to plan your perfect day

ISLAY WALK WEEK
10 – 16 April 2010
If you enjoy walking, the guided excursions of Islay Walk Week are a great way to see Islay and Jura. Walks are rated as easy, moderate, challenging or strenuous and suitable footwear and clothing are recommended for all. The Visitors' Welcome Evening, enjoying local music over a dram, makes you feel right at home.
walkislay.co.uk

ISLE OF BUTE JAZZ FESTIVAL
29 April – 3 May 2010
Since its first event in 1988, the Isle of Bute Jazz Festival has certainly grown in size and reputation. The festival continues to attract top class UK and international talent to this small Scottish island. It is also a great supporter of young jazz musicians, who feature prominently in the annual programme.
butejazz.com

COWAL HIGHLAND GATHERING
26 – 28 August 2010
The Cowal Highland Gathering is billed as 'the largest and most spectacular Highland Games in the world'. The weekend is filled with events like a classic car parade, pipe bands, a ceilidh tent, traditional heavy athletics and the Scottish National Championships for Highland dancing. There's also a Food Tent for even more local flavour.
cowalgathering.com

COWALFEST
8 – 17 October 2010
More than 80 different walks and a host of arts and social events make up Scotland's largest walking festival. Walks of varying lengths and levels encompass forests, shores and lochsides. Themes include wildlife, history, culture and the marine environment. Arts, drama, film and music widen the appeal even further.
cowalfest.org

WEST HIGHLANDS & ISLANDS

am

A82
Glen Orchy
Dalmally
To Stirling
ochaweside
A83
Ardgartan
To Glasgow
omond
Trossachs
nal Park
on
To Glasgow
Firth of Clyde
A78
ilchattan
ay
To Ayr

VisitScotland Information Centres

To help you plan and book your trip to Scotland email our travel experts at info@visitscotland.com. When you arrive call into one of our Information Centres where our friendly experts can offer advice on all things local as well as sharing their wider knowledge of Scotland. We don't just advise either. We can sort out your accommodation and all your travel needs, as well as tickets for events across Scotland. So if you're looking to get the most from your visit, there really is only one place to go.

WEST HIGHLANDS

Bowmore	The Square, Bowmore, Isle of Islay, PA43 7JP
Campbeltown	Mackinnon House, The Pier, Campbeltown, PA28 6EF
Craignure	The Pier, Craignure, Isle of Mull, PA65 6AY
Dunoon	7 Alexandra Parade, Dunoon, PA23 8AB
Inveraray	Front Street, Inveraray, PA32 8UY
Rothesay	Winter Gardens, Victoria Street, Rothesay, Isle of Bute, PA20 0AH
Oban	Argyll Square, Oban, PA34 4AN

- LOCAL KNOWLEDGE
- WHERE TO STAY
- ACCOMMODATION BOOKING
- PLACES TO VISIT
- THINGS TO DO
- MAPS AND GUIDES
- TRAVEL ADVICE
- ROUTE PLANNING
- WHERE TO SHOP AND EAT
- LOCAL CRAFTS AND PRODUCE
- EVENT INFORMATION
- TICKETS

West Highlands & Islands: Hotels

Dunoon

Abbot's Brae Hotel

Open: All year **Map Ref: 1F**

★★★★
SMALL HOTEL

55 Bullwood Road, Dunoon, PA23 7QJ
T: 01369 705021 E: info@abbotsbrae.co.uk W: abbotsbrae.co.uk

Indicated Prices:

Single	from £60.00 per room	Twin	from £110.00 per room
Double	from £90.00 per room	Family	from £125.00 per room
		Suite	from £130.00 per room

 752

Kilchrenan, Taynuilt

Ardanaiseig Hotel

Open: All year **Map Ref: 1F**

In a remote place of quiet tranquility and almost surreal natural beauty, where the slopes of Ben Cruachan fall into the clear waters of Loch Awe, there is a small, luxurious and wildly romantic old country house hotel. It sits alone overlooking the mysterious islands and crannogs of the loch in deeply wooded gardens teeming with wildlife...it's Ardanaiseig Hotel.

★★★★
COUNTRY HOUSE HOTEL

Kilchrenan, Taynuilt, Argyll, PA35 1HE
T: 01866 833333 E: ardanaiseig@clara.net W: ardanaiseig.com

Indicated Prices:

Single	from £76.00 per room	Twin	from £152.00 per room
Double	from £152.00 per room		

 1263

 PRICES STATED ARE ESTIMATES AND MAY BE SUBJECT TO CHANGE. PRICES ARE PER PERSON PER NIGHT UNLESS OTHERWISE STATED. AWARDS CORRECT AS OF BEGINNING OF OCTOBER 2009

West Highlands & Islands: Guest Houses and B&Bs

enderloch, Oban

lawthorn

Open: All year **Map Ref: 1E2**

★★★★
BED AND BREAKFAST

5 Keith Croft, Benderloch, Oban, PA37 1QS
T: 01631 720452 E: june@hawthorncottages.com W: hawthorncottages.com

Indicated Prices:

Single	from £35.00 per person	Twin	from £30.00 per person
Double	from £30.00 per person	Family	from £30.00 per person

V

29746

ıveraray

udha-Na-Craige

Open: All year **Map Ref: 1F3**

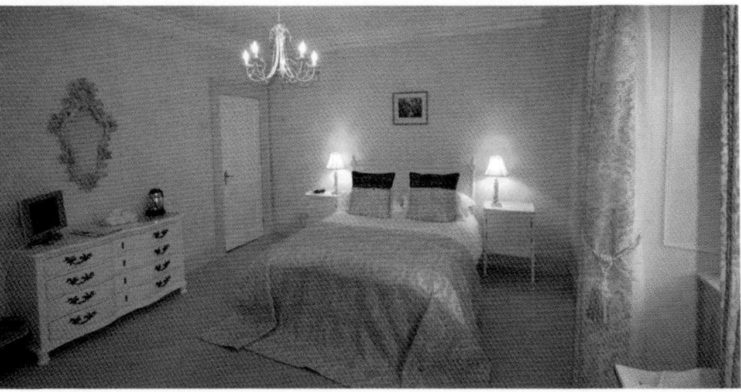

san and Howard Spicer welcome u to our beautiful and historical me where the Duke of Argyll's cestors once lived. Exceptional commodation, great food, stunning ch Fyne views, Inveraray centre arby. An individual experience with high standard of hospitality and mfort. Excellent base for touring gyll and the Highlands.

★★★★
GUEST HOUSE

The Avenue, Inveraray, PA32 8YX
T: +44(0)1499 302668 E: enquiries@rudha-na-craige.com W: www.rudha-na-craige.com

Indicated Prices:

Single	from £60.00 per room	Twin	from £118.00 per room
Double	from £90.00 per room	Suite	from £118.00 per room

V

75916

Isle of Islay, Ballygrant

Kilmeny Country House

Open: All year excl Xmas & New Year **Map Ref: 1C**

★★★★★ GOLD
GUEST HOUSE

Ballygrant, Islay, PA45 7QW
T: 01496 840668 E: info@kilmeny.co.uk W: kilmeny.co.uk

Indicated Prices:

Double	from £115.00 per room	Twin	from £125.00 per room
		Suite	from £145.00 per room

3385

Isle of Islay, by Port Ellen, Kilnaughton Bay

Samhchair

Open: Apr-Oct **Map Ref: 1C**

★★★★
BED AND BREAKFAST

Kilnaughton Bay, by Port Ellen, Isle of Islay, PA42 7AX
T: 01496 302596 E: info@samhchair.co.uk W: samhchair.co.uk

Indicated Prices:

Single	from £65.00 per room	Twin	from £40.00 per person
Double	from £40.00 per person		

8129

Lochgilphead

The Corran

Open: All year **Map Ref: 1E**

★★★★
BED AND BREAKFAST

Poltalloch Street, Lochgilphead, Argyll, PA31 8LR
T: 01546 603866 E: lamonthoy@tiscali.co.uk W: lamonthoy.co.uk

Indicated Prices:

Single	from £40.00 per room	Twin	from £60.00 per room
Double	from £60.00 per room	Family	from £80.00 per room

5861

Isle of Mull, Bunessan

An Caladh Bed & Breakfast

Open: All year excl Xmas & New Year **Map Ref: 1C**

★★★★
BED AND BREAKFAST

Ardtun, Bunessan, Isle of Mull, Argyll, PA67 6DH
T: 01681 700115 E: enquiries@ancaladhmull.co.uk W: ancaladhmull.co.uk

Indicated Prices:

Single	from £45.00 per room	Twin	from £70.00 per room
Double	from £60.00 per room		

8143

 PRICES STATED ARE ESTIMATES AND MAY BE SUBJECT TO CHANGE. PRICES ARE PER PERSON PER NIGHT UNLESS OTHERWISE STATED. AWARDS CORRECT AS OF BEGINNING OF OCTOBER 2009

Isle of Mull, Tobermory
Glengorm Castle
Open: Mar-Nov **Map Ref: 1C1**

Situated on the northern tip of Mull, Glengorm overlooks the Atlantic. The castle was built in 1860 and is set in dramatic scenery. The interior is warm and inviting. Enjoy log fires and a complimentary whisky watching amazing sunsets from the library. The perfect way to end a day.

★★★★
BED AND BREAKFAST

Tobermory, Isle of Mull, PA75 6QE
T: 01688 302321 E: enquiries@glengormcastle.co.uk W: glengormcastle.co.uk

Indicated Prices:

Single	from £120.00 per room	Twin	from £120.00 per room
Double	from £120.00 per room	Family	from £135.00 per room

28192

Oban
Aros Ard
Open: Mar-Oct **Map Ref: 1E2**

★★★★
BED AND BREAKFAST

Croft Road, Oban, PA34 5JN
T: 01631 565500 E: maclean@arosard.freeserve.co.uk W: arosard.co.uk

Indicated Prices:

Single	from £70.00 per room	Twin	from £70.00 per room
Double	from £70.00 per room		

12933

Oban
Briarbank Guest House
Open: All year **Map Ref: 1E2**

★★★★
BED AND BREAKFAST

Glencruitten Road, Oban, PA34 4DN
T: 01631 566549 E: juliegrove56@hotmail.com W: briarbank-oban.co.uk

Indicated Prices:

Single	from £35.00 per room
Double	from £55.00 per room

76179

Oban

Corriemar House

Open: All year **Map Ref: 1E**

'A legend in the very heart of the Highlands.' Situated on Oban's select Esplanade seafront. Internally, no expense has been spared to provide furnishing and decor to recapture the splendour and elegance so characteristic of its period. King size and four-poster rooms, sea view rooms, suite rooms. Delicious varied breakfasts. AA ★★★★

★★★★
GUEST HOUSE

Esplanade, Oban, PA34 5AQ
T: 01631 562476 E: info@corriemarhouse.co.uk W: corriemarhouse.co.uk

Indicated Prices:

Single	from £30.00 per room	Twin	from £50.00 per room
Double	from £50.00 per room	Family	from £85.00 per room
		Suite	from £70.00 per room

205

Oban

Glenburnie House

Open: Mar-Nov **Map Ref: 1E**

★★★★
GUEST HOUSE

Corran Esplanade, Oban, PA34 5AQ
T: 01631 562089 E: graeme.strachan@btinternet.com W: glenburnie.co.uk

Indicated Prices:

Single	from £40.00 per person	Twin	from £40.00 per person
Double	from £40.00 per person		

280

by Oban, Connel

Ronebhal Guest House

Open: Apr-Oct **Map Ref: 1E**

★★★★
GUEST HOUSE

Connel, by Oban, Argyll, PA75 6QY
T: 01631 710310 E: info@ronebhal.co.uk W: ronebhal.co.uk

Indicated Prices:

Single	from £30.00 per room	Twin	from £60.00 per room
Double	from £60.00 per room	Family	from £90.00 per room

520

 PRICES STATED ARE ESTIMATES AND MAY BE SUBJECT TO CHANGE. PRICES ARE PER PERSON PER NIGHT UNLESS OTHERWISE STATED. AWARDS CORRECT AS OF BEGINNING OF OCTOBER 2009

y Oban, Connel

rds House

Open: All year excl festive season **Map Ref: 1E2**

ly five miles from Oban in a truly llic location with breathtaking ws and incredible sunsets. ds House combines modern ilities and comforts with the ditional ambience of a Victorian a. An excellent base to explore st Highlands or simply relax d unwind. Exclusively for non-okers. AA five stars.

★★★★ GOLD
GUEST HOUSE

Connel, Oban, Argyll, PA37 1PT
T: 01631 710255 E: info@ardshouse.com W: ardshouse.com

Indicated Prices:

Single	from £55.00 per room	Twin	from £76.00 per room
Double	from £76.00 per room		

12673

aynuilt

anglewood Lodge

Open: All year excl Xmas week **Map Ref: 1F2**

★★★★
BED AND BREAKFAST

Tanglewood, Otter Creek, Taynuilt, Argyll, PA35 1HP
T: 01866 822114 E: carol@tanglewoodlodge.co.uk W: tanglewoodlodge.co.uk

Indicated Prices:

Single	from £60.00 per room	Twin	from £75.00 per room
Double	from £75.00 per room	Family	from £75.00 + £20-£25 per child*
			*Under 3 are free

81440

West Highlands & Islands: Self Catering

Appin

Appin House Lodges

Open: 6 Feb-31 Oct 2010; 19 Dec 2010-3 Jan 2011 **Map Ref: 1E**

★★★★
SELF CATERING

Appin House, Appin, Argyll, PA38 4BN
T: 01631 730207 E: denys@appinhouse.co.uk W: appinhouse.co.uk

2 Houses | 3 Bedrooms | Sleeps 2-8

Prices – House:
£565.00-£950.00 Per Week

Short breaks available

123

Appin

Inverboat House

Open: All year **Map Ref: 1E**

Spectacular building and picturesque setting on sea loch/mountain. Private beach, slipway, spa bath, sauna, logfires. Walking, sailing, diving, wildlife, fishing, skiing. Surrounded by nature reserve, Glasdrum wood (slopes of Ben Churalain) and Loch Creran with its biogenic reefs (Special Area of Conservation). See www.inverboathouse.co.uk for activities. Sleeps 4-14 plus cot.

★★★ UP TO ★★★★
SELF CATERING

Loch Creran, Appin, Argyll, PA38 4BQ
T: 0131 550 1180 E: bookings@mackays-scotland.co.uk W: mackays-scotland.co.uk

1 Cottage | 2 Bedrooms | Sleeps 4
1 House | 4 Bedrooms | Sleeps 8-10

Prices – Cottage:
£272.00-£642.00 Per Week

Prices – House:
£555.00-£1998.00 Per Week

318

 PRICES STATED ARE ESTIMATES AND MAY BE SUBJECT TO CHANGE. PRICES ARE PER UNIT PER WEEK UNLESS OTHERWISE STATED. AWARDS CORRECT AS OF BEGINNING OF OCTOBER 2009

le of Bute

rranview

Open: All year **Map Ref: 1F5**

★★★★★ SELF CATERING

Stewart Hall, Isle of Bute, PA20 0QS
T: 01700 500006 E: donald@stewarthall-isle-of-bute.co.uk W: visitbute.co.uk

1 Cottage 3 Bedrooms Sleeps 2-6

Prices – Cottage:
£500.00-£850.00 Per Week

Short breaks available

12996

le of Bute, Kilchattan Bay

ykenamar

Open: All year **Map Ref: 1F6**

★★★★ SELF CATERING

Dykenamar, Shore Road, Kilchattan Bay, Isle of Bute, PA20 9NW
T: 01483 772506/07712 667316 E: bookings@bute-haven.com W: bute-haven.com

1 Bungalow 3 Bedrooms Sleeps 1-6

Prices – Bungalow:
£450.00-£740.00 Per Week

23938

le of Bute, Rothesay

rdencraig House Apartments

Open: All year **Map Ref: 1F5**

★★★★ SELF CATERING

Ardencraig Road, High Craigmore, Rothesay, Isle of Bute, PA20 9EP
T: 01700 505077 E: ebdan10@aol.com W: ardencraig.org.uk

4 Apartments 1-2 Bedrooms Sleeps 1-7

Prices – Apartment:
£325.00-£575.00 Per Week

Short breaks available

12529

raobh Haven, by Lochgilphead

he Deckhouse

Open: All year **Map Ref: 1E3**

★★★★ SELF CATERING

Craobh Haven Self Catering, No 10 The Green, Craobh Haven, by Lochgilphead, Argyll, PA31 8UB
T: 07808 781464 E: info@craobhhavenselfcatering.com W: craobhhavenselfcatering.com

1 Cottage 2 Bedrooms Sleeps 1-4

Prices – Cottage:
£330.00-£700.00 Per Week

77320

Dunoon
Clyde Cottage
Open: All year **Map Ref: 1E**

★★★★
SELF CATERING

25 East Bay, Dunoon
T: 01546 510316 E: gordon@ri-cruin.freeserve.co.uk

1 House 3 Bedrooms Sleeps 1-

Prices – House:
£215.00-£563.00 Per Week

Short breaks available

197

Glen Orchy
The Old House
Open: All year **Map Ref: 1G**

★★★★
SELF CATERING

Arichastlich, Glen Orchy, Argyll, PA33 1BD
T: 01838 200399 E: theoldhouse@glen-orchy.co.uk W: glen-orchy.co.uk

1 House 3 Bedrooms Sleeps 1-

Prices – House:
£385.00-£1000.00 Per Week

Short breaks available

597

Kilchrenan, by Taynuilt
Ardabhaigh
Open: All year **Map Ref: 1F**

★★★★
SELF CATERING

Kilchrenan, by Taynuilt, Argyll, PA35 1NE
T: 01499 302736 E: gmoncrieff@btinternet.com

1 Bungalow 4 Bedrooms Sleeps 2-

Prices – Bungalow:
£350.00-£890.00 Per Week 15%-10% reduction for 2-3/4 persons respectively

124

Kilmartin, by Lochgilphead
The Bullock Shed and The Stable
Open: All year **Map Ref: 1E**

★★★★
SELF CATERING

Ri Cruin, Kilmartin, by Lochgilphead, PA31 8QF
T: 01546 510316 E: gordon@ri-cruin.freeserve.co.uk W: ri-cruin.co.uk

1 Cottage 2 Bedrooms Sleeps 1-4
1 Wing of house 3 Bedrooms Sleeps 1-6

Prices – Cottage:
£215.00-£563.00 Per Week

Prices – Wing of house:
£234.00-£667.00 Per Week

Short breaks available

197

 PRICES STATED ARE ESTIMATES AND MAY BE SUBJECT TO CHANGE. PRICES ARE PER UNIT PER WEEK UNLESS OTHERWISE STATED. AWARDS CORRECT AS OF BEGINNING OF OCTOBER 2009

ilmelford, by Oban
earnach Bay House
Open: All year **Map Ref: 1E3**

uxurious holiday home in an :eptional loch side position Melfort, Argyll. Spectacular ws, private fishing, stunning nery, renowned restaurant thin walking distance – what ore could you ask for? This is the imate self catering destination d offers the very best in five star mfort and luxury.

★★★★★
SELF CATERING

Kilmelford, by Oban, Argyll, PA34 4XD
T: 01852 200263 E: holiday@argyllholidaycottage.co.uk W: argyllholidaycottage.co.uk

1 House 4 Bedrooms Sleeps 2-8

Prices – House:
£945.00-£1900.00 Per Week

Short breaks available

85291

Imelford, by Oban
lelfort Village
Open: All year excl middle two weeks in Jan **Map Ref: 1E3**

★★★★
SELF CATERING

Kilmelford, by Oban, Argyll, PA34 4XD
T: 01852 200257 E: rentals@melfortvillage.co.uk W: melfortvillage.co.uk

32 Cottages 1-3 Bedroom Sleeps 2-8

Prices – Cottages:
£370.00-£1210.00 Per Week

Short breaks available

38024

le of Mull, Aros
uffer Aground Self Catering
Open: Easter-end Dec **Map Ref: 1D1**

★★★★
SELF CATERING

Smiddy Ho, Aros, Isle of Mull, PA72 6JB
T: 01680 300389 E: ellis-g@btconnect.com W: isleofmullcottageflats.co.uk

2 Cottages 1 Bedroom Sleeps 2+sofabed

Prices – Cottage:
£195.00-£380.00 Per Week

Short breaks available

60122

Isle of Mull, Craignure

Craignure Bay House

Open: All year **Map Ref: 1D**

SELF CATERING

Craignure, Isle of Mull, PA65 6AY
T: 07719 627500 E: enquiries@craignurebayhouse.co.uk W: craignurebayhouse.co.uk

1 Cottage 4 Bedrooms Sleeps 4-8

Prices – Cottage:
£500.00-£950.00 Per Week

Short breaks available

735

Isle of Mull, Dervaig

Alan and Emma Gardiner

Open: All year **Map Ref: 1C**

★★★★
SELF CATERING

Cocklaw Farm, Biggar, ML12 6RD
T: 01899 220473 E: info@self-catering-mull.com W: self-catering-mull.com

2 Houses 4 Bedrooms (per house) Sleeps 2-18

Prices – House:
£400.00-£900.00 Per Week

Short breaks available

205

Isle of Mull, Tobermory

Tralee

Open: Mar-Oct **Map Ref: 1C**

★★★★
SELF CATERING

Breadalbane Street, Tobermory, Isle of Mull, PA15 6PE
T: 01922 624091 E: royhands@talktalk.net

1 Cottage 3 Bedrooms Sleeps 5

Prices – Cottage:
£380.00-£495.00 Per Week

618

Isle of Seil, Ellenabeich

The Bolt Hole

Open: All year **Map Ref: 1D**

★★★★
SELF CATERING

Tramway Cottages, Ellenabeich, Isle of Seil, Oban, PA34 4RQ
T: 01904 492111 E: oktc@acsemail.co.uk W: cowtonscottage.co.uk

1 Cottage 2 Bedrooms Sleeps 4

Prices – Cottage:
£255.00-£525.00 Per Week

Short breaks available

786

 PRICES STATED ARE ESTIMATES AND MAY BE SUBJECT TO CHANGE. PRICES ARE PER UNIT PER WEEK UNLESS OTHERWISE STATED. AWARDS CORRECT AS OF BEGINNING OF OCTOBER 2009

ayvallich

he Steadings

Open: All year **Map Ref: 1D4**

★★★★
SELF CATERING

Inchjura, Carsaig Bay, Tayvallich, Argyll, PA31 8PN
T: 01546 870294/698 E: jamesb@riddellj.freeserve.co.uk W: the-steadings-tayvallich.co.uk

1 Cottage 3 Bedrooms Sleeps 6

Prices – Cottage:
£350.00-£575.00 Per Week

Short breaks available

60522

West Highlands & Islands: Food & Drink

le of Mull, Tobermory

ighland Cottage

Open: Mar-Oct **Map Ref: 1C1**

★★★★
SMALL HOTEL

Culinary Type:
SCOTTISH

Breadalbane Street,
Tobermory, Isle of Mull, PA75 6PD
T: 01688 302030
E: davidandjo@highlandcottage.co.uk
W: highlandcottage.co.uk

Best For:
- Romantic Meals
- Special Occasion

Prices:
Three courses from £45

Opening Times:
Dinner from 1900-2030

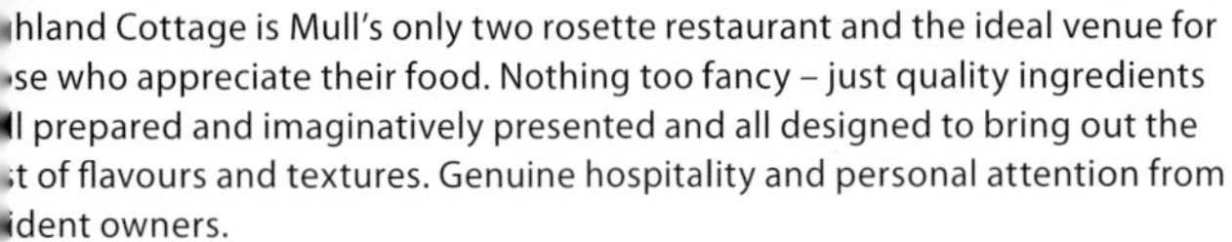

hland Cottage is Mull's only two rosette restaurant and the ideal venue for se who appreciate their food. Nothing too fancy – just quality ingredients l prepared and imaginatively presented and all designed to bring out the t of flavours and textures. Genuine hospitality and personal attention from ident owners.

30309

West Highlands & Islands: EatScotland Gold and Silver establishments

Taynuilt

Ardanaiseig Hotel

SILVER

Kilchrenan,
Taynuilt,
PA35 1HE
T: 01866 833 333

The Ardanaiseig Restaurant is noted for its imaginative use of fresh produce, particularly seafood, for which the West of Scotland is famous.

Oban

Coast

104 George Street,
Oban, Argyll & Bute,
PA34 5NT
T: 01631 569 900

A contemporary restaurant housed in a former bank building, the modern mix of wood, calming colours and music create a relaxed setting to enjoy the best local shellfish, fish and Scottish meats.

Campbeltown

Dunvalanree in Carradale

Port Righ, Carradale,
Campbeltown,
PA28 6SE
T: 01583 431 226

A founding member of The Seafood Trail, the Dunvalanree provides locally produced meals cooked with care and passion. Local produce is a feature at this friendly, family-run establishment.

Isle of Mull

Highland Cottage

Breadalbane Street,
Tobermory, Isle of Mull,
PA75 6PD
T: 01688 302 030

Occupying an elevated position overlooking Tobermory Bay, this cosy restaurant and conservatory lounge offers a friendly, homely atmosphere.

A solitary canoeist paddles his canoe on the calm waters of Loch Lubnaig. North of Callander, Stirlingshire

The Falls of Edinample –a waterfall in the course of the Burn of Ample, near Lochearnhead, Stirling

STIRLING, FORTH VALLEY & THE TROSSACHS

The Wallace Monument, Stirling

Welcome to Stirling, Forth Valley & the Trossachs

Stirling, Forth Valley & the Trossachs encapsulate the best of Scotland. The variety of scenery and activities in this area is as wide as the region is large, from historic towns and villages to a vast National Park.

Stirling is one of Scotland's oldest towns and now its newest city. The imposing castle at its heart and the city's Old Town recall stories of William Wallace and Robert the Bruce. The National Wallace Monument stands high above the trees on the skyline. Theatres, galleries and live music bring a lively cultural vibe to this university city.

Stirling is at the gateway to the Trossachs, as Scotland ascends into the Highlands. The National Park protects many of Scotland's best known species of wildlife and sealife within a stunning setting of lochs and mountains.

Take time to explore historic hamlets, picturesque villages and ancient castles, Doune and Blackness among them. Plan an overnight stay in a luxurious mansion house or castle and seek out regional and seasonal favourites in restaurants and at local food events.

01 The Pineapple summerhouse, Dunmore

02 SS Sir Walter Scott, Loch Katrine

03 Medieval priory on Inchmahome Island, Lake of Menteith

04 Castle Campbell, Dollar Glen, Clackmannanshire

Inspired ideas for you to indulge

DUNMORE PINEAPPLE

The Pineapple is an elaborate two-storey summerhouse built for the 4th Earl of Dunmore in 1761. South-east of Stirling, this eccentric folly with its stony fruit centrepiece and immense walled garden are owned by the National Trust for Scotland. You can stay inside The Pineapple itself in an elegant self-catering room.
landmarktrust.org.uk

SHOPPING IN BRIDGE OF ALLAN

Just three miles from Stirling, you'll find shops like they used to be in Bridge of Allan. This picturesque Victorian spa town hosts a range of interesting boutiques and galleries, traditional butchers, whisky merchants and renowned deli, Clive Ramsay. Plenty of great eating places let you make a day of it.
bridgeofallan.org

GLENBERVIE GOLF CLUB

Since it opened in 1932, Glenbervie has become one of Scotland's foremost golf clubs. Renowned course architect, James Braid, who also built The King's Course at Gleneagles, set this parkland course amidst mature trees with outstanding views of the Ochil Hills. Glenbervie often features in the Top 100 courses list.
glenberviegolfclub.com

LOCH KATRINE CRUISES

Loch Katrine inspired Sir Walter Scott to pen his famous poem 'The Lady of the Lake', first published in 1810. Two hundred years on, you can sail the loch on Steamship Sir Walter Scott to find your own inspiration in the landscape of the loch. Sailings depart April to October from Trossachs Pier or Stronachlachar.
lochkatrine.com

LAKE OF MENTEITH

South of Callander sits the Lake of Menteith, the only major body of water in Scotland not to be called a loch. From Port of Menteith village, you can take a summer ferry to the 13th century island priory of Inchmahome. It was here that the four-year-old Mary, Queen of Scots found refuge in 1547.
portofmenteith.org.uk

CASTLE CAMPBELL

Near Dollar you'll find the imposing ruins of 15th century Castle Campbell, one of Scotland's best-preserved tower-house castles, in dramatic isolation overlooked by the Ochil Hills. Once known as Castle Glume, it was the home of the Campbells for 200 years until they moved to Argyll's Lodging beside Stirling Castle.
historic-scotland.gov.uk

01 Monachyle Mhor Hotel – a foodies' heaven!

02 Creagan House Restaurant, Strathyre

03 Exquisite desserts at the Monachyle Mhor Hotel

04 Celebrity chef Nick Nairn

Savour the real taste of Scotland

MONACHYLE MHOR

Foodies flock to this boutique hotel in the Trossachs to savour dishes made with the best of what its restaurant can gather within a 30-mile radius. The family running this boutique hotel also manages the surrounding farmland, so the venison, beef, lamb, pork and organic greens all come from the farm.

EatScotland Gold Award

mhor.net

NICK NAIRN COOK SCHOOL

Sharpen up your cooking skills or learn new techniques at the Nick Nairn Cook School near Port of Menteith. From tips for easy entertaining to masterclasses on shellfish, classes cover a wide range of topics and skill levels. Book a one-day cooking experience with the school's top chefs or with the man himself, Nick Nairn.

nicknairncookschool.com

CREAGAN HOUSE RESTAURANT

This cosy farmhouse in Strathyre is a renowned five-star restaurant with rooms. Chef and owner Gordon Gunn finds local sources for his quality ingredients; meat from Perthshire, fish from Scottish ports, free-range eggs from a neighbour and herbs from the garden. Round off an excellent dinner with one of Creagan House's selection of more than 50 malts.

EatScotland Silver Award

www.creaganhouse.co.uk

AA

Something a little bit different

AIRTH CASTLE HOTEL & SPA RESORT

Airth Castle, on the shores of the River Forth near Stirling, once belonged to the family of Robert the Bruce. Today it's a luxury hotel with twelve individually-designed bedrooms. You can indulge in a range of treatments in the hotel's Cloud Nine Leisure and Beauty Spa or even arrange exclusive use of the Castle.
airthcastlehotel.com

FAIRY TRAIL

Aberfoyle will be associated forever with local Reverend Robert Kirk's 'The Secret Commonwealth', written in 1691 about the lives of fairies. Kirk died on a walk on Doon Hill, the sacred place of fairies, and is said to have entered the fairy realm there. You can decide for yourself on what is a pleasant stroll.

CHAMPAGNE AFTERNOON TEA

The Roman Camp Hotel in Callander is an ideal country-house setting for a relaxing afternoon tea. Sip a glass of champagne in the elegant Drawing Room with its open fire before enjoying sandwiches, home-baked scones, shortbread and fruit loaf with a choice of teas.
roman-camp-hotel.co.uk

LOCH LOMOND & THE TROSSACHS NATIONAL PARK

From its woods and mountains to its lochs and coasts, this National Park is home to diverse populations of wildlife. Park Rangers organise year-round wildlife activities and events. Watch out for red squirrels and deer in forest parks. Ospreys are summer visitors to some lochs, while others are home to seals and porpoises.
lochlomond-trossachs.org

Time to plan your perfect day

A SCOTT'S LAND

June – September 2010

During a Trossachs family holiday in 1810, Sir Walter Scott was inspired to write 'The Lady of the Lake'. The poem was an instant global hit and initiated a tourism boom and enduring affection for the area's natural beauty. Scott's Land marks the poem's 200th anniversary with events including evening cruises and a literary trail.

TROSSACHS MUSHROOM FESTIVAL

21 – 24 October 2010

The Trossachs region is home to a rich variety of wild fungi. You can find out more about them on guided fungus forays and pick up some mushroom recipes at cookery demonstrations by local chefs. Theatre, woodland walks, whisky tastings, ceilidhs and live music add to the festival atmosphere.
trossachsmushroomfestival.co.uk

CALLANDER JAZZ & BLUES FESTIVAL

1 – 3 October 2010 (tbc)

Jazz up the Trossachs at the fifth annual festival of live jazz and blues in the heart of Loch Lomond and Trossachs National Park. Callander and Aberfoyle are hosts to a lively weekend of everything from big band jazz to boogie and blues. There's even a jazz cruise on Loch Katrine.
callanderjazz.com

TROSSACHS BEER FESTIVAL

27 August – 6 September 2010

From the Scottish Borders to the Shetlands, Scotland produces a wonderful range of real ales. Held annually in Kilmahog's Lade Inn near Callander, this beer festival celebrates the work of Scotland's many small brewers. Ingredients include heather, seaweed, red berries, malt whisky and even porridge. You can buy your favourite at the neighbouring Scottish Real Ale Shop.
theladeinn.com

STIRLING HOGMANAY

31 December 2010

Bring in the New Year at the Hogmanay celebrations on Stirling Castle's esplanade. Live acts get the party started in the run-up to midnight. As 2010 becomes 2011, Scottish pipers and drummers cross the castle drawbridge while a fireworks display illuminates the night sky. A rousing start to the year!
stirlinghogmanay.co.uk

01 Roman Camp Country House Hotel, Callander

02 The banks of Loch Lomond

03 SS Sir Walter Scott, Loch Katrine

04 Callander Jazz and Blues Festival

05 A rich variety of wild fungi can be found in the Trossachs

STIRLING, FORTH VALLEY & THE TROSSACHS

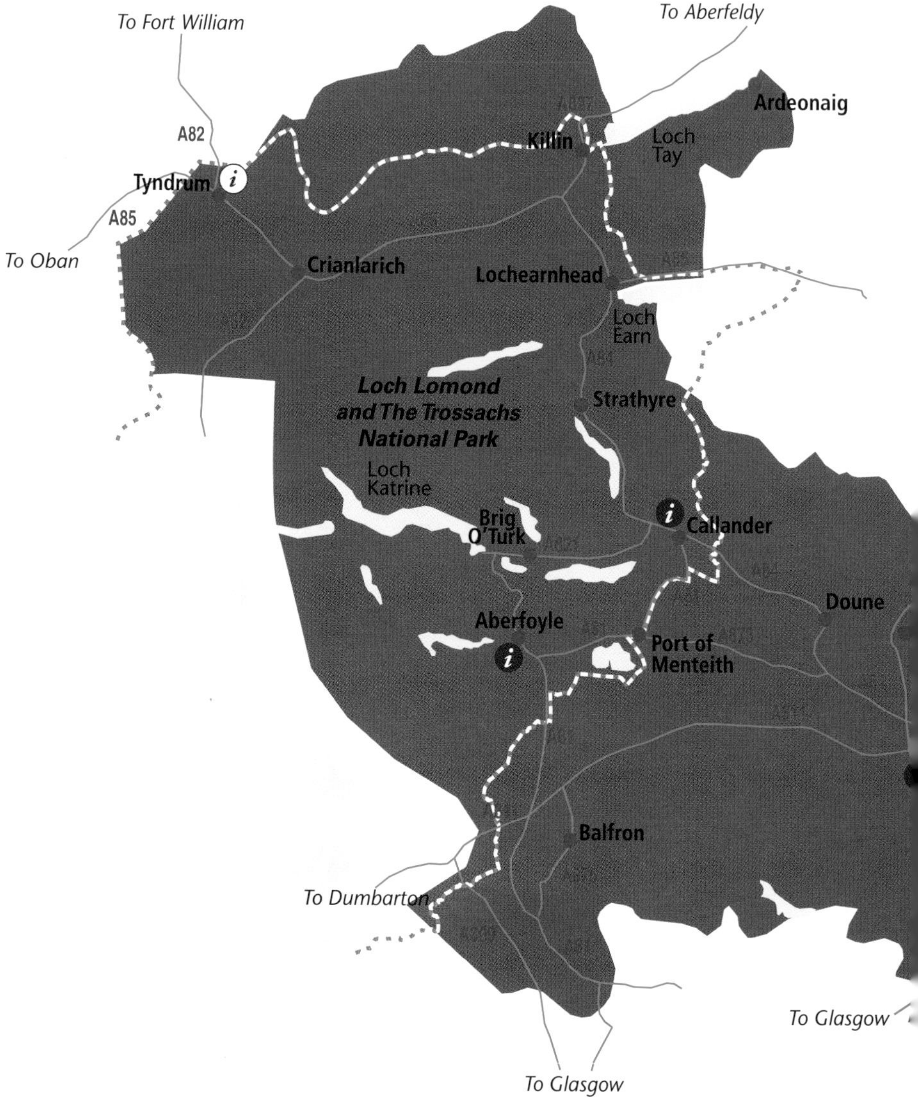

To Fort William
To Aberfeldy
A82
Tyndrum
A85
To Oban
Killin
Ardeonaig
Loch Tay
Crianlarich
Lochearnhead
Loch Earn
Strathyre
Loch Lomond and The Trossachs National Park
Loch Katrine
Brig O'Turk
Callander
Doune
Aberfoyle
Port of Menteith
Balfron
To Dumbarton
To Glasgow
To Glasgow

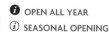

OPEN ALL YEAR
SEASONAL OPENING

To Perth
To Kinross
logie Alva
Tillicoultry
wayhead
A91
A907
ING
nnockburn
M9
M876
Bo'ness
nny
Falkirk
Redding
M9
To Edinburgh

VisitScotland Information Centres

To help you plan and book your trip to Scotland email our travel experts at info@visitscotland.com. When you arrive call into one of our Information Centres where our friendly experts can offer advice on all things local as well as sharing their wider knowledge of Scotland. We don't just advise either. We can sort out your accommodation and all your travel needs, as well as tickets for events across Scotland. So if you're looking to get the most from your visit, there really is only one place to go.

STIRLING

Aberfoyle	Trossachs Discovery Centre, Main Street, Aberfoyle, FK8 3UQ
Callander	Ancaster Square, Callander, FK17 8ED
Falkirk	The Falkirk Wheel, Lime Road, Tamfourhill, Falkirk, FK1 4RS
Stirling (Dumbarton Road)	41 Dumbarton Road, Stirling, FK8 2QQ
Stirling (Pirnhall), MOTO	M9 Motorway Services Area, Pirnhall Roundabout, Stirling, FK7 8ET

- LOCAL KNOWLEDGE
- WHERE TO STAY
- ACCOMMODATION BOOKING
- PLACES TO VISIT
- THINGS TO DO
- MAPS AND GUIDES
- TRAVEL ADVICE
- ROUTE PLANNING
- WHERE TO SHOP AND EAT
- LOCAL CRAFTS AND PRODUCE
- EVENT INFORMATION
- TICKETS

Stirling & Trossachs: Hotels

Callander

Creagan House Restaurant with Accommodation

Open: All year excl Wed & Thurs, 20 Jan-4 Mar, 10 Nov-25 Nov, 24-26 Dec Map Ref: 1

★★★★★ RESTAURANT WITH ROOMS

Strathyre, Callander, Perthshire, FK18 8ND
T: 01877 384638 E: eatandstay@creaganhouse.co.uk W: creaganhouse.co.uk

Indicated Prices:

Single	from £70.00 per room	Twin	from £120.00 per room
Double	from £120.00 per room	Family	from £145.00 per room

211

Callander

Roman Camp Country House and Restaurant

Open: All year Map Ref: 1H

Set in 20 acres of secluded gardens overlooking the River Teith, in the heart of the Trossachs. This beautiful hunting lodge was built in 1625. Warm, atmospheric and complimented by wonderful food, it could be your perfect hideaway.

★★★★ COUNTRY HOUSE HOTEL

Callander, Perthshire, FK17 8BG
T: 01877 330003 E: mail@romancamphotel.co.uk W: romancamphotel.co.uk

Indicated Prices:

Single	from £85.00 per room	Twin	from £135.00 per room
Double	from £135.00 per room		

519

unblane

oubletree by Hilton Dunblane Hydro

Open: All year **Map Ref: 2A3**

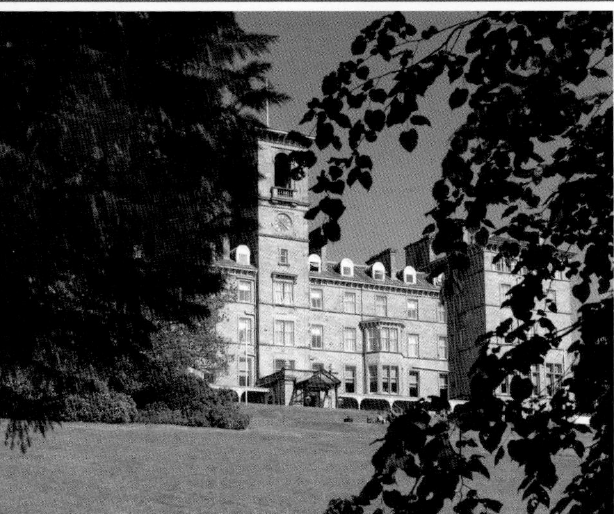

★★★★
HOTEL

Perth Road,
Dunblane, FK15 0HG
T: 01786 822551
E: reservations.dunblane@hilton.com
W: doubletreedunblane.com

Features:

- Recently undergone £12 million refurbishment
- The Kailyard restaurant by Nick Nairn
- 200 beautifully appointed bedrooms and suites
- Timeless elegance of the Stewart Lounge
- Pool and leisure facilities
- Convenient location for touring the area

Indicated Prices:

Single	from £99.00 per room B&B
Double	from £109.00 per room B&B
Twin	from £109.00 per room B&B
Family	from £159.00 per room B&B
Suite	from £209.00 per room B&B

30612

: within 10 acres of landscaped ›unds, the Victorian style ubletree by Hilton Dunblane dro offers breathtaking views :he Trossachs and Campsie ls. Keep fit in the Livingwell ure club, indulge in traditional ottish fayre in the Kailyard staurant and enjoy an after-dinner drink in the stylish cocktail bar. An extensive multi-million pound refurbishment has added contemporary style and world-class facilities to Doubletree Dunblane Hydro. You'll find our service as impressive as our surrounds though far less imposing.

by Killin, Ardeonaig

Ardeonaig Hotel and Restaurant

Open: All year **Map Ref: 1H**

Where else can you stay in a luxury African-influenced Rondawel or loch view lodge on the banks of one of Scotland's most spectacular lochs? Eat Michelin-standard food surrounded by the most extensive South African wine collection in Europe? Only one place, Ardeonaig Hotel & Restaurant, an idyllic hideaway well worth the journey.

★★★★
SMALL HOTEL

South Road Loch Tay, Ardeonaig, Perthshire, FK21 8SU
T: 01567 820400 E: info@ardeonaighotel.co.uk W: ardeonaighotel.co.uk

Indicated Prices:

Double	from £147.00 per room	Twin	from £147.00 per room
		Suite	from £297.00 per room

125

Stirling & Trossachs: Guest Houses and B&Bs

Callander

Annfield Guest House

Open: Mar-Dec **Map Ref: 1H**

★★★★
GUEST HOUSE

18 North Church Street, Callander, Perthshire, FK17 8EG
T: 01877 330204 E: reservations@annfieldguesthouse.co.uk W: annfieldguesthouse.co.u

Indicated Prices:

Single	from £40.00 per room	Twin	from £60.00 per room
Double	from £60.00 per room	Family	from £75.00 per room

748

 PRICES STATED ARE ESTIMATES AND MAY BE SUBJECT TO CHANGE. PRICES ARE PER PERSON PER NIGHT UNLESS OTHERWISE STATED. AWARDS CORRECT AS OF BEGINNING OF OCTOBER 2009

allander

Vesterton Bed and Breakfast

Open: Feb-Oct **Map Ref: 1H3**

★★★★
BED AND BREAKFAST

Westerton, Leny Road, Callander, Perthshire, FK17 8AJ
T: 01877 330147 E: westerton.callander@tiscali.co.uk W: westerton.co.uk

Indicated Prices:

Double from £75.00 per room

63838

illin

)all Lodge Country House

Open: Apr-Oct **Map Ref: 1H2**

★★★★
GUEST HOUSE

Main Street, Killin, Perthshire, FK21 8TN
T: 01567 820217 E: connor@dalllodge.co.uk W: dalllodge.co.uk

Indicated Prices:

Single from £32.00
Double from £27.00 per person
Twin from £30.00 per person
Family from £38.00 per person
Suite from £38.00 per person

22048

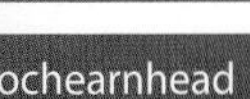

ochearnhead

Aansewood Country House

Open: All year **Map Ref: 1H2**

★★★★
GUEST HOUSE

Lochearnhead, Stirling, FK19 8NS
T: 01567 830213 E: stay@mansewoodcountryhouse.co.uk W: mansewoodcountryhouse.co.uk

Indicated Prices:

Single from £45.00 per room
Double from £66.00 per room
Twin from £66.00 per room

75801

tirling

Ars Moira Stewart

Open: All year excl 15 Dec-15 Jan **Map Ref: 2A4**

★★★★
BED AND BREAKFAST

West Plean House, Denny Road, Stirling, FK7 8HA
T: 01786 812208 E: moira@westpleanhouse.com W: westpleanhouse.com

Indicated Prices:

Single from £50.00 per person
Double from £40.00 per person
Twin from £40.00 per person
Children under 12 half price

63729

Stirling & Trossachs: Self Catering

Callander

Leny Estate Self Catering Ltd

Open: All year **Map Ref: 1H**

Leny Estate is a small family run business offering luxury self catering properties. Our 16th century castle conversion 'The North Wing' is on three levels and retains many original features but is fully modernised. Our self-contained two bedroom lodges all have elevated panoramic views over the countryside with large private balconies and bbq area.

AWAITING GRADING

Leny Estate, Callander, Perthshire, FK17 8HA
T: 01877 331078 E: res@lenyestate.com W: lenyestate.com

2 Cottages	2 Bedrooms	Sleeps 6
5 Cabins	2 Bedrooms	Sleeps 6
1 Apartment	2 Bedrooms	Sleeps 4

Prices – Cottage: £560.00-£880.00 Per Week
Prices – Cabin: £450.00-£775.00 Per Week
Prices – Apartment: £975.00-£1305.00 Per Wee

Short breaks available

838

by Killin, Morenish

Morenish Mews

Open: All year **Map Ref: 1H**

★★★★
SELF CATERING

by Killin, Perthshire, FK21 8TX
T: 01567 820527 E: stay@morenishmews.com W: morenishmews.com

2 Cottages	1 Bedroom	Sleeps 1-2
1 Apartment	1 Bedroom	Sleeps 1-2

Prices – Cottage: £225.00-£375.00 Per Week
Prices – Apartment: £225.00-£375.00 Per Week

Short breaks available

725

tirling

ewholme House

Open: All year **Map Ref: 2A4**

ewholme is a large six bedroomed lwardian house standing in its wn mature and secluded gardens. ving room, drawing room, large ning room and modern recently furbished kitchen and large off ad secluded parking. Satellite TV. x bedrooms and three bathrooms. ternet connection, heating and ectric included. 40 mins from linburgh and Glasgow airports.

★★★★
SELF CATERING

19 Birkhill Road, Stirling, FK7 9LA
T: 01786 442001 E: newholme1@btconnect.com W: newholme.co.uk

1 House | 6 Bedrooms | Sleeps 1-12

Prices – House:
£500.00-£1500.00 **Per Week**

Short breaks available

47268

Stirling & Trossachs: EatScotland Gold and Silver establishments

quhidder

onachyle Mhor Hotel

GOLD

lquhidder,
rling,
9 8PQ
1877 384 622

The restaurant prides itself on using the best of what it can gather within 30 miles. The farm surrounding the hotel provides the beef, lamb, venison and pork whenever possible.

drum

e Real Food Café

SILVER

in Street,
ndrum,
21 8RU
1838 400 235

The Real Food Cafe has won numerous awards for its unique, great quality, great tasting food using locally sourced, sustainable produce.

Outdoor spa, The Gleneagles Hotel, Auchterarder

Welcome to Perthshire, Angus & Dundee

Perthshire, where lowland meets Highland, is a region for rural relaxation. Known as Big Tree Country, you'll not only find Europe's oldest tree but one of Britain's tallest and the world's highest hedge all in this area. The beauty of the unspoilt landscape extends to moors, lochs and the famous peak of Schiehallion. The Queen's View over Loch Tummel towards Glencoe is one of Scotland's most breathtaking.

Relax in The Spa at The Gleneagles Hotel, or play a round on its championship courses. The resort is an easy drive to Perth, where you can enjoy concerts and theatre or browse its boutiques.

Further east is Angus, a contrasting mix of craggy coastline, romantic castles and the Angus Glens, as well as golf greats like Carnoustie. Look out for wildlife, both inland and offshore, as well as glorious gardens across the region.

Dundee, Scotland's fourth largest city, has its own Cultural Quarter with galleries, theatre, live music and speciality shopping. Dundee is also the permanent home of Captain Scott's famous ship, RRS Discovery.

01 Loch Tummel from the Queen's View, Perthshire

02 Scone Palace, Perthshire

03 Atholl Highlanders, Europe's only private army, at Blair Castle

04 The cellar, Gleneagles Hotel, Auchterarder

Inspired ideas for you to indulge

SCONE PALACE

Scone Palace (pronounced Skoon) was the crowning place of Scottish kings and home to the Stone of Destiny. Now home to the Earls of Mansfield, the palace opens its magnificent State Rooms to visitors every April to October. After your tour, drop into the Gift Shop for exclusive ranges in silk and wool, tapestries and samplers.
scone-palace.co.uk

THE FAMOUS GROUSE EXPERIENCE

Glenturret, just outside Crieff, is Scotland's oldest malt whisky distillery. It is also the most visited thanks to The Famous Grouse Experience. Get to know this renowned tipple on a variety of tours. Then sit back for a grouse's eye view of Scotland, soaring over many of the country's landmarks.
thefamousgrouse.com

PERTH 800

This year is a big one for Perth as it celebrates the 800th anniversary of being granted a Royal Burgh Charter by King William the Lion of Scotland. Look out for heritage, sport, arts and cultural activities as part of Perth 800's year-long programme of events to mark the occasion.
perth800.com

GLAMIS CASTLE

Famed for its Macbeth connections, Glamis Castle is arguably Scotland's finest fairytale castle. Glamis was the birthplace of Princess Margaret and the Queen Mother's childhood home. Against the backdrop of the Grampian Mountains, Glamis Castle is host to the Grand Scottish Proms in August, where rousing music combines with a spectacular fireworks display.
glamis-castle.co.uk

THE HOUSE OF BRUAR

Close to Blair Atholl, The House of Bruar is 'The Home of Country Clothing'. Choose from the UK's largest collection of cashmeres in the Knitwear Hall or pick up a wicker hamper of Scottish fine foods in the Food Hall. There's also The Gallery, Country Living Hall and more to explore.
houseofbruar.com

01 Exceptional dining at 63 Tay Street Restaurant, Perth

02 Applying the finishing touches at Gordon's Restaurant, Inverkeilor

03 The famous Arbroath Smokies

04 The finest local ingredients presented to perfection

Savour the real taste of Scotland

ANDREW FAIRLIE AT GLENEAGLES

Andrew Fairlie at Gleneagles is Scotland's first restaurant to gain two Michelin stars. This mecca of culinary excellence serves simple food brilliantly prepared within the five-star Gleneagles Hotel. Order à la carte or try the menu du marché or menu dégustation. The ultimate luxury treat.
EatScotland Gold Award
andrewfairlie.com

ARBROATH SMOKIE

Just like champagne, the Arbroath Smokie is safeguarded by the EU. Haddock is smoked using traditional methods dating back to the late 1800s. The Arbroath Smokie originated in the small fishing village of Auchmithie. The But 'n' Ben Restaurant there is renowned for its seafood with the Smokie pancake a speciality.

63 TAY STREET

The emphasis of this Perth restaurant is on sourcing the best of what is both local and seasonal. Dishes include home-cured Scottish salmon, Aberdeen Angus steak and East Perthshire summer berries. Enjoy lunch in the restaurant's bright modern interior or relax over dinner in a sophisticated evening atmosphere.
EatScotland Silver Award
63taystreet.com

CASTLETON HOUSE HOTEL

This traditional country house hotel near Glamis finds the most local of sources for its highly-rated cuisine – its vegetable garden. Castleton also has free-range chickens and home-rears its own Tamworth pork, fed on the orchard's windfall apples. In summer, guests can buy free-range eggs from the hotel.
castletonglamis.co.uk

GORDON'S RESTAURANT

Gordon's is a destination restaurant tucked away in the tiny Angus village of Inverkeilor. It's a family-run business, with father and son the experienced chefs. Together they create stylish dishes using regional ingredients like Scotch lamb and Arbroath Smokie. You can also stay overnight in one of the restaurant's five bedrooms.
EatScotland Award
gordonsrestaurant.co.uk

Something a little bit different

HIGHLAND SAFARIS

Get closer to the rugged beauty of Highland Perthshire on a wildlife tour with Highland Safaris. Your driver takes you off-road in a 4x4 vehicle to explore the Perthshire estate. Keep your eyes peeled and camera ready for red deer, mountain hare and golden eagles on the popular Mountain Safari. highlandsafaris.net

YU SPA

Within the stylish surroundings of the Apex City Quay Hotel you'll find the sanctuary that is Yu Spa. Its holistic approach to wellbeing lets you relax in herbal-infused steam rooms or de-stress with a hot stone therapy. Elemis treatments for men and women get you looking and feeling your best. yuspa.co.uk

OPEN ROAD HIRE

Take to the open road in an open-top sports car. It's a great way to enjoy the quiet and scenic roads of the Scottish Highlands. Perth-based Open Road Hire offers self-drive in the Caterham Super Seven, a modern classic and the ultimate fun car. This is a real treat for all motor enthusiasts. openroadhire.co.uk

TAY DOLPHIN WATCHING

In recent years, bottle nose dolphins have started to appear in the River Tay. They are thought to be part of the Moray Firth bottle nose dolphin population. It remains to be seen whether they are setting up a new Tay Estuary home or just on extended holidays from March to September. mvstay.org

01 RRS Discovery

02 The majestic golden eagle

03 Blair Castle, Perthshire

04 Vintage cars at the Scottish Transport Extravaganza

05 Bottle nose dolphins have been spotted in the Tay Estuary

Time to plan your perfect day

PERTH FESTIVAL OF THE ARTS
20 – 30 May 2010
Perth's annual 11-day festival is a real celebration of the arts, from opera and classical music to rock, jazz, dance and the visual arts. This year, you can enjoy English Touring Opera performing three operas, including "The Marriage of Figaro". Manchester's Halle Orchestra and The Moscow State Symphony Orchestra are also appearing.
perthfestival.co.uk

THE SCOTTISH TRANSPORT EXTRAVAGANZA
10 – 11 July 2010
Glamis Castle grounds provide a suitably period setting for what is Scotland's premier vintage motoring event. Over 1,000 vehicles are expected over the two days of the annual extravaganza. There are more than 150 stalls of motor-related items and antiques to browse, as well as a craft tent where you can see artists crafting their own goods.
glamis-castle.co.uk

DUNDEE FLOWER & FOOD FESTIVAL
3 – 5 September 2010
Head to Dundee for one of Scotland's tastiest and most vibrant festivals. The Floral Marquee is a riot of colour and fragrance. And you can pick up some hot tips from the area's top chefs in the Food Fair, as well as the best local home-baking.
dundeeflowerandfoodfestival.com

GAME CONSERVANCY SCOTTISH FAIR
2 – 4 July 2010
Set in the grounds of Scone Palace, this annual fair is one of Scotland's main countryside events. It's a full weekend celebration of all things country, including falconry and sheepdog displays, clay pigeon shooting, gundog and fishing competitions. There's also a Food Hall with local produce and a Cookery Theatre.
scottishfair.com

BLAIR CASTLE INTERNATIONAL HORSE TRIALS
26 – 29 August 2010
Scotland's most visited historic house is host for four days to international equestrian sport. Two days of elegant dressage are followed by cross-country and show-jumping. There's a popular Food Hall, as well as more than 200 trade stands. On Saturday and Sunday, you can enjoy displays and demonstrations at the Country Fair.
blairhorsetrials.co.uk

PERTHSHIRE, ANGUS & DUNDEE

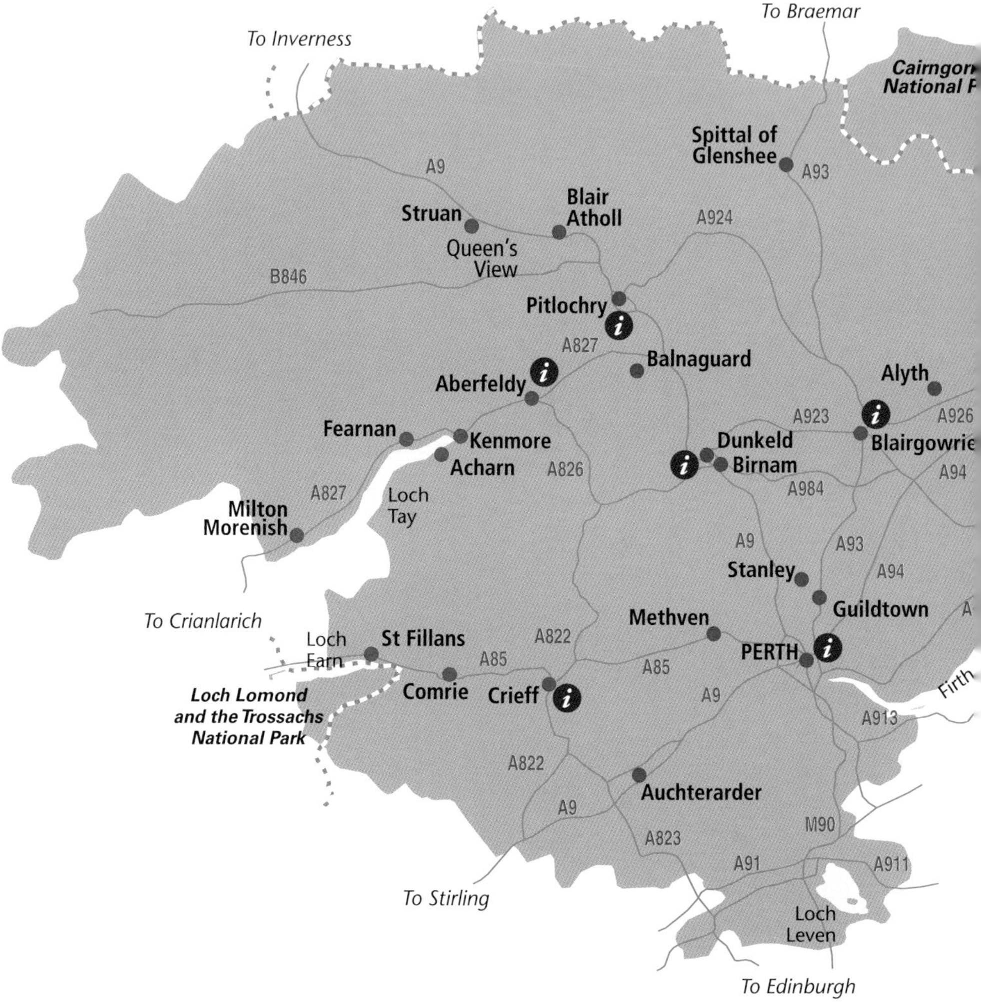

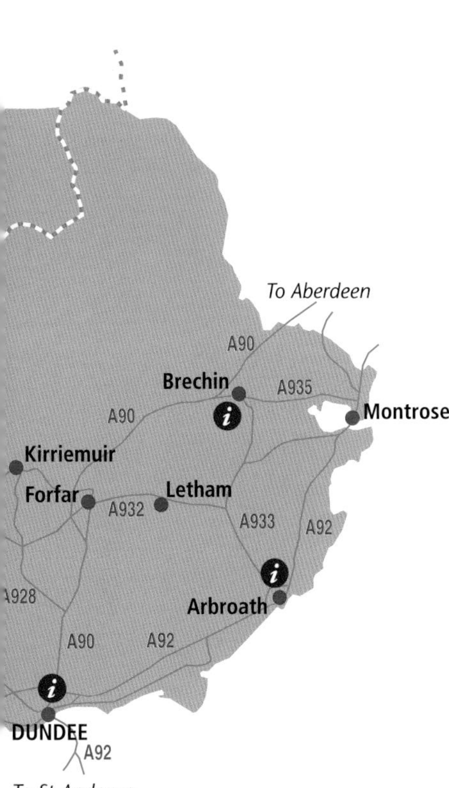

© Collins Bartholomew Ltd 2009

VisitScotland Information Centres

To help you plan and book your trip to Scotland email our travel experts at info@visitscotland.com. When you arrive call into one of our Information Centres where our friendly experts can offer advice on all things local as well as sharing their wider knowledge of Scotland. We don't just advise either. We can sort out your accommodation and all your travel needs, as well as tickets for events across Scotland. So if you're looking to get the most from your visit, there really is only one place to go.

ANGUS & DUNDEE

Arbroath	Harbour Visitor Centre, Fishmarket Quay, Arbroath, DD11 1PS
Brechin	Pictavia Centre, Haughmuir, Brechin, DD9 6RL
Dundee	Discovery Point, Riverside Drive, Dundee, DD1 4XA

PERTHSHIRE

Aberfeldy	The Square, Aberfeldy, PH15 2DD
Blairgowrie	26 Wellmeadow, Blairgowrie, PH10 6AS
Crieff	High Street, Crieff, PH7 3HU
Dunkeld	The Cross, Dunkeld, PH8 0AN
Perth	Lower City Mills, West Mill Street, Perth, PH1 5QP
Pitlochry	22 Atholl Road, Pitlochry, PH16 5BX

- LOCAL KNOWLEDGE
- WHERE TO STAY
- ACCOMMODATION BOOKING
- PLACES TO VISIT
- THINGS TO DO
- MAPS AND GUIDES
- TRAVEL ADVICE
- ROUTE PLANNING
- WHERE TO SHOP AND EAT
- LOCAL CRAFTS AND PRODUCE
- EVENT INFORMATION
- TICKETS

Perthshire: Hotels

Aberfeldy

Fortingall Hotel

Open: All year **Map Ref: 2A**

Fortingall is a traditional country house hotel with a modern twist, offering a warm and friendly welcome. There are ten stylish bedrooms, a bar with a wide selection of whisky and a two AA rosette restaurant that offers locally-sourced and delicious cuisine.

★★★★ SMALL HOTEL

Fortingall, by Aberfeldy, PH15 2NQ
T: 01887 830367 E: hotel@fortingallhotel.com W: fortingall.com

Indicated Prices:

Double	from £80.00 per person	Family	from £105.00 per person
Twin	from £80.00 per person	Suite	from £105.00 per person

266

 PRICES STATED ARE ESTIMATES AND MAY BE SUBJECT TO CHANGE. PRICES ARE PER PERSON PER NIGHT UNLESS OTHERWISE STATED. AWARDS CORRECT AS OF BEGINNING OF OCTOBER 2009

ıchterarder

ıe Gleneagles Hotel

Open: All year **Map Ref: 2A3**

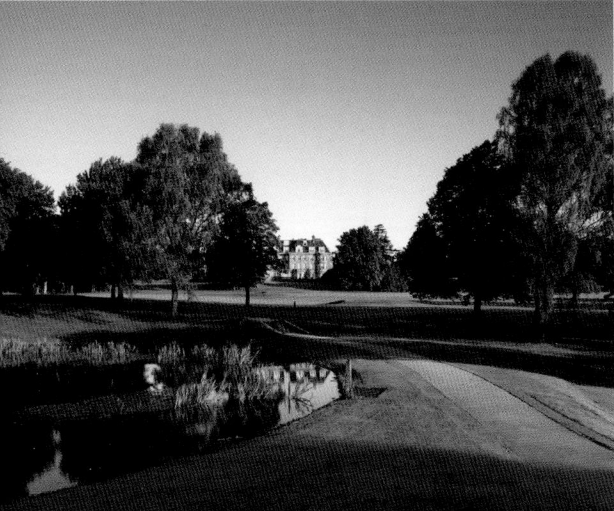

★★★★★ GOLD HOTEL

Auchterarder,
Perthshire, PH3 1NF
T: 01764 662231
E: resort.sales@gleneagles.com
W: gleneagles.com

Features:

- Three world-class championship golf courses
- Award-winning destination spa by ESPA
- Andrew Fairlie's two Michelin Star restaurant
- Nine two-bedroom top floor Spirit Suites
- Wide range of outdoor leisure pursuits

in a magnificent 850-acre ate. Gleneagles® 5 Red Star ɔrt is one hour's drive from sgow and Edinburgh.

ː hotel is a byword for style, gance and comfort, with three ımpionship golf courses and a ːt of outdoor activities.

To relax there's an award-winning spa by ESPA, as well as a range of bars and restaurants, including the Michelin starred Andrew Fairlie. Gleneagles is a sanctuary from the modern world, offering the best of Scotland every day of the year.

Indicated Prices:

Double	from £410.00 per room
Twin	from £410.00 per room
Family	from £490.00 per room
Suite	from £945.00 per suite

59091

Pitlochry

Pine Trees Hotel

Open: All year **Map Ref: 2A**

★★★★ COUNTRY HOUSE HOTEL

Strathview Terrace, Pitlochry, PH16 5QR
T: 01796 472121 E: info@pinetreeshotel.co.uk W: pinetreeshotel.co.uk

Indicated Prices:

Single	from £47.00 per room	Twin	from £94.00 per room
Double	from £94.00 per room		

498

Perthshire: Guest Houses and B&Bs

Crieff

Merlindale B&B

Open: mid Jan-mid Dec **Map Ref: 2A**

★★★★ BED AND BREAKFAST

Perth Road, Crieff, PH7 3EQ
T: 01764 655205 E: merlin.dale@virgin.net W: merlindale.co.uk

Indicated Prices:

Single	from £45.00	Twin	from £70.00 per room
Double	from £70.00 per room		

381

Dunkeld

Letter Farm

Open: May-Nov **Map Ref: 2B**

★★★★ FARM HOUSE

Letter Farm, Dunkeld, Perthshire, PH8 0HH
T: 01350 724254 E: letterfarm@btconnect.com W: letterfarm.co.uk

Indicated Prices:

Single	from £40.00	Twin	from £64.00 per room
Double	from £64.00 per room		

353

erth
chnacarry Guest House
Open: All year **Map Ref: 2B2**

GUEST HOUSE

3 Picullen Crescent, Perth, PH2 7HT
T: 01738 621421 E: info@achnacarry.co.uk W: www.achnacarry.co.uk

Indicated Prices:

Single	from £30.00	Twin	from £27.50 per person
Double	from £27.50 per person	Family	from £65.00 per room

10981

erth
ckinnoull Guest House
Open: All year excl Xmas & New Year **Map Ref: 2B2**

★★★★
GUEST HOUSE

5 Pitcullen Crescent, Perth, PH2 7HT
T: 01738 634165 E: ackinnoull@yahoo.com W: ackinnoull.com

Indicated Prices:

Single	from £30.00 per room	Twin	from £50.00 per room
Double	from £50.00 per room	Family	from £60.00 per room

11010

erth
alvey
Open: All year excl Xmas & New Year **Map Ref: 2B2**

★★★★
BED AND BREAKFAST

55 Dunkeld Road, Perth, PH1 5RP
T: 01738 621714 E: info@dalvey-perth.co.uk W: dalvey-perth.co.uk

Indicated Prices:

Single	from £35.00 per room	Twin	from £60.00 per room
Double	from £60.00 per room		

22130

Perth

Halton House B&B

Open: All year **Map Ref: 2E**

Halton House is a delightfully decorated and comfortable arts and crafts house situated in a quiet central location in Perth. You will receive a warm welcome from your hosts Jody and David Brown. Fishing, shooting and golf parties a speciality and can be arranged or tailored to suit.

★★★★
BED AND BREAKFAST

Halton House, 11 Tullylumb Terrace, Perth, PH1 1BA
T: 01738 643446 E: jody@haltonhousebandb.co.uk W: haltonhousebandb.co.uk

Indicated Prices:

Single	from £50.00 per room	Twin	from £80.00 per room
Double	from £80.00 per room		

826

by Pitlochry, Balnaguard

Balbeagan

Open: Mar-Nov **Map Ref: 2B**

Ann and Paul welcome you to our friendly B&B in tranquil Balnaguard, six miles from Pitlochry. Traditionally produced foods for full Scottish breakfasts; smoked fish; platters (photo) or Balbeagan pancakes. Bargain weekly rates (£150-£175). Advice given on walking (routes provided), historical sites, landscape and wildlife locations. You'll love staying here!

★★★★
BED AND BREAKFAST

Balbeagan, Balnaguard, Pitlochry, PH9 0PY
T: 01796 482627 E: paulscroft@aol.com W: balbeagan.com

Indicated Prices:

Single	from £25.00 per room	Twin	from £50.00 per room

121

Perthshire: Self Catering

ılyth

'he Steadings

Open: All year **Map Ref: 2C1**

ɔur VIP cottages for dog lovers in
ɐe pastoral valley of Strathmore.
ı hour and a half from Edinburgh,
ıen Prosen, Glen Isla, Glen Clova
 star) and Glen Doll (4 star) are
ɋuipped to the highest standard.
ɔmfortable beds with Egyptian
ɔtton linen, attention to details,
ɘsh mountain air.

★★★★ UP TO ★★★★★
SELF CATERING

Auchteralyth, Alyth, PH11 8JT
T: 01575 530474 E: anne@auchteralythsteadings.com W: auchteralythsteadings.com

4 Cottages 1-2 Bedrooms Sleeps 2-12

Prices – Cottage:
£250.00-£700.00 Per Week

Short breaks available

72316

Ɔomrie

ɜlenbuckie House – Lawers Estate

Open: All year **Map Ref: 2A2**

★★★★
SELF CATERING

The Estate Office, Lawers House, Comrie, Perthshire
T: 01764 670050 E: estate.office@lawers.co.uk

1 House 7 Bedrooms Sleeps 12

Prices – House:
£700.00-£2000.00 Per Week

Short breaks available

74223

by Kenmore, Acharn

Bracken Lodges

Open: All year **Map Ref: 1H**

★★★★ SELF CATERING

Loch Tay, Acharn, by Kenmore, Aberfeldy, Perthshire, PH15 2HX
T: 01567 820169 E: info@bracken-lodges.com W: bracken-lodges.com

8 Lodges | 1-3 Bedrooms | Sleeps 2-6

Prices – Lodge:
£375.00-£750.00 Per Week

Short breaks available

1594

by Kenmore, Fearnan

Mrs Morag Pugh

Open: All year **Map Ref: 2A**

★★★★ SELF CATERING

Tigh Na Clachan, Fearnan, Aberfeldy, Perthshire, PH15 2PF
T: 01670 772234 E: moragpugh@hotmail.com

1 Bungalow | 4 Bedrooms | Sleeps 7

Prices – Bungalow:
£500.00-£800.00 Per Week

Short breaks available

6116

by Kenmore, Glenlyon

Innerwick Estate

Open: All year **Map Ref: 1H**

Three charming traditional stone cottages on a family run farm/ sporting estate. Fully modernised, log fires, panoramic views and varied walks. National Scenic Area with special interest for botanists and bird watchers. Fishing, tennis on site. Golf, riding, watersports within 30 minutes. Weekly prices £325-£1230 inc of heating. Pets welcome. Brochure available.

★★★★ UP TO ★★★★★ SELF CATERING

Glenlyon, Aberfeldy, Perthshire, PH15 2PP
T: 01887 866222 E: enquiries@innerwick.com W: innerwick.com

1 Cottage | 2 Bedrooms | Sleeps 4
2 Houses | 3-4 Bedrooms | Sleeps 6-8

Prices – Cottage:
£325.00-£540.00 Per Week

Prices – House:
£360.00-£1230.00 Per Week

Short breaks available

3168

 PRICES STATED ARE ESTIMATES AND MAY BE SUBJECT TO CHANGE. PRICES ARE PER UNIT PER WEEK UNLESS OTHERWISE STATED. AWARDS CORRECT AS OF BEGINNING OF OCTOBER 2009

'erth

'ome from Home

Open: All year **Map Ref: 2B2**

uiet peaceful location yet
:ntrally situated with private
arking. Personally supervised by
wner you are assured of a warm
elcome. Within walking distance
' railway and bus stations,
umerous restaurants, shops and
tractions, making an ideal base
r a break at any time of year.

★★★★
SELF CATERING

South Inch Court, Perth, PH2 8BG
T: 01577 863367/07790 071757 E: home46fromhome@aol.com W: homefromhome.uk.net

1 Apartment 2 Bedrooms Sleeps 1-4

Prices – Apartment:
£315.00-£500.00 **Per Week**

Short breaks available

44330

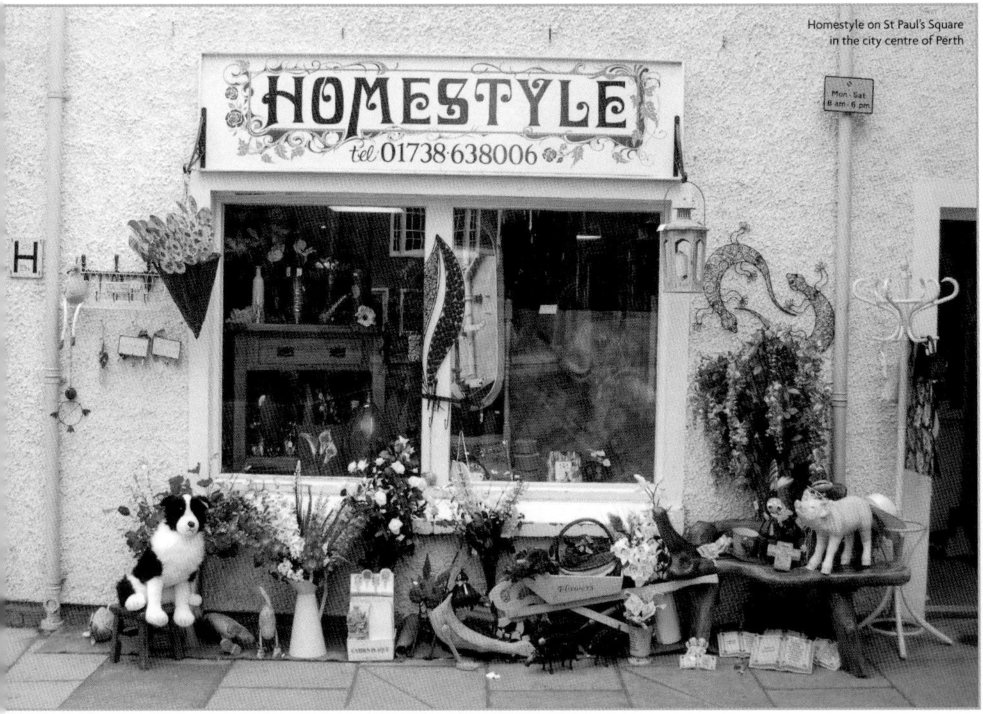

Homestyle on St Paul's Square in the city centre of Perth

Angus & Dundee: Hotels

The RRS Discover
Discovery Point, Dun

undee

pex City Quay Hotel & Spa

Open: All year **Map Ref: 2D2**

★★★★ HOTEL

1 West Victoria Dock Road, Dundee, DD1 3JP
T: 0845 365 0000
E: reservations@apexhotels.co.uk
W: apexhotels.co.uk

Features:

- 152 luxurious and contemporary bedrooms
- Yu Spa
- Elemis treatment rooms
- Metro Brasserie and Bar
- Free wi-fi and local calls

Indicated Prices:

Double	from £75.00 per room
Twin	from £75.00 per room
Family	from £75.00 per room
Suite	from £175.00 per room

12301

ndee is a vibrant and smopolitan city on the east ast of Scotland, which has more an earned its reputation as a ty of Discovery' – an ideal base touring Scotland's east coast. otland's fourth largest city, it's me to the Apex City Quay Hotel pa, perfectly placed to enjoy stunning views of the Quay and Tay River and Bridge. A stylish contemporary hotel surrounded by businesses, thriving nightlife and some of the city's best shopping.

Angus & Dundee: Guest Houses and B&Bs

Arbroath

Brucefield Boutique B&B

Open: All year **Map Ref: 2E**

Brucefield is Arbroath's only boutique B&B, offering contemporary and stylish accommodation in a 1920's manor house within walking distance to the centre of Arbroath. We offer four modern en-suite bedrooms with luxurious features such as flat screen TVs, DVDs, in-room fridges and wireless broadband. Our gourmet breakfasts are legendary!

★★★★★
BED AND BREAKFAST

Brucefield, Cliffburn Road, Arbroath, Angus, DD11 5BS
T: 01241 875393 E: info@brucefieldbandb.com W: brucefieldbandb.com

Indicated Prices:

Single	from £75.00 per room	Twin	from £80.00 per room
Double	from £80.00 per room	Suite	from £90.00 per room

8678

by Kirriemuir, Kingoldrum

Falls of Holm Bed and Breakfast

Open: All year **Map Ref: 2C**

★★★★
BED AND BREAKFAST

Falls of Holm, Kingoldrum, by Kirriemuir, Angus, DD8 5HY
T: 01575 575867 E: fallsofholm@btinternet.com W: fallsofholm.com

Indicated Prices:

Single	from £35.00	Twin	from £30.00 per person
Double	from £30.00 per person	Family	from £30.00 per person

2558

 PRICES STATED ARE ESTIMATES AND MAY BE SUBJECT TO CHANGE. PRICES ARE PER PERSON PER NIGHT UNLESS OTHERWISE STATED. AWARDS CORRECT AS OF BEGINNING OF OCTOBER 2009

Iontrose

skview Farm B&B

Open: All year **Map Ref: 4F12**

★★★★
BED AND BREAKFAST

St Cyrus, Montrose, Angus, DD10 0AQ
T: 01674 830890 E: kathsdanes@aol.com W: eskviewfarm.co.uk

Indicated Prices:

Single	from £35.00 per room	Twin	from £55.00 per room
Double	from £55.00 per room	Family	from £70.00 per room

C V

25115

Scurdie Ness Lighthouse
by Montrose, Angus

Perthshire, Angus & Dundee: EatScotland Gold and Silver establishments

Perth

63 Tay Street Restaurant

SILVER

63 Tay Street,
Perth,
PH2 8NN
T: 01738 441 451

This highly rated restaurant, located in the heart of historic Perth, uses produce sourced locally and from fine suppliers a little further afield.

Perth

Acanthus, Parklands Hotel

2 St Leonards Bank,
Perth,
PH2 8EB
T: 01738 622 451

Acanthus is a small, intimate restaurant in a friendly and cosy hotel in the centre of Perth, enjoying excellent views and serving dishes using top quality local produce.

Auchterarder

Andrew Fairlie @ Gleneagles

Gleneagles Hotel,
Auchterarder,
PH3 1NF
T: 01764 694 267

Andrew Fairlie creates signature dishes in his intimate, two Michelin-starred restaurant, where every detail has been carefully planned to create a truly special experience.

Ardeonaig, Loch Tay

Ardeonaig Hotel and Restaurant

South Road Loch Tay,
Ardeonaig, Perthshire,
FK21 8SU
T: 01567 820 400

Ardeonaig is dedicated to providing the freshest, local seasonal produce, cooked with care and flair, to bring out its full flavour.
A menu dictated by what's best in season.

Stanley

Ballathie House Hotel

Kinclaven, Stanley,
Perthshire,
PH1 4QN
T: 01250 883 268

Ballathie Country House is in an idyllic picturesque setting on its own Perthshire Estate. The ambience is warm, the staff are exceptionally welcoming and the food is exemplary.

Callander

Creagan House Restaurant

Strathyre, Callander,
Perthshire,
FK18 8ND
T: 01877 384 638

Personally run by the owners. The accent is firmly on fresh, high quality, local ingredients, interestingly presented.

Perth

Deans at Let's Eat

77-79 Kinnoull Street,
Perth,
PH1 5EZ
T: 01738 643 377

Willie Deans describes his cooking as vibrant modern Scottish, with a focus on flavour and seasonality. Prime Scotch beef, fresh fish and seafood are delivered daily.

Perthshire

Deseo

The Gleneagles Hotel,
Auchterarder,
Perthshire, PH3 1NF
T: 0800 704 705

The lively Deseo restaurant at the Gleneagles Hotel offers fine food from the Mediterranean. The food emporium is like a bustling market, full of fresh ingredients.

Perth

Opus One at The New County Hotel

New County Hotel,
22-30 New County Place,
Perth, PH2 8EE
T: 01738 623 355

Enjoy fine dining at its very best in Opus One, a contemporary restaurant which produces meals using only fresh, local ingredients.

Bridge of Earn

The Roost Restaurant

Forgandenny Road, Kintillo,
Bridge of Earn,
Perthshire, PH2 9AZ
T: 01738 812 111

Husband and wife team, Tim and Anna Dover extend a warm welcome at The Roost Restaurant. This intimate little restaurant is open for breakfasts, lunches and weekend evening meals.

By Forfar

Victorian Kitchen Restaurant

Glamis Castle,
By Forfar, Angus,
DD8 1RJ
T: 01307 475 305

The spires, turrets, towers and statues demand attention as you approach the castle. This is a popular visitor attraction, enhanced further by the Victorian Kitchen Restaurant.

The City of Perth and the River Tay photographed at dusk

ST ANDREWS & THE KINGDOM OF FIFE

The world famous Old Course, St Andrews

Welcome to St Andrews & the Kingdom of Fife

The Kingdom of Fife: the very title hints at its important past, when Dunfermline was Scotland's ancient capital. Fife hugs the east coastline of Scotland, bordered by the Forth and Tay estuaries and the North Sea. It combines rich agricultural land with coastal scenery and enchanting villages like Culross.

A country drive brings you to a royal palace, thriving fishing villages and communities of local artists and craftspeople. Arguably Fife's biggest claim to fame is as the Home of Golf. More than 45 courses, from links to parkland, spread across the region.

The Old Course at St Andrews is a mecca for most golfers and is host to The Open Championship in 2010. St Andrews has more to offer than just golf, of course. Harbour walks, individual boutiques, regular theatre and concerts all add to its appeal.

With so much produce grown or raised in the region, the local Fife larder is particularly strong. Markets regularly appear in Fife's towns and villages while restaurants throughout the area offer the best of Fife on a plate.

Inspired ideas for you to indulge

01 West Sands, St Andrews, Fife

02 Falkland Palace, Fife

03 Luxurious spa at Fairmont St Andrews Hotel

04 St Andrews Castle, Fife

05 The harbour at St Monans in Fife's East Neuk

06 Aberdour Golf Club, Fife

FALKLAND PALACE

Falkland Palace was a royal lodge for Stuart kings and queens hunting deer and wild boar in the forests of Fife. The palace was also a favourite childhood playground of Mary, Queen of Scots. Built in the 1500s, it houses the original Royal Tennis Court, the oldest in Britain still in use.

nts.org.uk

HOME OF GOLF

As the Home of Golf, Fife has more than 45 golf courses to play. St Andrews stands out but elsewhere in Fife are courses with their own charm and challenges. Ladybank and Kingsbarns are both qualifying venues for the Open Championship in 2010. Golfers of all levels can enjoy playing at Cupar, reputedly the world's oldest nine-hole.

visitfife.com/golf

PERSONAL SPAS

St Andrews has two five-star hotel resorts to its name, each with destination spa facilities. The Old Course Hotel Resort & Spa overlooks the famous golf course. The Fairmont St Andrews makes the most of its tranquil coastal location. You can book into either for an hour or a day of pampering pleasure.

oldcoursehotel.kohler.com
fairmont.com/standrews

AWARD-WINNING BEACHES

Scotland's Blue Flag award scheme recognises beaches for their clean sands, fresh water and good facilities. Fife has four such beaches at Aberdour Silver Sands, Burntisland, Leven East and St Andrews West Sands. They're great places for peaceful strolls, quiet contemplation or just for their marvellous views.

THE EAST NEUK VILLAGES

The picturesque villages of the East Neuk are a highlight of a trip to Fife. Each village has remained largely untouched over the centuries and provides a reminder of a bygone age. Discover the cobbled streets and harbour of Crail, Anstruther with its Fisheries Museum, as well as Elie, St Monans and the arts community of Pittenweem.
eastneukwide.co.uk

THE FIFE COASTAL PATH

The Fife Coastal Path begins at the Forth Bridges north of Edinburgh and ends at Dundee's Tay Bridge. The 93 miles (150km) in between provide a great stretch of walking for all levels of walker. Spend a day wandering part of the route to take in sandy beaches, coastal wildlife and local villages.
fifecoastalpath.co.uk

Savour the real taste of Scotland

THE INN AT LATHONES
This charming 400-year-old coaching inn close to St Andrews has a well-earned reputation for good food. The atmosphere is relaxed, the menu is fresh, organic and locally-sourced and there's an extensive wine list. You can also spend the night in one of the Inn's 21 suites and bedrooms.
theinn.co.uk

THE VINE LEAF RESTAURANT
You'll discover this family-run restaurant down a winding close in the centre of St Andrews. The menu's emphasis is very much on fresh local produce such as beef, game, lamb and seafood, as well as creative vegetarian dishes. The Vine Leaf is a new addition to the Good Food Guide 2010.
vineleafstandrews.co.uk

ANSTRUTHER FISH BAR & RESTAURANT
Fish and chips never tasted better and that's official. The Anstruther Fish Bar and Restaurant has won many accolades over the years, including UK Fish & Chip Shop of the Year 2008/09. Watch local fishermen bring in their catch to the harbour as you tuck into freshly-caught seafood or fish.
EatScotland Award
anstrutherfishbar.co.uk

OSTLER'S CLOSE
Tucked up an alleyway, Ostler's Close Restaurant is a real find in the market town of Cupar. Chef Jimmy Graham gives a modern twist to classic dishes of seafood, fish, meat and game while wife Amanda looks after everyone in the intimate restaurant. Definitely leave room for dessert!
EatScotland Silver Award
ostlersclose.co.uk

SANGSTER'S
Sangster's in Elie on the East Neuk coast is a culinary gem run by husband and wife team, Bruce and Jackie Sangster. Bruce was named Chef of the Year 2009 and Sangster's gained a Michelin star in the same year. Booking is recommended to sample Sangster's inventive menu.
sangsters.co.uk

01 The Inn at Lathones

02 Fresh lobster, the Vine Leaf Restaurant, St Andrews

03 The famous Anstruther Fish Bar

04 Sangster's Restaurant, Elie, East Neuk

05 Pittenweem, East Neuk

03

Something a little bit different

RAPTOR WORLD
Raptor World's series of Experience Days offers an affordable and memorable way of getting close to some of Scotland's birds of prey. Enjoy a one-hour Nose to Beak session or a whole day with these magnificent birds, at Raptor World's base in Fife, set in the Scottish hills and countryside.
raptorworld.co.uk

KINGARROCK HICKORY CLUB
Enjoy a round of golf as it used to be played at Kingarrock Hickory Club. You play the nine-hole course off Reddy Tees with original hickory-shafted clubs carried in a canvas and leather bag. There's a nip of whisky before teeing off and ginger beer and shortbread at the end.
kingarrock.com

CAMERON TOURS
Rather than struggle with maps and directions you can enjoy a private escorted tour of Fife with Cameron Tours. Their local knowledge introduces you to lesser-known aspects of the Kingdom, as well as the best places to eat, shop and visit. Each tour is tailor-made to your own individual tastes and interests.
camerontoursofscotland.co.uk

BALBIRNIE HOUSE HOTEL
Balbirnie House is one of the finest privately-owned luxury hotels in Scotland. Set in 416 acres of parkland, this Georgian country mansion house dates back to 1777. The Balbirnie Craft Centre, housed in the original stable block, is the place to find local jewellery, pottery, glassworks and leather goods.
balbirnie.co.uk

Time to plan your perfect day

01 Culross, Fife

02 Balbirnie House Hotel, Markinch, Fife

03 Golf from a bygone era at Kingarrock Hickory Club, Fife

04 Scotland's birds of prey

05 The St Andrews Festival

STANZA POETRY FESTIVAL
17 – 21 March 2010
Scotland's only regular festival dedicated to poetry is an annual opportunity to celebrate poetry in all its forms. Well-known poets read from their works and there are performances mixing poetry with music, film and dance, including poetry and music from Shetland. Join in the festival ceilidh for some rousing Scottish country dancing.
stanzapoetry.org

EAST NEUK FESTIVAL
30 June – 4 July 2010
The villages of the East Neuk combine for their annual summer festival of music and literature. Some of the area's beautiful churches provide evocative settings for classical recitals. Other venues can include Scout huts and even St Fillan's Cave in Pittenweem.
eastneukfestival.com

THE OPEN CHAMPIONSHIP
15 – 18 July 2010
The Open Championship returns to the Home of Golf for the twenty-eighth time in 2010. The Old Course, St Andrews sets the challenge for some of the greatest golfers to play for one of the world's most coveted trophies. See golf played at the highest level at this unmissable event.
visitfife.com/open2010

ST ANDREWS FESTIVAL
26 – 30 November 2010
It is fitting that the town that takes its name from Scotland's patron saint should hold a festival which celebrates Scotland's rich culture. Around St Andrew's Day, St Andrews hosts a lively programme of events, from live music and theatre to art exhibitions.
standrewsfestival.co.uk

02
LENOBLE

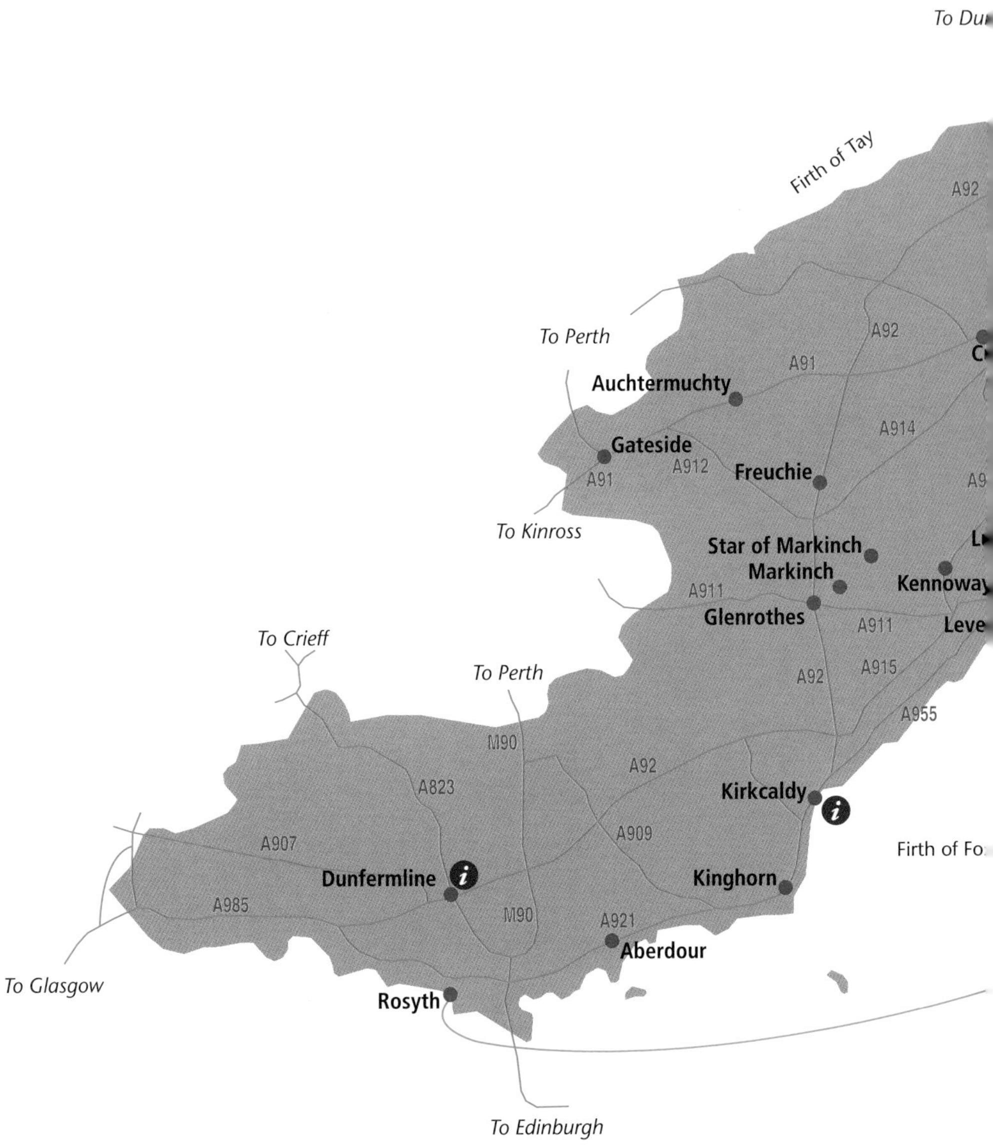

To Du
Firth of Tay
A92
To Perth
A92
A91
Auchtermuchty
A914
Gateside
A912
A91
Freuchie
A9
To Kinross
Star of Markinch
Markinch
Kennoway
A911
Glenrothes
A911
Leve
To Crieff
To Perth
A92
A915
A955
M90
A92
A823
Kirkcaldy
A909
A907
Firth of Fo
Dunfermline
Kinghorn
A985
M90
A921
Aberdour
To Glasgow
Rosyth
To Edinburgh

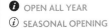

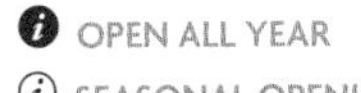

A92
A914
A919
A91
St Andrews
Strathkinness
A917
Kingsbarns
A915
Crail
A917
Upper Largo
East Neuk
Anstruther
A917
Pittenweem
A917
Elie

To Belgium

VisitScotland Information Centres

To help you plan and book your trip to Scotland email our travel experts at info@visitscotland.com. When you arrive call into one of our Information Centres where our friendly experts can offer advice on all things local as well as sharing their wider knowledge of Scotland. We don't just advise either. We can sort out your accommodation and all your travel needs, as well as tickets for events across Scotland. So if you're looking to get the most from your visit, there really is only one place to go.

FIFE

Dunfermline	1 High Street, Dunfermline, KY12 7DL
Kirkcaldy	The Merchant's House, 339 High Street, Kirkcaldy, KY1 1JL
St. Andrews	70 Market Street, St. Andrews, KY16 9NU

- LOCAL KNOWLEDGE
- WHERE TO STAY
- ACCOMMODATION BOOKING
- PLACES TO VISIT
- THINGS TO DO
- MAPS AND GUIDES
- TRAVEL ADVICE
- ROUTE PLANNING
- WHERE TO SHOP AND EAT
- LOCAL CRAFTS AND PRODUCE
- EVENT INFORMATION
- TICKETS

Kingdom of Fife: Hotels

St Andrews

Old Course Hotel, Golf Resort & Spa

Open: All year **Map Ref: 2D2**

Bordering the 17th 'Road Hole' of the world's most famous golf course in St Andrews. A Leading Hotel of the World, the five red star resort truly lives up to its reputation as Scotland's finest. Every guest who stays at the Old Course hotel receives a personal level of service.

★★★★★ HOTEL

St Andrews, Fife, KY16 9SP
T: 01334 474371 E: reservations@oldcoursehotel.co.uk W: oldcoursehotel.co.uk

Indicated Prices:

Single	from £205.00	Twin	from £235.00
Double	from £235.00	Family	from £285.00
		Suite	from £680.00

TV P C £ V

4825

by St Andrews

The Peat Inn

Open: All year excl Sun & Mon, 17-21 Nov, 24-27 Dec, 1-14 Jan 2010 **Map Ref: 2D3**

The Peat Inn is a five star restaurant with eight luxury suites situated just six miles from St Andrews. Dating from 1700's, this old coaching inn continues to attract guests from far and wide to dine in the award-winning restaurant or to stay in the luxury accommodation.

★★★★★
RESTAURANT WITH ROOMS

Peat Inn, nr St Andrews, Fife, KY15 5LH
T: 01334 840206 E: stay@thepeatinn.co.uk W: thepeatinn.co.uk

Indicated Prices:

Single	from £115.00 per room	Twin	from £175.00 per room
Double	from £175.00 per room	Family	from £225.00 per room
		Suite	from £175.00 per room

TV P C £ V

74837

Kingdom of Fife: Guest Houses and B&Bs

by Glenrothes, Star of Markinch

Priory Star B&B

Open: All year excl 16 Dec 2009-16 Jan 2010 **Map Ref: 2C3**

★★★★
BED AND BREAKFAST

East End, Star of Markinch, Glenrothes, Fife, KY7 6LQ
T: 01592 754566 E: priorystarbb@aol.com W: priorystar.com

Indicated Prices:

Single	from £28.00	Twin	from £26.00 per person
Double	from £26.00 per person	Family	from £26.00 per person

TV P

 **60113**

Kingsbarns, St Andrews
Cambo Estate
Open: All year excl Xmas & New Year **Map Ref: 2D3**

Unwind in the informal restful atmosphere of this historic family home with magnificently furnished bedrooms and bathrooms nestling on the seashore by Kingsbarns Golf Links among acres of gardens and woodlands. Close to St Andrews, picturesque fishing villages and an abundance of golf courses. Arrive a guest, leave a friend.

★★★★
BED AND BREAKFAST

Cambo House, Cambo Estate, Kingsbarns, St Andrews, KY16 8QD
T: 01333 450313 E: cambo@camboestate.com W: camboestate.com

Indicated Prices:

Single	from £62.00 per person	Twin	from £52.00 per person
Double	from £52.00 per person		

 1770

St Andrews
Six Murray Park
Open: All year **Map Ref: 2D2**

Six Murray Park is an elegant Victorian townhouse which has been transformed into a boutique styled bed and breakfast. It is set in an area of conservation right in the hub of St Andrews. It is just 250 metres from the famous Old Course and the stunning West Sands beach.

★★★★
GUEST HOUSE

6 Murray Park, St Andrews, Fife, KY16 9AW
T: 01334 473319 E: info@sixmurraypark.co.uk W: sixmurraypark.co.uk

Indicated Prices:

Single	from £40.00 per room	Twin	from £70.00 per room
Double	from £70.00 per room		

8558

by St Andrews, Strathkinness
Hawthorne House B&B
Open: All year **Map Ref: 2D2**

★★★★
BED AND BREAKFAST

33 Main Street, Strathkinness, St Andrews, Fife, KY16 9RY
T: 01334 850855 E: hawthornehouse@onetel.com W: thehawthornehouse.co.uk

Indicated Prices:

Single	from £40.00 per room	Twin	from £50.00 per room
Double	from £50.00 per room		

TV P V

29764

by Upper Largo, Drumeldrie
Bayview
Open: All year **Map Ref: 2D3**

★★★★
BED AND BREAKFAST

Drumeldrie, Upper Largo, Fife, KY8 6JD
T: 01333 360454 E: margaret@bayviewfife.com W: bayviewfife.com

Indicated Prices:

Single	from £55.00 per room	Twin	from £70.00 per room
Double	from £70.00 per room	Family	from £75.00 per room

TV P C V

72218

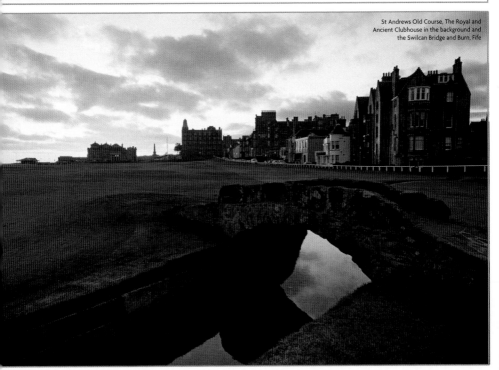

St Andrews Old Course, The Royal and Ancient Clubhouse in the background and the Swilcan Bridge and Burn, Fife

Kingdom of Fife: Self Catering

Aberdour

Capital View Lodge Cabin

Open: All year

Map Ref: 2C4

From a family holiday to a romantic escape for two, Capital View Lodge is the perfect getaway. Centrally located with easy access to Edinburgh, Glasgow and the north. Alternatively just relax in the hot tub where the view over the River Forth to Edinburgh is breathtaking. Aberdour Station one mile away.

★★★ UP TO ★★★★
SELF CATERING

Mr N Clegg, Capital View Lodge Cabin, Pleasants Farm, Aberdour, Fife, KY3 0RR
T: 01383 860661 E: info@bookselfcateringfife.co.uk W: capital-view.net

1 Cabin | 3 Bedrooms | Sleeps 5

Prices – Cabin:
£400.00-£650.00 Per Week

Short breaks available

6430

by Auchtermuchty

Pitcairlie House

Open: All year

Map Ref: 2C3

★★★★
SELF CATERING

Pitcairlie Leisure Business, Pitcairlie House, by Auchtermuchty, Newburgh, KY14 6EU
T: 01337 827418/07831 646157 E: reservations@pitcairlie-leisure.co.uk W: pitcairlie-leisure.co.uk

1 Cottage | 2 Bedrooms | Sleeps 4
4 Apartments | 2-3 Bedrooms | Sleeps 2-6

Prices – Cottage:
£290.00-£1000.00 Per Week

Prices – Apartment:
£290.00-£1000.00 Per Week

Prices vary depending on time of year and whether short break or more nigh

Short breaks available

4989

ateside

denshead Cottage Open: All year Map Ref: 2C3

★★★★ SELF CATERING

Edenshead House, Gateside, Fife, KY14 7ST
T: 01337 868210 E: gillym@totalise.co.uk or info@edenshead.co.uk W: edenshead.co.uk

1 Cottage 1 Bedroom Sleeps 1-3

Prices – Cottage:
£150.00-£300.00 Per Week

Short breaks available

24386

ingsbarns, St Andrews

ambo Estate Open: All year Map Ref: 2D3

xuriate in an awesome apartment th magnificent furniture, savouring ace and tranquillity or chill out in stylish country cottage. Nestling the seashore by Kingsbarns Golf ıks among acres of gardens and odlands, this historic family home ten minutes drive from St Andrews d picturesque fishing villages.

★★★★ SELF CATERING

Cambo House, Kingsbarns, St Andrews, Fife, KY16 8QD
T: 01333 450313 E: cambo@camboestate.com W: camboestate.com

2 Cottages	1-2 Bedrooms	Sleeps 2-4
1 Apartment	2 Bedrooms	Sleeps 4

Prices – Cottages: £290.00-£535.00 Per Week
Prices – Apartment: £510.00-£780.00 Per Week

Short breaks available

17700

Pittenweem

Sue Foan

Open: All year **Map Ref: 2D**

A charming character cottage. Luxuriously appointed. Dating back to around 1740, situated in the centre of the delightful fishing village of Pittenweem, renowned for its annual arts festival. Lovingly refurbished. Furnished to the highest standards by an interior designer. Delightful garden with barbecue. Ten miles from St Andrews.

★★★★★
SELF CATERING

18 Cecil Avenue, Queens Park, Bournemouth, BH8 9EH
T: 01202 257914 E: sue@spindlecottage.com W: spindlecottage.com

1 Cottage 3 Bedrooms Sleeps 4

Prices – Cottage:
£575.00-£1100.00 Per Week

Short breaks available

794

St Andrews

Albany Apartments

Open: All year **Map Ref: 2D**

★★★★★
SELF CATERING

28 Albany Place, North Street, St Andrews, Fife
T: 0131 346 8662 E: alastair.loudon@btconnect.com W: albany-apartments.com

1 House 3 Bedrooms Sleeps 5

Prices – House:
£840.00-£1260.00 Per Week

Short breaks available

114

St Andrews

Dr John Murchison Lovett

Open: June-mid Sept **Map Ref: 2D**

★★★★
SELF CATERING

The Auld Hoose, 1 Shorehead, St Andrews, Fife, KY16 9RG
T: 0774 8700458/0141 943 1990 E: johnlovett@johnlovett.plus.com

1 House 3 Bedrooms Sleeps 1-6

Prices – House:
£650.00-£910.00 Per Week

795

Kingdom of Fife: Food & Drink

t Andrews

ld Course Hotel, Golf Resort & Spa

Open: All year **Map Ref: 2D2**

ıds Grill offers a menu inspired by a traditional grill house whilst promoting ɔtland's finest seasonal ingredients. The menu offers 12 different cuts of ɔttish beef provided by a local butcher with meat sourced from local farms d delicious local seafood from the East Neuk of Fife.

Culinary Type:
SCOTTISH

St Andrews,
Fife, KY16 9SP
T: 01334 474371
E: reservations@oldcoursehotel.co.uk
W: oldcoursehotel.co.uk

Best For:
- Romantic Meals
- Special Occasion

Prices:

Starter from:	£6.25
Main Course from:	£12.50
Dessert from:	£6.95

Opening Times:
Lunch from 1200-1430
Dinner from 1800-2200

48257

Kingdom of Fife: EatScotland Gold and Silver establishments

St Andrews
Esperante

Fairmont St Andrews Hotel,
St Andrews,
KY16 8PN
T: 01334 837 000

Located at the Fairmont St Andrews Hotel. The menu provides a combination of the flavours and cooking styles of the finest, local Scottish ingredients to create a fine dining experience.

Cupar
Ostlers Close Restaurant

SILVER

25 Bonnygale,
Cupar,
KY15 4BU
T: 01334 655 574

Ostler's Close is an exceptional find. The service is friendly and attentive and the food is exceptionally well presented and expertly cooked.

Anstruther
Spindrift Private Hotel

SILVER

Pittenweem Road,
Anstruther,
KY10 3DJ
T: 01333 310 573

This friendly dining room offers quality locally sourced produce, with a local variety of speciality foods ranging from Pittenween oatcakes to Aberdeen Smokies.

Nr St Andrews
The Inn at Lathones

SILVER

Largoward,
Nr St Andrews,
KY9 1JE
T: 01334 840 494

The Inn at Lathones has an inviting charm. The lounge and restaurant have a warm, relaxed and comfortable ambience. The chef uses local produce where possible and the speciality is the sea food platter (requires 24 hours to prepare).

Kincardine
The Unicorn Inn

The Unicorn Inn,
15 Excise Street,
Kincardine, FK10 4LN
T: 01259 739 129

The restaurant has a contemporary feel with simple but tasteful decoration. The staff are pleasant and efficient, which complements the impressive food that is served.

A pedestrianised street where diners enjoy a meal outside

ABERDEEN CITY & SHIRE

Dunnottar Castle, Aberdeenshire

Welcome to Aberdeen City & Shire

Aberdeen City and the surrounding Shire give you the best of both worlds. There's all you'd expect from a cosmopolitan city while magnificent mountains and glens await on its doorstep.

This is very much castle country with several grand stately homes to explore as well. It's an area in touch with its culture, as year-round events display, from Highland Games to annual Hogmanay rituals.

The region is rich in agricultural land, perfect for cultivating the very best Aberdeen Angus beef, organic fruit and vegetables. Seafood and fish arrive on restaurant menus fresh from local rivers and fishing ports.

The distinctive sparkling stone of many of the buildings in Aberdeen explain its title as The Granite City. It's a lively place full of museums, galleries, theatre, concerts and 'The Granite Mile' of shops on Union Street. It's also an ideal base from which you can tour the coast and countryside all around you.

01 Stonehaven Golf Course, Aberdeenshire

02 A stained glass portrait of Sir Robert Burnett of Leys at Crathes Castle

03 Balmoral Castle, the River Dee and Dee Valley

04 Crathes Castle, Aberdeenshire

Inspired ideas for you to indulge

THE CONNOISSEURS' EXPERIENCE

GlenDronach Distillery lies near Huntly just north of Aberdeen. Join the GlenDronach Discovery Tour to follow its whisky's journey. From malting floor to maturation warehouses, traditional methods used remain unchanged in nearly 200 years. Book ahead for The Connoisseurs' Experience giving a more in-depth distillery tour, rounded off with an expert tutored tasting.
glendronachdistillery.com

CAIRNGORMS NATIONAL PARK

Combine natural beauty with regal splendour in Royal Deeside. The Cairngorms National Park has vast expanses of colourful grouse moors, Scots pine forests, dramatic mountains and rushing rivers. Arrange a Land Rover safari for an off-road adventure or wander the grounds and gardens of nearby Balmoral Castle, the Royal Family's summer home.
discoverroyaldeeside.com

STONEHAVEN GOLF CLUB

Stonehaven Golf Club is renowned as much for its scenic beauty as its velvety greens. You play against the backdrop of the North Sea, Dunnottar Castle and the town of Stonehaven. Look out, too, for porpoises, dolphins and seals. The course challenges you with dramatic holes played over gullies and cliffs so take a few extra balls!
stonehavengolfclub.com

CRATHES CASTLE AND ESTATE

Crathes Castle is one of Scotland's most beautiful and best preserved castles. You can tour its wonderful interiors in summer months. The estate gardens, shop, bookshop and Courtyard café are open all year. The Milton Restaurant on the banks of the River Dee makes a great lunch stop.
nts.org.ukthemilton.co.uk

DUNNOTTAR CASTLE SUNSETS

One of Scotland's most impressive ruins, Dunnottar Castle has a commanding cliff-top presence looking out to the North Sea. It has associations with famous figures like William Wallace, Mary Queen of Scots and the future King Charles II. Time your visit, if you can, near sunset to see the castle's rugged outline against an orange sea.
dunnottarcastle.co.uk

01 Whisky nosing – getting to know a good dram!

02 The Silver Darling Restaurant, Aberdeen

03 Fishing in Clunie Water, Glen Clunie

04 Aberdeen Angus beef – a favourite throughout the world

Savour the real taste of Scotland

REGIONAL TASTES

Aberdeen and the surrounding area are home to Scotland's largest concentration of food and drink producers. Four generations of the Mackie family have farmed in Aberdeenshire. Their ice cream is a local treat worth seeking out. Aberdeen hosts regular street markets and you can find farmers' markets across the whole region.
scottishfarmersmarkets.co.uk

THE MARCLIFFE HOTEL AND SPA

The five-star Marcliffe Hotel and Spa is set in wooded grounds on the western fringe of Aberdeen. Chefs here use the best Grampian produce, like Aberdeen Angus beef and fish from local rivers, to create wonderful dishes. Dine in the Conservatory Restaurant, before retiring to The Drawing Room bar, stocked with more than 100 malts.
EatScotland Silver Award
marcliffe.com

WHISKY TASTING AT THE MAL

Other cities may have a Mal, but only in Malmaison Aberdeen can you arrange a tasting of the finest malts from the comfort of an armchair in the hotel's Whisky Snug. If wine is more to your taste, private wine tastings with the hotel's sommelier are also available.
malmaisonaberdeen.com

THE CARRON RESTAURANT

Step back in time to the glamorous 1930s at The Carron Restaurant in Stonehaven. Carefully restored to its former glory, it's one of the UK's finest examples of Art Deco. The nine-foot mirror at the entrance is rumoured to be by Picasso. You can decide for yourself over Chef's crab soup or pot-roasted venison.
carron-restaurant.co.uk

THE COCK AND BULL INN

Work up an appetite on a stroll along the golden sand dunes of Balmedie Country Park before a meal at the nearby Cock and Bull Inn. Dine in nooks of the intimate bar, the newly-refurbished restaurant or the bright conservatory. Specialities include local fish and prawn stew, North Sea mackerel and turbot, and Aberdeenshire steak.
thecockandbull.co.uk

04

05

Something a little bit different

CHAMPAGNE BALLOON FLIGHT

Set your sights high for a balloon trip over Aberdeenshire's magnificent scenery. Taking off from the grounds of Castle Fraser, near Inverurie, you can help inflate the balloon before an hour's gentle flight, glass of champagne in hand. A flight certificate signed by your pilot and Sir Richard Branson is a great reminder of your trip.
virginballoonflights.co.uk

AFTERNOON DELIGHTS

With its tranquil setting and sumptuous interior, Macdonald Pittodrie House Hotel near Inverurie is a wonderful place to relax. Enjoy Sunday lunch in the restaurant or afternoon tea in the drawing room. Equally relaxing are the spa treatments at the Mercure Ardoe House Hotel and Spa, a baronial mansion inspired by Balmoral Castle.
macdonaldhotels.co.uk
mercure.com

GLEN TANAR ESTATE

You can get to the very heart of some of Scotland's most stunning scenery with a stay on the Glen Tanar Estate. Your luxurious cottage is set in a beautiful glen within the Cairngorms National Park. And if you don't feel like cooking, Glen Tanar's housekeeper offers homemade bread, jams, chutneys, home-baking and delicious oven-ready meals.
glentanar.co.uk

01 Castle Fraser, Inverurie, Aberdeenshire

02 King's College, University of Aberdeen

03 Lonach Highland Gathering and Games, Strathdon

04 Pittodrie House Hotel, Inverurie

05 Bedroom suite at Pittodrie House Hotel, Inverurie

06 Baronial dining room, Castle Fraser, Aberdeenshire

Time to plan your perfect day

WORD 2010

14 – 16 May 2010

Word is the University of Aberdeen Writers' Festival centred round the 500-year old King's College campus. From crime writers to poets, you can enjoy a rich and packed festival programme. Author readings, writing workshops and book events across the city are joined by music, art exhibitions and film screenings. A word perfect weekend!

abdn.ac.uk/word

TASTE OF GRAMPIAN

5 June 2010

Based at the Thainstone Centre in Inverurie, this one-day food and drink festival marks its eleventh successful year in 2010. You can spend a glorious gourmet day tasting and buying the finest Scottish smoked salmon, buttery shortbread, creamy fudge and malts from the region's distilleries. The programme also includes cookery demonstrations and celebrity chef cook-offs.

tasteofgrampian.co.uk

BRAEMAR GATHERING

4 September 2010

The first Saturday in September is traditionally the date for the Braemar Gathering. Braemar is one of Scotland's oldest and largest Highland gatherings and The Royal Family attend every year while staying at nearby Balmoral. Book a grandstand seat for the best view of pipe bands, Highland dancing and tossing the caber.

braemargathering.org

STONEHAVEN FIREBALL FESTIVAL

31 December 2010

Stonehaven welcomes in the New Year in its own special way. In the run-up to midnight, locals parade up and down the Old Town, swinging flaming balls of fire around their heads. They then head for the harbour and throw the fireballs into the sea. It's quite a sight!

stonehavenfireballs.co.uk

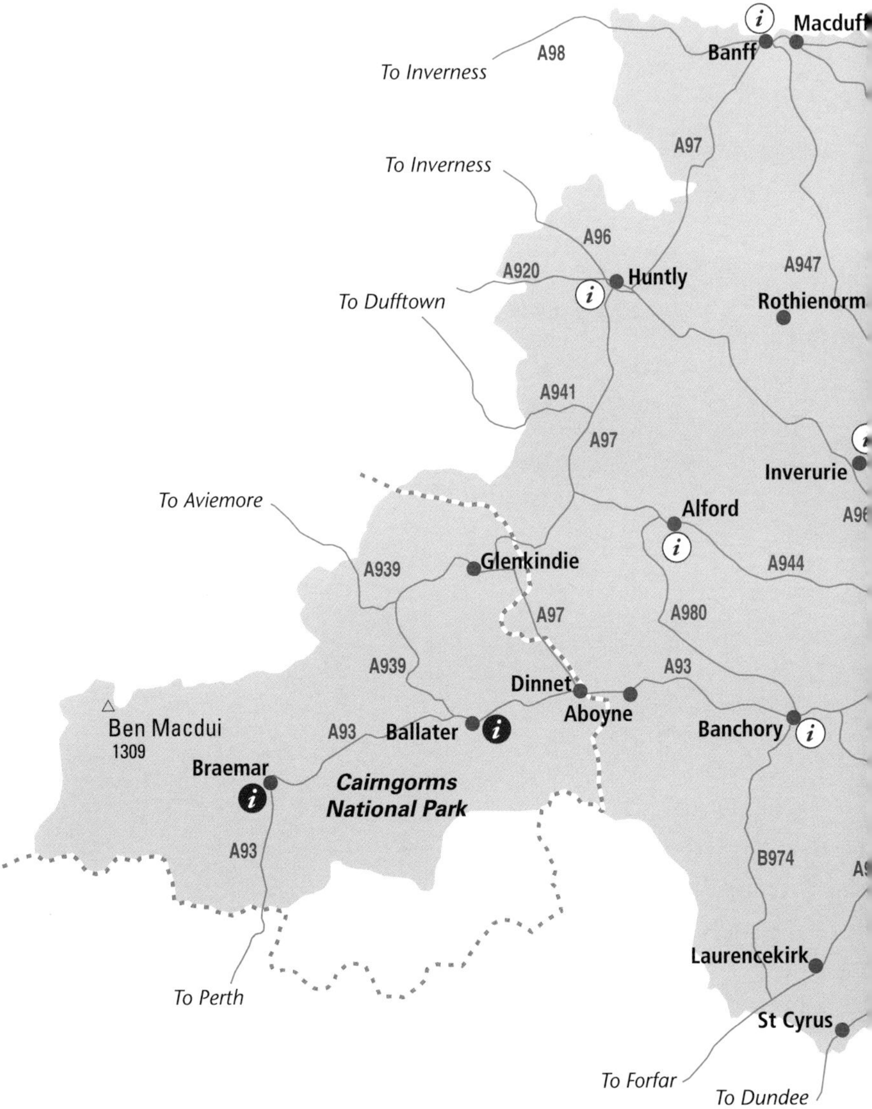

ABERDEEN CITY & SHIRE

To Inverness
A98
Banff
Macduff
A97
To Inverness
A96
A920
Huntly
To Dufftown
A947
Rothienorm
A941
A97
Inverurie
To Aviemore
Alford
A96
A939
Glenkindie
A944
A97
A980
A939
Dinnet
A93
Aboyne
Ben Macdui
1309
A93
Ballater
Banchory
Braemar
Cairngorms National Park
A93
B974
Laurencekirk
To Perth
St Cyrus
To Forfar
To Dundee

OPEN ALL YEAR

SEASONAL OPENING

Fraserburgh
A98
New Leeds
A90
A950
A952
To Kirkwall and Lerwick
lmeldrum
A90
Craibstone
ksburn
ABERDEEN
Altens
Stonehaven

VisitScotland Information Centres

To help you plan and book your trip to Scotland email our travel experts at info@visitscotland.com. When you arrive call into one of our Information Centres where our friendly experts can offer advice on all things local as well as sharing their wider knowledge of Scotland. We don't just advise either. We can sort out your accommodation and all your travel needs, as well as tickets for events across Scotland. So if you're looking to get the most from your visit, there really is only one place to go.

ABERDEEN

Aberdeen	23 Union Street, Aberdeen, AB11 5BP
Ballater	The Old Royal Station, Station Square, Ballater, AB35 5RB
Braemar	Unit 3, The Mews, Mar Road, Braemar, AB35 5YL

- LOCAL KNOWLEDGE
- WHERE TO STAY
- ACCOMMODATION BOOKING
- PLACES TO VISIT
- THINGS TO DO
- MAPS AND GUIDES
- TRAVEL ADVICE
- ROUTE PLANNING
- WHERE TO SHOP AND EAT
- LOCAL CRAFTS AND PRODUCE
- EVENT INFORMATION
- TICKETS

Aberdeen & Grampian: Hotels

Aberdeen

Hilton Aberdeen Treetops

Open: All year **Map Ref: 4G10**

★★★★
HOTEL

161 Springfield Road, Aberdeen, AB15 7AQ
T: 01224 313377 E: reservations.aberdeen@hilton.com W: hilton.co.uk/aberdeen

Indicated Prices:

Single	from £65.00 per room	Twin	from £65.00 per room
Double	from £65.00 per room	Family	from £65.00 per room
		Suite	from £100.00 per room

TV P C V

3060

Aberdeen

The Marcliffe Hotel and Spa

Open: All year **Map Ref: 4G10**

The Marcliffe Hotel and Spa is ideally located for visiting Scotland's scenic North East. Within two hours of the hotel there are over fifteen castles, thirty malt whisky distilleries and sixty golf courses. VisitScotland 5 star hotel and member of Small Luxury Hotels of the World and Connoisseurs Scotland.

★★★★★
HOTEL

North Deeside Road, Aberdeen, AB15 9YA
T: 01224 861000 W: marcliffe.com

Indicated Prices:

Single	from £140.00 per room	Twin	from £150.00 per room
Double	from £150.00 per room	Family	from £165.00 per room
		Suite	from £275.00 per room

TV P V

 59622

 PRICES STATED ARE ESTIMATES AND MAY BE SUBJECT TO CHANGE. PRICES ARE PER PERSON PER NIGHT UNLESS OTHERWISE STATED. AWARDS CORRECT AS OF BEGINNING OF OCTOBER 2009

berdeen
lorwood Hall Hotel

Open: All year **Map Ref: 4G10**

ırwood Hall is a truly wonderful :reat yet only 10 minutes from e heart of the city. Roaring fires, /eeping staircases and secluded rdens, Norwood Hall offers the :st of Scottish hospitality. Enjoy me of life's little luxuries – ternoon tea in the library d award-winning food in the staurant.

★★★★
HOTEL

Garthdee Road, Aberdeen, AB15 9FX
T: 01224 868951 E: reservations@norwood-hall.co.uk W: norwood-hall.co.uk

Indicated Prices:

Single	from £85.00 per room	Family	from £135.00 per room
Double	from £95.00 per room	Suite	from £200.00 per room

C £ V

65289

ıberdeen
;impson's Hotel, Bar & Restaurant

Open: All year excl Xmas & New Year **Map Ref: 4G10**

★★★★
HOTEL

59-63 Queens Road, Aberdeen, AB15 4YP
T: 01224 327777 E: reservations@simpsonshotel.co.uk W: simpsonshotel.co.uk

Indicated Prices:

Single	from £90.00 per room	Twin	from £110.00 per room
Double	from £110.00 per room	Family	from £110.00 per room
		Suite	from £160.00 per room

£ V

60418

Aberdeen & Grampian: Guest Houses and B&Bs

Aberdeen

St Elmo Guest House

Open: All year **Map Ref: 4G1**

★★★★
GUEST HOUSE

64 Hilton Drive, Aberdeen, AB24 4NP
T: 01224 483065 E: stelmo@ensuitedreams.com W: ensuitedreams.com

Indicated Prices:

Single	from £45.00 per room	Twin	from £70.00 per room
Double	from £60.00 per room	Family	from £90.00 per room

C V

5583

Macduff

Monica and Martin's B&B

Open: All year **Map Ref: 4F**

★★★★
BED AND BREAKFAST

21 Gellymill Street, Macduff, Aberdeenshire, AB44 1TN
T: 01261 832336 E: gellymill@talktalk.net

Indicated Prices:

Single	from £25.00	Twin	from £23.00 per person
Double	from £23.00 per person		

C V

3884

Oldmeldrum

Cromlet Hill Guest House

Open: All year **Map Ref: 4G**

BED AND BREAKFAST

South Road, Oldmeldrum, Aberdeenshire, AB51 0AB
T: 01651 872315 E: johnpage@cromlethill.co.uk W: cromlethill.co.uk

Indicated Prices:

Single	from £40.00	Twin	from £28.00 per person
Double	from £28.00 per person	Family	from £70.00 per room

V

2141

Aberdeen & Grampian: Self Catering

allater

nvercauld Lodges

Open: All year

Map Ref: 4E11

autifully set in a secluded rden only 400 yards from the ntre of the village, Invercauld dges offer a peaceful quiet cation where guests of all ages turn year after year. Our policy of ntinually investing in the lodges eans you will thoroughly enjoy ur relaxing break.

★★★★
SELF CATERING

12 Invercauld Road, Ballater, Royal Deeside, AB35 5RP
T: 013397 55015 E: info@invercauldlodges.co.uk W: invercauldlodges.co.uk

6 Cabins | 2 Bedrooms | Sleeps 3-5

Prices – Cabins:
£250.00-£495.00 Per Week

Short breaks available

79176

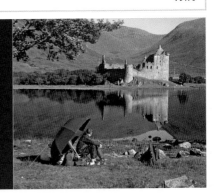

Aberdeen & Grampian: EatScotland Gold and Silver establishments

Banchory
Banchory Lodge Hotel

SILVER

Off Dee Street,
Banchory,
AB31 5HS
T: 01330 822 625

Banchory Lodge Hotel is situated by the River Dee, with traditional furnishings, log fires and a rosetted restaurant using finest quality, locally sourced ingredients.

Nr Ellon
Eat on the Green

SILVER

Udny Green,
Nr Ellon,
AB41 7RS
T: 01651 842 337

Eat on the Green offers innovative lunch and dinner menus with contemporary and classic dishes, using the finest fresh and local produce.

Inverurie
Fjord Inn

SILVER

Fisherford,
Inverurie,
AB51 8YS
T: 01464 841 232

The Fjord Inn at Fisherford promises a warm welcome and the best in fresh local produce. Chef/owner Norman Mundie enjoys creating an interesting menu which keeps customers coming back for more.

Nr Aberdeen
Marcliffe of Pitfodels

SILVER

North Deeside Road,
Pitfodels, Nr Aberdeen,
AB15 9YA
T: 01224 861 000

Eating at the Marcliffe is an experience not to be missed. You will taste some of the finest ingredients from the Grampian area, cooked and presented with style and flare.

Maryculter
Maryculter House Hotel

South Deeside Road,
Maryculter,
AB12 5GB
T: 01224 732 124

Experience the lifestyle of Scottish nobility in one of Scotland's finest Country House Hotels. Choose from bar suppers in the Poachers Pocket, or a la carte in the Priory Restaurant.

Ballater
The Auld Kirk

SILVER

31 Braemar Road,
Ballater,
AB35 5RQ
T: 01339 755 762

Dine in style and comfort, sampling local produce freshly cooked to order in the dramatic Spirit Restaurant. First class friendly service is assured.

Ballater

The Green Inn

SILVER

9 Victoria Road,
Ballater,
AB35 5QQ
T: 01339 755 701

An intimate, multi award winning restaurant with rooms offering a fine dining experience utilising the very best of fresh locally sourced ingredients.

Ballater

The Oaks

SILVER

Hilton Craigendarroch,
Braemar Road, Ballater,
AB35 5XA
T: 01339 755 858

Enjoy local specialities such as chicken with haggis and smoked Scottish salmon at the Hilton Craigendarroch Hotel, set against panoramic views of the Dee valley.

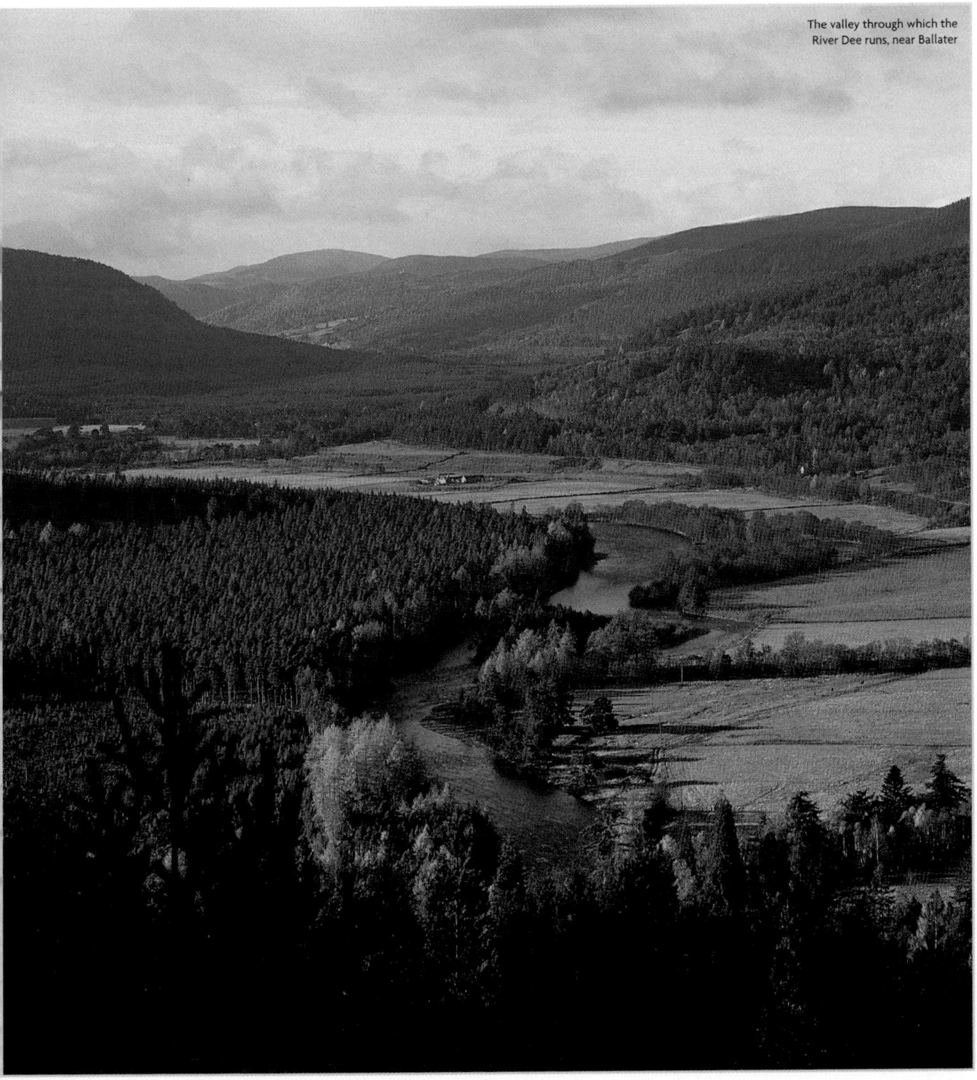

The valley through which the River Dee runs, near Ballater

THE HIGHLANDS & ISLANDS

Faraid Head, Balnakeil Bay, near Durness

Welcome to the Highlands & Islands

The vast expanse of the Scottish Highlands, from mainland to islands, gives you plenty of opportunity to really get away from it all. The still natural beauty extends from the silent majesty of Glencoe and the stark wilderness of the Cairngorms to island life on the Outer Hebrides, Orkney & Shetland.

Walking here is full of unexpected rewards. In some areas you may not see another soul all day, save for some local wildlife. Look out for red squirrels in trees, deer tentatively exploring the forest edge, ospreys and eagles soaring overhead and dolphins and whales swimming just off the coast.

This is a region rich in natural resources. Restaurant chefs let the freshness and quality of local produce speak for itself. You'll develop a taste, too, for some of the regional flavours, from Speyside whiskies to Orkney cheeses.

The Highlands are a natural playground where you can make the most of fishing rivers or seas, golfing on links courses or just strolling along golden sandy beaches.

NORTHERN HIGHLANDS, INVERNESS, LOCH NESS & NAIRN

You'll quickly be won over by the vast wilderness, dramatic coastlines and spectacular mountains of Scotland's most northerly mainland area.

Loch Ness is a perennial pull for visitors intrigued by its deepest mysteries. Nearby is the expanding city of Inverness, the lively, modern Capital of the Highlands set amidst stunning scenery.

This is an ancient land with a culture to match. The long history of East Sutherland and Caithness is evident in the brochs and cairns that dot their dramatic coastlines.

Head as far north as mainland allows to John O'Groats or spot whales and dolphins from Chanonry Point on the Black Isle. Picturesque towns and villages like Ullapool have their own charms to discover.

Days can be as active or as relaxed as you like, from woodland walks and rounds of golf to seaside strolls and wildlife cruises. And evenings can include impromptu live Scottish music with your supper.

Inspired ideas for you to indulge

THE NORTHWEST HIGHLANDS GEOPARK

Scotland's first Geopark has an incredible blend of wildlife, deserted sandy beaches, mountainous ridges and three-million-year-old geology. The sense of the wild nature and grandeur of the scene all around you is captivating. Relish the perfect peace of this most sparsely populated corner of Europe on a variety of walks.
northwest-highlands-geopark.org.uk

CASTLE STUART GOLF LINKS

Seven miles from Inverness, Castle Stuart Golf proved an immediate hit with golfers when it opened in July 2009. The setting is magical, with views of the Kessock Bridge, Chanonry Lighthouse and the Moray Firth. 'Rumples', a bumpy feature of many a links course, and riveted bunkers may add some unpredictability to your game.
castlestuartgolf.com

REELIG GLEN

Drive west of Beauly on the A862 for eight miles and follow the road signposted Reelig and Moniack. After a mile, a Forestry Commission sign will lead you on an easy short walk through woodland of spectacular old conifer and broad-leaved trees along gentle paths. Look out for Dughall Mor, one of Britain's tallest trees.
forestry.gov.uk

THIRLE DOOR AND THE STACKS OF DUNCANSBY

Not far from John O'Groats you'll find dramatic coastline and a vast nesting colony for thousands of seabirds. As you walk across the clifftop fields, a stunning and changing view unfolds to the south of Thirle Door, a rocky arch, and the Stacks of Duncansby, a group of large, jagged sea stacks.
www.undiscovered.co.uk

ASSYNT

Assynt is an area dominated by spectacular mountains in the far north-west of Scotland. The Assynt Visitor Centre is the best place for local information on attractions like Ardvreck Castle, the ruined ancient stronghold of the MacLeods of Assynt. Watch potters at work at Lochinver's Highland Stoneware or take a boat trip to remote Kerracher Gardens.
assynt.info

ROYAL DORNOCH

Five times Open Champion Tom Watson famously remarked it was the most fun he'd ever had on a golf course. The Royal Dornoch course was originally designed by golfing legend Tom Morris. Records show golf played in this beautifully natural landscape as early as 1616. Today it's regarded as one of the world's finest links courses.
royaldornoch.com

HIGHLANDS ARTS AND CRAFTS

You'll discover an eclectic mix of arts and crafts in the Inverness area. Admire local art in Leakey's second-hand bookshop in Inverness and in galleries in Wick and Durness. There's glassblowing in Fort Augustus, woodturning at Farr and pottery in Lochinver. And near Tain, you can indulge in luxury Scottish brand, Anta.

01 Ardvreck Castle, Loch Assynt

02 Royal Dornoch Golf Club, Sutherland

03 Lochinver overlooked by the mountain of Quinag

Savour the real taste of Scotland

LOCHINVER PIES

Lochinver Larder makes some of the best pies in Scotland. The relaxing bistro in Lochinver provides a perfect excuse to stop for a while and plan the next part of your journey over a succulent pie. Flavour combinations include venison and cranberry, haggis, neeps and tatties and fresh poached salmon.
lochinverlarder.co.uk

CHEZ ROUX AT ROCPOOL

Chez Roux at Rocpool is the epitome of quality food and service in Inverness. With the Gallic influence of Albert Roux, Chef Davey Aspin creates indulgent Scottish dishes with a French twist. If time is tight, try the Rouxpress lunch or Bar Bites for light snacks. À la carte menus change monthly to reflect seasonality.
rocpool.com

THE CAPTAIN'S GALLEY

The Captain's Galley is set within a sympathetically renovated former ice house in Scrabster. Its menu offers about 20 different species of seafood each week and up to 10 every night. The menu changes daily according to the fresh catches which chef and owner Jim Cowie selects from Scrabster fish market or directly from the fishing boats.
captainsgalley.co.uk

SUTOR CREEK CAFÉ

Cromarty's Sutor Creek Café specialises in local seafood and fresh pizzas cooked in a wood-fired oven. Each Saturday evening the oven is also used overnight to slow-roast local meats infused with home-grown herbs ready for Sunday. The Independent lists Sutor Creek as one of the UK's fifty best places for Sunday lunch.
sutorcreek.co.uk

01 Lochinver with the view to Suilven

02 The harbour, Scrabster, Thurso Bay

03 The art of salmon smoking

DONALD C. MACADIE
THURSO
DISTRIBUTOR
OF
FISONS FERTILISERS
WK230
Saffron

Time to plan your perfect day

THE SPIRIT OF SPEYSIDE WHISKY FESTIVAL

29 April – 3 May 2010

This festival is as much about the food, heritage and culture of the area as it is about its wonderful whiskies. Join music events, dance at ceilidhs and enjoy Speyside's best. Of course, the packed programme features plenty of nosings and tastings of local malts and the chance to buy your favourites to take home.

spiritofspeyside.com

BELLADRUM TARTAN HEART FESTIVAL

6 – 7 August 2010

Belladrum's Tartan Heart Festival near Beauly is a home-grown celebration of music and the arts. Indie and blues music join Celtic rock and everything in between. The diversity is echoed in the performing arts events, embracing everything from dance, theatre and cabaret to poetry and literature. All in a beautiful Highland setting.

tartanheartfestival.co.uk

Something a little bit different

01 Cliffs alive with seabirds, island of Handa, Sutherland

02 A Jacobite Cruise on Loch Ness

03 A whisky tasting masterclass at the Glenlivet Distillery

04 The Pass of the Cattle, the highest road in Scotland

HANDA ISLAND

Each summer the northwest of Handa Island comes alive with more than 200,000 breeding seabirds. From April to September, you can take a boat trip with the aid of a ranger for a close-up view of the precipitous cliffs and famous stack bird sanctuary. Breeds include skuas, puffins, guillemots and razorbills.

swt.org.uk

HEBRIDEAN WHALE CRUISES

From its base in the west coast fishing community of Gairloch, Hebridean Whale Cruises offers two boats and different cruises to match what you want to see and the range you wish to cover. Cruises take you to areas frequented by whales and dolphins. You may also see gannets fishing or seals sunning themselves.

hebridean-whale-cruises.com

JACOBITE EXPERIENCE

You can choose from a number of cruises on Loch Ness with the Jacobite team. You can really appreciate the vastness of the loch as you sail towards Urquhart Castle. There you can step ashore to explore the castle ruins and the exhibition outlining the fortress's history.

jacobite.co.uk

GLEN MORAY DISTILLERY

Glen Moray in Elgin is known for producing whisky with a distinctly smooth flavour. Its Single Malt Whisky has been produced here since 1897 by a small team of dedicated distillers. Find out how whisky is made on a distillery tour or, for something more in-depth, tutored tastings are also available.

glenmoray.com

FORT WILLIAM, LOCHABER, SKYE & LOCHALSH

You don't have to look far to see why Fort William is called the Outdoor Capital of the UK. The area hosts the annual Mountain Bike World Cup, as thrilling for spectators as competitors. The majesty of the Highlands and the lure of the coast have inspired all manner of ways to enjoy these great outdoors.

You'll find some of Scotland's best known icons and attractions in this region. It's home to Ben Nevis, the UK's highest mountain, and the scenic beauty of Glencoe and Rannoch Moor. And Eilean Donan Castle, Scotland's most famous postcard image is even more beautiful in real life.

You'll find splendid seclusion at Ardnamurchan Point, as far west as the British mainland allows. You're also well-placed here to island hop. Just board a ferry to the isles of Eigg, Rum, Canna or Muck. And just like Bonnie Prince Charlie, you can take a boat to Skye. There you can discover the white coral beach and castle at Dunvegan, dine at The Three Chimneys and sample the whisky at Talisker Distillery.

Inspired ideas for you to indulge

JACOBITE STEAM TRAIN

Wanderlust magazine voted this the "Top Railway Journey in the World 2009". You'll understand why with its scenic views, including the UK's highest mountain, Ben Nevis. You also cross the Glenfinnan Viaduct, famed for its role in the Harry Potter films. The train is a thrilling way to reach Mallaig, en route to Skye and the Small Isles.
steamtrain.info

GLENELG

The secluded coastal village of Glenelg is a great place to discover ancient brochs, whales and cormorants. A seasonal car ferry takes you across to Kylerhea on Skye. There you'll find the Forestry Commission's otter haven and the Brightwater Visitor Centre, which tells the story of Gavin Maxwell, author of Ring of Brightwater.
lochalsh.co.uk

BEACHES

The shoreline stretching between Arisaig and Mallaig is renowned for its beautiful beaches, among them Camusdarach, Traigh and the Silver Sands of Morar. Each provides a peaceful setting for a picnic or a wander, with the Small Isles of Eigg and Rum as your wonderful backdrop. The changing light also picks out the coastline's numerous skerries.

GLENCOE VISITOR CENTRE

Glencoe is known for its geology and wildlife as much as its history and heritage. The National Trust for Scotland's Glencoe Visitor Centre addresses each in turn through interactive displays and activities. You also gain an insight into the ongoing conservation issues facing the National Trust for Scotland today.
glencoe-nts.org.uk

KNOYDART

If you really want to get away from it all, the Knoydart peninsula is recognised as the remotest part of mainland Britain. Only accessible by boat from Mallaig or a 20-mile walk from Kinlochhourn, Knoydart is one of the country's best hiking spots and ideal for watching wildlife, fishing or locally-run special interest breaks.
road-to-the-isles.org.uk

01 Loch Duich and Eilean Donan Castle

02 The Old Drovers Road and The Three Sisters, Glencoe

03 Jacobite steam train crosses the Glenfinnan Viaduct

04 Dun Telve, one of the Glenelg Brochs

05 Loch Scavaig and the Black Cuillin, Elgol, Isle of Skye

06 The Silver Sands at Morar

Savour the real taste of Scotland

01 Seafood platter, Crannog Restaurant, Fort William

02 Sunset over the islands of Rum and Eigg

03 The Three Chimneys Restaurant, Isle of Skye

04 The Glenelg to Kylerhea ferry (Easter to October sailings)

THE THREE CHIMNEYS RESTAURANT

Food lovers regularly travel to Skye specifically to eat here. This converted crofter's cottage in Colbost on Loch Dunvegan's shores features in Restaurant Magazine's list of the World's Top 50 Restaurants. The setting, the views, the food and the restaurant's six bedrooms: all are superb. Book yourself a real treat.

EatScotland Gold Award

threechimneys.co.uk

THE GLENELG INN

This former coaching mews has views to Skye. Menus take full advantage of the fresh local langoustine, scallops, venison and hill lamb. The wine list is extensive, as is the range of malt whiskies. Six guest bedrooms, a morning room and garden terrace encourage you to relax and absorb the perfectly tranquil surroundings.

glenelg-inn.com

CRANNOG SEAFOOD RESTAURANT

Crannog in Fort William has been serving fantastic West Highland seafood for almost 20 years. Chefs prepare fish and seafood from Crannog's own smokehouse and the freshest daily catches directly from the owner's boat. Choose from a menu of firm favourites like mussels, salmon and langoustine, as well as meat and vegetarian dishes.

crannog.net

MACDONALD'S SMOKED PRODUCE

Glenuig lies near Ardnamurchan Point, mainland Britain's most westerly spot. Here you'll discover a smokehouse well-known for the quality of its smoked seafood and fish. You can try freshly-smoked Scottish salmon, rainbow trout, more exotic game meats and smoked cheeses like creamy Lochaber. Buy while you're there or have your order delivered.

smokedproduce.co.uk

Something a little bit different

THE ICE FACTOR
Kinlochleven is home to the world's biggest indoor ice-climbing facility. The Ice Factor includes ice and rock climbing walls, tutored indoor and outdoor activity courses and a relaxing sauna and steam room. The views of Loch Leven and hearty food have made the bar and bistro here popular draws in their own right.
ice-factor.co.uk

LOCH CORUISK
Board the 'Misty Isle' at Elgol on Skye for a boat trip to isolated Loch Coruisk, inspiration for a Turner painting and the writings of Sir Walter Scott. Your guide will point out the large seal colony as you sail, as well as any dolphins, whales or basking sharks. Hot drinks with shortbread await your return.
mistyisleboattrips.co.uk

ORBOST GALLERY
Near Dunvegan on the shore of Loch Brackadale, Skye, Orbost Gallery exhibits works which celebrate the landscape of Skye and the surrounding Highlands. All works are by professional artists and include watercolours, calligraphy, prints and wood engravings. If there's a favourite Skye view you'd like captured on canvas, the gallery accepts commissions.
orbostgallery.co.uk

01 View across Rannoch Moor

02 Loch Dunvegan and the Black Cuillin, Isle of Skye

03 Gondola cable car, Nevis Range, near Fort William

04 The Ice Factor, the world's biggest indoor ice climbing centre, Kinlochleven, Lochaber

Time to plan your perfect day

LIME TREE GALLERY

This private gallery in Fort William holds regular exhibitions of contemporary art. You can also view the paintings of artist-in-residence David Wilson, who draws on the striking Highland scenery for inspiration. The gallery has hosted shows from the National Art Collections and also gives contemporary artists a platform to display and sell their art.
limetreefortwilliam.co.uk

THE BLAS FESTIVAL

3 – 11 September 2010

The Blas Festival is a nine-day celebration of Gaelic language and culture through the distinctive lilt of traditional music. It's a Highland-wide programme with main events around Fort William and on the Isle of Skye. If you want to experience the best of Gaelic culture in an authentic atmosphere, this is the festival for you.
blas-festival.com

SCOTTISH FOOD AND DRINK FORTNIGHT

4 – 19 September 2010

Each September, as part of this Scotland-wide event, food producers on Skye open their doors to show how they make and rear their produce. From restaurants to retailers, it's a rare chance for you to discover, sample and enjoy food and drink produced and prepared on and around Skye.
scottishfoodanddrinkfortnight.co.uk

MORAY, AVIEMORE & THE CAIRNGORMS

The variety of scenery and the range of ways to enjoy it ensure the continued popularity of this northern region. Active types make for Aviemore and the outdoor challenges of the Cairngorms. The Malt Whisky Trail informs and entertains as it wends its way through Speyside.

Ranger-guided walks give you the best chance of spotting the diverse wildlife of the Cairngorms National Park. Catch a glimpse of dolphins from the golden beaches of the Moray coast or on a wildlife cruise.

Spectacular surroundings at courses like Aviemore and Boat of Garten add to your golfing pleasure. Networked trails encourage you to enjoy leisurely strolls at various locations, including the Rothiemurchus and Glenlivet estates, Culbin Forest and Craigellachie National Nature Reserve. The rapid River Spey and charming River Findhorn offer some excellent fishing during the salmon run. Alternatively, watch the wonderful Cairngorm views glide by over lunch on board a steam train from Aviemore to Boat of Garten and Broomhill.

01 Loch Morlich, Cairngorms National Park

02 Insh Marshes, national nature reserve, Strathspey

03 Malt whisky country

04 Elgin Cathedral, Moray

05 Golden eagle

Inspired ideas for you to indulge

MALT WHISKY TRAIL

See if you can pick out the different subtleties of aroma and taste on the Malt Whisky Trail. Eight Speyside distilleries, including Glenfiddich and The Glenlivet, make up the trail, as well as the Speyside Cooperage, where you can watch traditional construction of the all-important oak whisky casks.
maltwhiskytrail.com

CAIRNGORMS NATIONAL PARK

Cairngorms National Park is Britain's largest and home to a quarter of the UK's endangered bird, animal and plant species. Try to spy a Scottish Crossbill, the only bird unique to Britain. Ospreys and eagles all share the air here. Pine martens, red squirrels and wildcats are just some of the other wildlife to spot.
cairngorms.co.uk

ELGIN'S HISTORICAL SITES

The impressive 13th century ruin of Elgin Cathedral is the site of Scotland's tallest gravestone and finest octagonal chapter house. People & Place, a new exhibition at the town's museum, gives you an insight to 1,000 years of Scottish and Moray history, including Pictish stones and a Roman hoard discovered on a local dig.

INSH MARSHES NATIONAL NATURE RESERVE

Insh Marshes Reserve near Kingussie is a great place for bird-watching. About half of Britain's golden-eyes nest here in spring, as do lapwings, redshanks and curlews. When this important wetland floods in winter, it heralds the arrival of flocks of whooper swans and greylag geese while roe deer and wildcats explore the marsh edges.
rspb.org.uk

JOHNSTONS CASHMERE

Johnstons of Elgin is the only Scottish mill still to carry out all processes from raw fibre to finished garment. You can learn the whole story in the new Heritage Centre. You can also tour the mill and browse the shop for softest cashmere, woollen and tweed products, now including the new Johnstons Home range.
johnstonscashmere.com

HIGHLAND FOLK MUSEUM

The Highland Folk Museum in Newtonmore lets you explore more than 400 years of domestic and working Highland life. Step back in time with the reconstruction of an 18th century Highland township and a 20th century working croft. You can also see traditional skills and crafts in action through live demonstrations and activities.
highlandfolk.museum

Savour the real taste of Scotland

ORD BÀN RESTAURANT CAFÉ

Within the Rothiemurchus Centre, Ord Bàn is a friendly and relaxed café by day and an intimate dining space in the evening. It makes its own bread each morning by hand and there's a tempting selection of home-baking, too. Lunch, brunch and supper menus feature dishes like potted salmon, sea trout and venison stew.

ordban.com

THE OLD BRIDGE INN

After a day in the open air, The Old Bridge Inn on the outskirts of Aviemore is a haven of good food and drink. There's a daily blackboard menu or try a marinated venison steak from the chargrill menu. Watch ospreys in summer from the veranda and in winter, settle in front of the roaring log fire.

oldbridgeinn.co.uk

THE QUAICH BAR

Within the Craigellachie Hotel, the Quaich Bar is something of a favourite with whisky connoisseurs. The bar has won plaudits and praise for its range of nearly 700 different single malt whiskies. Prices range from a modest sum to £275 for a rare and much prized nip! The extremely knowledgeable staff will even conduct impromptu nosings in the bar.

craigellachie.com

GORDON AND MACPHAIL

From 1895, Gordon and MacPhail have sold malt whisky from distilleries throughout Scotland. The firm is renowned in the industry and from its location in Elgin this tradition continues. The extensive range of malt whiskies is now supplemented by a mouthwatering deli, a personalised label service and a selection of decadent gift hampers.

gordonandmacphail.com

01 After a day on the slopes, a welcoming drink and roaring fire at the Cas Bar, Cairngorm Mountain Ski Centre

02 The famous Quaich Bar, Craigellachie Hotel

THE BALVENIE
PortWood

Something a little bit different

SPEYSIDE COOPERAGE

Appropriately enough, the UK's only working cooperage in Craigellachie is in the very heart of Malt Whisky Country. You'll see the age-old craft of whisky cask-making carried out with traditional tools and skills. You'll also pick up lots of unusual facts to make you see whisky and casks in a whole new light.
speysidecooperage.co.uk

LOCH AN EILEIN WALK

Rothiemurchus Forest surrounds one of Scotland's most beautiful lochs. Start at Loch an Eilein car park to tour its edge. A castle, sitting proudly on an island in the loch, was once a stronghold connected to the shore by causeway until the 1800s when the water level was raised.
walkhighlands.co.uk

SPEYSIDE WILDLIFE

Wildlife spotting comes down to knowing where to look. Speyside Wildlife organises wildlife-watching holidays, all fully-guided, for casual to serious enthusiasts. Tours can also be tailored to your interests and available time. From comfortable hides in Cairngorms National Park, you'll get a close-up and personal view of birds and mammals in their natural habitats.
speysidewildlife.co.uk

DOLPHIN CRUISES

The Moray Firth is home to large numbers of dolphins, porpoises, seals, whales and seabirds. Join the crew aboard MV Top Cat for a close-up view. Regular two-hour dolphin cruises, some with guides, leave from Findhorn. New for 2010 is an onboard remotely-operated vehicle to give you a diver's-eye view under the surface.
moraydiving.com

Time to plan your perfect day

THE SPIRIT OF SPEYSIDE WHISKY FESTIVAL
29 April – 3 May 2010
This festival is as much about the food, heritage and culture of the area as it is about its wonderful whiskies. Join music events, dance at ceilidhs and enjoy Speyside's best. Of course, the packed programme features plenty of nosings and tastings of local malts and the chance to buy your favourites to take home.
spiritofspeyside.com

THE CAIRNGORMS FARMERS' MARKET
Various dates
Farmers' markets set up shop in venues across Britain's largest national park throughout the year. As well as a selection of the best local produce, cookery and craft demonstrations and craft stalls also appear. Look out for hand-made jewellery, pottery, glass and even chainsaw carvings. Check dates of where and when on the website.
cairngorms-farmers-market.com

01 Speyside Cooperage, Craigellachie, Moray

02 The annual Spirit of Speyside Whisky Festival

03 Duffus Castle, near Elgin

04 The Still Room, Glenfiddich Distillery, Dufftown

05 Dolphin spotting on the Moray Firth

OUTER HEBRIDES

The Outer Hebrides allow you to escape to a different way of life. Remote they may be, distant they're not. The Hebridean way is to care for each other and share with everyone.

There are strong contrasts in the natural beauty of this archipelago of ten inhabited islands, and many uninhabited ones. Only a stream separates largely flat Lewis from more mountainous Harris. The east coast of Harris has a rocky edge, while the west has miles of soft golden sands.

The nature of North and South Uist makes them ideal homes for two nature reserves. Follow the road round the entire island of Barra to see more than 1,000 species of wild flower against a stunning coastal backdrop. The islands' connections to ancient history stand out at historic sites like the famous Callanish Stones and Kisimul Castle.

Daily return flights from Scotland's airports and inexpensive ferry crossings from three mainland ports to five islands make it easier than ever to reach these island paradises.

Inspired ideas for you to indulge

CALLANISH STANDING STONES

The Neolithic Standing Stones at Callanish have stood on the Isle of Lewis for thousands of years. Second only to Stonehenge, the towering stone circle is remarkable. Were they a lunar calendar system or heathen island giants turned to stone by St Kieran? Make up your own mind at the visitor centre's exhibition.
isle-of-lewis.com

LUSKENTYRE

Harris is famed for its beaches. The largest and most spectacular of these is Luskentyre, also regarded as one of the most beautiful beaches in Europe. Warmed by the Gulf Stream, its blue and turquoise waters blend with the golden-white sands and lush green countryside. Bring your camera to capture this picture perfect scene.

TAIGH CHEARSABHAGH

Originally built in 1741 in Lochmaddy, North Uist, Taigh Chearsabhagh was the first property in the area to have a slated roof. It's now a popular museum and arts centre. Exhibitions let you find out more about Uist heritage, culture and crafts. There's also a shop and a café with its own local artist exhibitions.
taigh-chearsabhagh.org

ERISKAY

Though an island of only three square miles, Eriskay was the inspiration for Whisky Galore and the haunting ballad, Eriskay Love Lilt. Bonnie Prince Charlie first stepped on Scottish soil here in 1745 from France. It's also home to the Eriskay pony, saved by locals from extinction. Since 2001, Eriskay has been linked by a causeway to South Uist.

THE OUTER HEBRIDES FOOD TRAIL

From the Butt of Lewis to Barra, you'll find a hamper full of Hebridean treats. As well as the famous Stornoway black pudding, you'll discover a rich supply of locally-reared beef and lamb, Hebridean haggis and freshly-caught scallops and langoustines. The trail also takes in regional beers, real ales, chocolates and confectionery.
outerhebridesfoodtrail.com

KISIMUL CASTLE

Known locally as 'the castle in the sea', Kisimul Castle was the home of the Clan Macneil and is now in the care of Historic Scotland. You'll find it just off Castlebay on Barra and there are boat trips to the castle in summer.
historic-scotland.gov.uk

01 Prince Charlie's Bay, Eriskay

02 The Sound of Taransay from Luskentyre Beach

03 Callanish Standing Stones, Isle of Lewis

04 Castlebay and Kisimul Castle, the Isle of Barra

05

Savour the real taste of Scotland

DIGBY CHICK RESTAURANT
Taking its name from an historic herring dish, Digby Chick in Stornoway offers an original and modern take on fish, shellfish and game like local Lewis venison. The restaurant offers lunch, early bird and dinner menus. Catch of the Day appears on the restaurant blackboard and can include monkfish, skate wing or herring.

Time to plan your perfect day

HARRIS ARTS FESTIVAL
May – September 2010
The Harris Arts Festival lets you get to the heart of Hebridean culture. Find out more about Harris Tweed and St Kilda, try a spinning workshop or just sit back and enjoy songs and stories of a bygone age. While the festival concentrates on traditional and folk music, classical music is also a major part.
harrisarts.net

CEÒLAS
4 – 9 July 2010
Set within the Gaelic-speaking community of South Uist, Ceòlas is a summer music and dance festival. It features expert tuition in piping, fiddling, singing, Scotch reels, quadrilles, step dancing and the Gaelic language. There's ample opportunity to get involved in all these art forms, both at ceilidhs and in homes.
ceolas.co.uk

HEBRIDEAN MARITIME FESTIVALS
12 – 17 July 2010
Whether you have a traditional or modern boat or just want to join in the fun, these friendly festivals in Stornoway are open to everyone. Both UK and international boats take part. Sail in company with others, learn the basics or just enjoy the food, music and camaraderie.
sailhebrides.info

NORTH UIST HIGHLAND GAMES
23 July 2010
Highland Games are a great tradition throughout Scotland and one of the mainstays of the events calendar in the Outer Hebrides. With strongman events, Highland dancing and a range of side-stalls and activities, this is one of a number of similar events taking place throughout the islands.

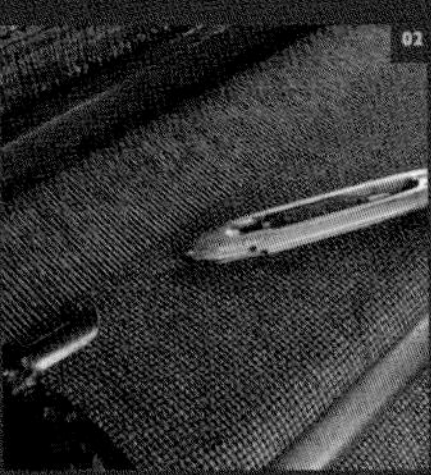

Something a little bit different

ST KILDA
For thousands of years, St Kilda was home to Europe's most remote community. The final residents chose to evacuate to the mainland in 1930. Today it is a UNESCO double World Heritage Site for both its natural and cultural significance. Local cruises let you visit this island treasure with its seabird population and Britain's highest sea cliffs.
kilda.org.uk

01 Village Bay, St Kilda archipelago nature reserve
02 Harris Tweed on the loom, Isle of Harris
03 Competing in the Maritime Festival
04 A detail of full Highland dress
05 Stornoway harbour, Isle of Lewis
06 Approaching the St Kilda archipelago

ORKNEY & SHETLAND

Orkney & Shetland effortlessly blend living history with outstanding natural beauty.

Orkney is made up of 70 or so islands and skerries, 21 of them inhabited, and is the site of Northern Europe's oldest houses at Papa Westray, dating back to 3800BC. Links to an ancient past and heritage are also evident at the Neolithic village of Skara Brae, the Standing Stones of Stenness, the Ring of Brodgar and the Broch of Gurness.

Shetland is part of Scotland, yet closer to Norway. You can see the Viking influence at events like the Up Helly Aa winter fire festival. Shetland has more than 100 islands, home to 22,000 people and more than one million seabirds.

Festivals celebrate both Shetland's and Orkney's cultural connections while local producers and chefs get the best from the land and sea. The almost tangible tranquillity provides you with an ideal setting to see wildlife across all the islands, either from quiet, sandy beaches or aboard a wildlife cruise.

01 Mucklebrick's Wick, Island of Foula, Shetland

02 Ring of Brodgar, Orkney

03 The Shetland Museum, Lerwick, mainland Shetland

04 The Italian Chapel built by Italian prisoners of war, Lamb Holm, Orkney

05 A peat fired kiln, Highland Park Distillery, Orkney

Inspired ideas for you to indulge

RING OF BRODGAR

The Ring of Brodgar in Stenness is an outstanding example of a circular stone ring and stands as an emblem of Orkney's ancient heritage. Twenty-seven stones remain standing today in strong relief against the Orcadian landscape. More than 4,000 years old, the stones are part of the Heart of Neolithic Orkney World Heritage Site. **visitorkney.com/brodgar**

ITALIAN CHAPEL

In 1942 some 550 Italian prisoners-of-war were brought to Lambholm on Orkney to overcome a labour shortage. They were housed in Camp 60, which the Italians improved with gardens and paths. Two Nissen huts were joined together to form a chapel, which the prisoners transformed into the outstanding work of art you see today.

HIGHLAND PARK DISTILLERY

One of the most well-known and respected single malts, Highland Park is a part of Orkney's heritage and has an unbroken tradition of whisky-making stretching back to 1798. Tour the world's northernmost Scotch whisky distillery and discover the influences that help create Highland Park's distinctively aromatic floral sweetness. **highlandpark.co.uk**

SHETLAND MUSEUM AND ARCHIVES

A striking modern building near Lerwick town centre brings together Shetland's museum and archive collections for the first time. Galleries cover such diverse subjects as Early Peoples and Textiles. Watch boats being worked on in the Boat Shed, see them suspended in the Boat Hall then grab a bowl of seafood chowder in the café. **shetland-museum.org.uk**

BONHOGA GALLERY

Opened in 1994, Bonhoga is the first purpose-built visual and applied art gallery in Shetland and the most northerly in the UK. Bonhoga, which means 'my spiritual home', lives up to its name by showcasing the best arts and crafts inspired by the islands and supporting a thriving touring programme. **shetlandarts.org/venues**

VALHALLA BREWERY TOUR

Unst on Shetland is home to the UK's most northerly brewery. The Valhalla Brewery currently produces six real ales, each with its own distinctive flavour and character and names like Island Bere and Old Scatness. You can pre-arrange a tour of the brewery and see the whole process from mash tun to bottling and labelling. **valhallabrewery.co.uk**

Savour the real taste of Scotland

THE FOVERAN HOTEL AND RESTAURANT
The Foveran Hotel combines a great base from which to explore Orkney with wonderful food to welcome you back at the end of each day. Chefs present the natural produce from Orkney's land and waters simply and stylishly in the hotel restaurant. Gaze out over Scapa Flow and the southern isles as you dine.
foveranhotel.co.uk

THE CREEL RESTAURANT
Cross Orkney's Churchill Barriers and you come to St Margaret's Hope and The Creel Restaurant with Rooms. Not surprisingly, fresh fish and seafood are always on the menu, though these include some species you may not know like megrim, torsk and sea-witch. There's also prime Orkney beef and local seaweed-fed lamb to try.
thecreel.co.uk

MONTY'S BISTRO
Informal and relaxed, Monty's Bistro is set amongst the wynds in Lerwick's port area. Popular with locals and visitors alike, fresh local fish and lamb are treated with the respect they deserve and the results speak for themselves – innovative and creative cooking at its best.
taste-of-scotland.com

BRAEWICK CAFÉ
The Braewick Café Restaurant overlooks the shore of Braewick Bay at Eshaness. The café has its own Shetland croft so the menu's pork, lamb and beef, as well as the vegetables, are all home-reared. Daytime snacks give way to à la carte dinners in the evening. The café also has a craft shop and gallery.
eshaness.shetland.co.uk

SHETLAND FOOD FESTIVAL
1 – 10 October 2010
Shetland produces some excellent food: from lamb and beef to fish and shellfish. There are also more unusual specialities like seawater oatcakes and Shetland Black potatoes. Through workshops, a food theatre and producers' market, this festival showcases the best of Shetland. Local eateries also take part by creating special festival menus.
shetlandfoodfestival.co.uk

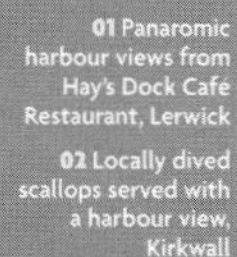

01 Panaromic harbour views from Hay's Dock Cafe Restaurant, Lerwick

02 Locally dived scallops served with a harbour view, Kirkwall

03 Rope grown mussels from Vaila Voe

Something a little bit different

PIER ARTS CENTRE

The Pier Arts Centre in Stromness, Orkney provides a home for an important collection of British fine art donated to be 'held in trust' for Orkney. Alongside this permanent collection, the Centre runs a year-round programme of changing exhibitions. The Centre building itself won Scotland's Best Building Award 2007.
pierartscentre.com

NORTHERN LIGHTS HOLISTIC SPA

On the small island of Bressay is Shetland's only residential, purpose-built spa. Choose from treatments including hydro spa, sauna, Turkish steam room and a flotation therapy room. The holistic approach extends to locally-sourced organic dishes prepared by the spa's chef. Book a longer pampering stay in one of only four bedrooms.
shetlandspa.com

NOSS AND BRESSAY BOAT TRIPS

Noss National Nature Reserve near Lerwick is where hundreds and thousands of seabirds including puffins, gannets and guillemots call home. Seabirds and Seals boat trips bring you unbelievably close to these birds. Trips also explore the island coastline of Bressay. An onboard underwater colour TV camera lets you see what's going on underwater as well.
seabirds-and-seals.com

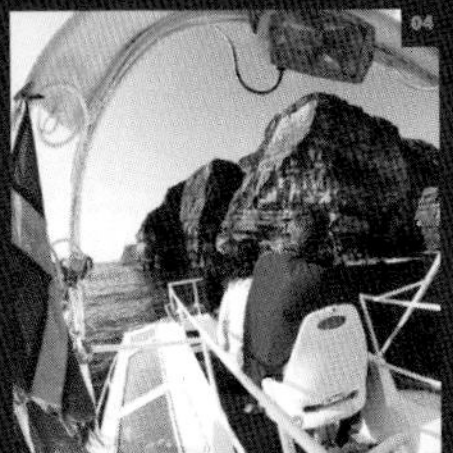

Time to plan your perfect day

UP HELLY AA
26 January 2010
On the last Tuesday of January every year, the town of Lerwick gives itself over to Europe's biggest fire festival. As well as a celebration of Shetland's Viking history, Up Helly Aa is a fun spectacle with a torchlight procession and galley burning. You can see the Up Helly Aa exhibition in Lerwick's Galley Shed.
visitshetland.com

SHETLAND FOLK FESTIVAL
29 April – 2 May 2010
The Shetland Folk Festival marks its 30th anniversary in 2010. It offers a foot-tapping mix of musicians from Shetland, the UK and wider afield. Expect plenty of Scottish fiddles and traditional dialect songs, as well as a variety of world folk music.
shetlandfolkfestival.com

ORKNEY FOLK FESTIVAL
27 – 30 May 2010
The Orcadian tradition of music and song is kept very much alive at the Orkney Folk Festival in Stromness. The festival combines well-established folk musicians and emerging talents from outwith Orkney with multi-talented local musicians, many themselves well-known in the folk music world.
orkneyfolkfestival.com

ST MAGNUS FESTIVAL
18 – 23 June 2010
Orkney's midsummer celebration of the arts is one of Britain's most highly regarded and adventurous arts events. The 2010 programme looks set to further enhance its reputation with appearances by, among others, Scottish violin virtuosa Nicola Benedetti, the BBC Scottish Symphony Orchestra and the Hebrides Ensemble.
stmagnusfestival.com

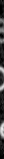

CREATIVE CONNECTIONS
9 – 15 August 2010
You can get involved in various ways with this week of cultural events on Shetland. There are summer courses in creative writing, Scottish fiddle-playing and contemporary knitting to try. Join a Shetland storytelling tour, visit an art exhibition or just enjoy the concerts and dances.
visitshetland.com

01 A craftsman at work, Weisdale Mill, Shetland

02 Up Helly Aa Fire Festival, Lerwick

03 Fiddlers – traditional folk music

04 Spotting the local wildlife on the Islands of Bressay and Noss

05 Trout fishing, Loch of Harray, Orkney

06 The Broch of Gurness, Eynhallow Sound

THE HIGHLANDS & ISLANDS

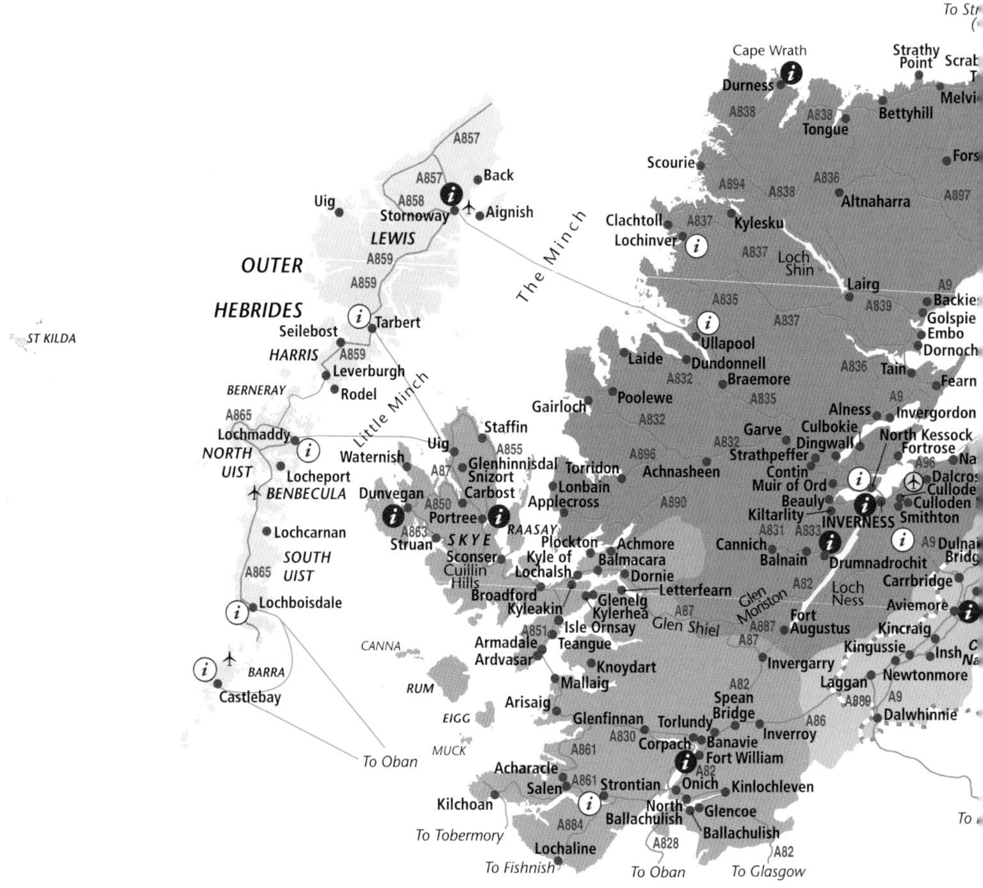

To Str
Cape Wrath
Strathy Point
Scrab
Durness
Melvi
A838
A838
Tongue
Bettyhill
Scourie
Fors
A894
A838
A836
Altnaharra
A897
A857
Back
A857
Uig
A858
Stornoway
Aignish
Clachtoll
A837
Kylesku
Lochinver
A837
Loch Shin
LEWIS
A859
OUTER
A859
The Minch
Lairg
A9
Backies
A835
A839
HEBRIDES
Golspie
Tarbert
A837
Embo
ST KILDA
Seilebost
Ullapool
Dornoch
HARRIS
A859
Laide
Dundonnell
A836
Tain
Leverburgh
A832
Braemore
Fearn
BERNERAY
Rodel
A835
A9
Little Minch
Alness
Invergordon
A865
Gairloch
Poolewe
A832
Lochmaddy
Staffin
Garve
Culbokie
North Kessock
NORTH UIST
Uig
A855
A832
Dingwall
Fortrose
Waternish
A896
Strathpeffer
A96
Na
Locheport
A87
Glenhinnisdal
Torridon
Achnasheen
Contin
Dalcros
Snizort
Lonbain
Muir of Ord
Cullode
BENBECULA
Dunvegan
Carbost
Applecross
A890
Beauly
Culloden
A850
Kiltarlity
INVERNESS
Smithton
Portree
RAASAY
A831
A833
Lochcarnan
A863
SKYE
Plockton
Achmore
Cannich
A9
Dulnai
SOUTH UIST
Struan
Sconser
Kyle of Lochalsh
Balmacara
Balnain
Drumnadrochit
Bridg
Cuillin Hills
Dornie
A865
Broadford
Letterfean
Glen Moriston
A82
Loch Ness
Carrbridge
Lochboisdale
Kyleakin
Glenelg
Kylerhea
A87
Fort Augustus
Aviemore
A851
Isle Ornsay
Glen Shiel
A887
Kincraig
CANNA
Armadale
Teangue
A87
Kingussie
Insh
Ardvasar
Knoydart
Invergarry
BARRA
Mallaig
Laggan
Newtonmore
RUM
Castlebay
A82
Spean Bridge
A889
A9
Arisaig
Dalwhinnie
EIGG
Glenfinnan
Torlundy
A86
A830
Corpach
Banavie
Inverroy
MUCK
To Oban
A861
Fort William
Acharacle
A82
A861
Strontian
Onich
Kinlochleven
Salen
Kilchoan
North Ballachulish
Glencoe
A884
To Tobermory
Ballachulish
Lochaline
A828
A82
To Fishnish
To Oban
To Glasgow
To

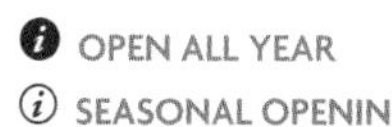

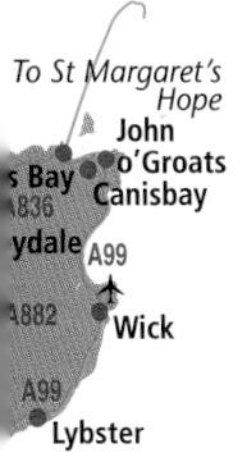

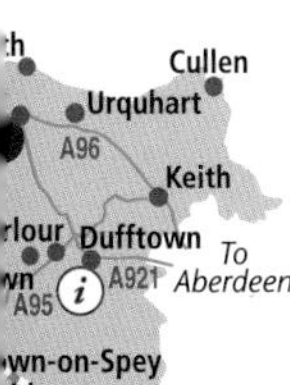

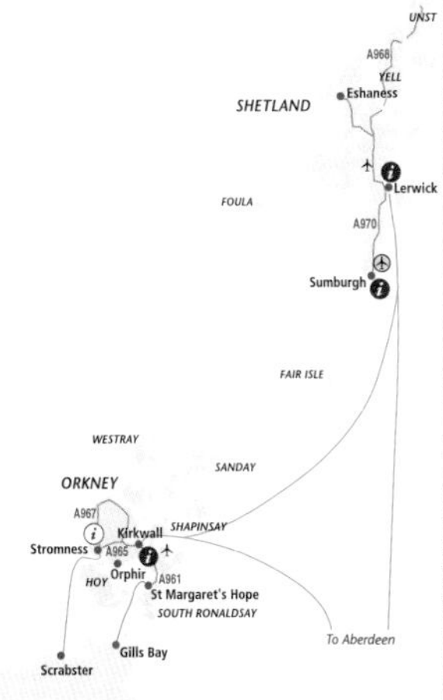

VisitScotland Information Centres

To help you plan and book your trip to Scotland email our travel experts at info@visitscotland.com. When you arrive call into one of our Information Centres where our friendly experts can offer advice on all things local as well as sharing their wider knowledge of Scotland. We don't just advise either. We can sort out your accommodation and all your travel needs, as well as tickets for events across Scotland. So if you're looking to get the most from your visit, there really is only one place to go.

FORT WILLIAM, LOCHABER, SKYE & LOCHALSH

Dunvegan	2 Lochside, Dunvegan, Isle of Skye, IV55 8WB
Fort William	15 High Street, Fort William, PH33 6DH
Portree	Bayfield Road, Portree, Isle of Skye, IV51 9EL

MORAY, AVIEMORE & THE CAIRNGORMS

Aviemore	No 7 The Parade, Grampian Road, Aviemore, PH22 1RH
Elgin	Elgin Library, Elgin, IV30 1HS

NORTH HIGHLANDS, INVERNESS, LOCH NESS & NAIRN

Drumnadrochit	The Car Park, Drumnadrochit, Inverness-shire, IV63 6TX
Durness	Sango, Durness, Sutherland, IV27 4PZ
Inverness	Castle Wynd, Inverness, IV2 3BJ

ORKNEY & SHETLAND

Kirkwall	The Travel Centre, West Castle Street, Kirkwall, Orkney, KW15 1GU
Lerwick	Market Cross, Lerwick, Shetland, ZE1 0LU
Sumburgh (Airport)	Wilsness Terminal, Sumburgh Airport, Shetland, ZE3 9JP

OUTER HEBRIDES

Stornoway	26 Cromwell Street, Stornoway, Isle of Lewis, HS1 2DD

- LOCAL KNOWLEDGE
- WHERE TO STAY
- ACCOMMODATION BOOKING
- PLACES TO VISIT
- THINGS TO DO
- MAPS AND GUIDES
- TRAVEL ADVICE
- ROUTE PLANNING
- WHERE TO SHOP AND EAT
- LOCAL CRAFTS AND PRODUCE
- EVENT INFORMATION
- TICKETS

Northern Highlands, Inverness, Loch Ness & Nairn: Hotels

Drumnadrochit

Glenurquhart House Hotel

Open: 1 Mar-14 Nov **Map Ref: 4A9**

Set in a scenic and tranquil location between Loch Ness and Glen Affric, with views of Loch Meiklie and Glen Urquhart, we offer six individually designed en-suite bedrooms, two with four poster beds, cosy lounge bar with log fire and intimate restaurant serving freshly cooked meals. A warm welcome awaits you from your hosts Ewan and Carol.

★★★★
RESTAURANT WITH ROOMS

Balnain, Drumnadrochit, Inverness, IV63 6TJ
T: 01456 476234 E: info@glenurquhart-house-hotel.co.uk W: glenurquhart-house-hotel.co.uk

Indicated Prices:

Single	from £55.00 per room	Twin	from £90.00 per room
Double	from £90.00 per room	Family	from £110.00 per room

 2837

nvergordon

Kincraig Castle Hotel

Open: All year **Map Ref: 4B7**

ncraig Castle Hotel offers 15 nsuite rooms, a number of which e newly created Premier and xecutive rooms. A refurbished à carte Restaurant and bar and a pacious oak panelled lounge offer perb character and comfort.

★★★★
COUNTRY HOUSE HOTEL

Invergordon, Ross-shire, IV18 0LF
T: 01349 852587 E: info@kincraig-castle-hotel.co.uk W: kincraig-castle-hotel.co.uk

Indicated Prices:

Single	from £100.00 per room	Twin	from £150.00 per room
Double	from £150.00 per room	Family	from £175.00 per room

33956

nverness

Glenmoriston Town House

Open: All year **Map Ref: 4B8**

tuated on the banks of the River ess, with its majestic setting, the lenmoriston Town House has verything to meet your needs hether your stay is for business r leisure. With an award winning ench Restaurant Abstract, a verside Brasserie Contrast, 30 xurious bedrooms and a Piano ar with live music every Friday nd Saturday.

★★★★
HOTEL

20 Ness Bank, Inverness, IV2 4SF
T: 01463 223777 E: reception@glenmoristontownhouse.com W: glenmoristontownhouse.com

Indicated Prices:

Single	from £95.00 per room	Twin	from £130.00 per room
Double	from £130.00 per room		

28283

Inverness

Kingsmills Hotel

Open: All year **Map Ref: 4B8**

Extensively refurbished in 2009, the four star Kingsmills Hotel offers a relaxing environment from our leisure club with pool and jacuzzi through to our lounge and conservatory restaurant. Spacious bedrooms equipped with full facilities, including some with their own garden patio compliment the overall hotel.

★★★★
HOTEL

Culcabock Road, Inverness, IV2 3LP
T: 01463 257100 E: reservations@kingsmillshotel.com W: kingsmillshotel.com

Indicated Prices:

Single	from £78.00 per room	Twin	from £88.00 per room
Double	from £88.00 per room	Family	from £98.00 per room
		Suite	from £108.00 per room

8099

by Inverness, Culloden

Culloden House

Open: All year excl Xmas **Map Ref: 4B8**

Steeped in history, this award-winning 18th century country house offers luxury accommodation and fine dining cuisine. Set in 40 acres of private grounds and gardens three miles east of Inverness. Easy access to Inverness Airport, visitor attractions and touring.

★★★★
COUNTRY HOUSE HOTEL

Culloden, Inverness, IV2 7BZ
T: 01463 790461 E: reservations@cullodenhouse.co.uk W: cullodenhouse.co.uk

Indicated Prices:

Single	from £95.00 per room	Twin	from £190.00 per room
Double	from £190.00 per room	Family	from £240.00 per room
		Suite	from £300.00 per room

 2168

Northern Highlands, Inverness, Loch Ness & Nairn: Guest Houses and B&Bs

Beauly
Cnocend Bed & Breakfast
Open: Mar-end Nov **Map Ref: 4A8**

★★★★
BED AND BREAKFAST

Cnocend, Croyard Road, Beauly, IV4 7DJ
T: 01463 782230 E: patcnocend@aol.com

Indicated Prices:

Single	from £30.00	Twin	from £25.00 per person
Double	from £25.00 per person		

19842

by Beauly, Kiltarlity
Cherry Trees
Open: 1 Mar-30 Nov **Map Ref: 4A9**

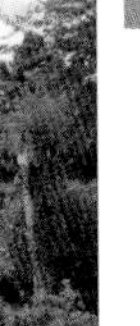

★★★★
FARM HOUSE

Kiltarlity, by Beauly, IV4 7JQ
T: 01463 741368 E: jessiematheson@btinternet.com

Indicated Prices:

Single	from £40.00 per person
Double	from £26.00 per person

19046

Culbokie, Black Isle
Ben Wyvis Views
Open: All year **Map Ref: 4B8**

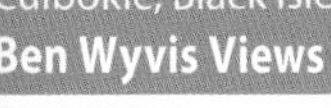

★★★★
BED AND BREAKFAST

Bydand, Culbokie, Ross-shire, IV7 8JH
T: 01349 877430 E: jane@culbokie.net W: culbokie.net

Indicated Prices:

Single	from £45.00 per room	Twin	from £35.00 per person
Double	from £35.00 per person		

67938

Dornoch

Hillview

Open: All year excl Xmas & New Year **Map Ref: 4B6**

★★★★
BED AND BREAKFAST

Evelix Road, Dornoch, IV25 3RD
T: 01862 810151 E: hillviewbb@talk21.com W: milford.co.uk/go/hillviewbb.html

Indicated Prices:

Single	from £45.00 per room	Twin	from £60.00 per room
Double	from £60.00 per room	Family	from £90.00 per room

3058

Drumnadrochit

Kilmore Farmhouse

Open: Apr-Oct **Map Ref: 4A9**

★★★★
BED AND BREAKFAST

Drumnadrochit, Inverness, IV63 6UF
T: 01456 450524 E: kilmorefarm@supanet.com W: visitdrumnadrochit.com

Indicated Prices:

Single	from £40.00 per room	Twin	from £58.00 per room
Double	from £58.00 per room	Family	from £65.00 per room

3386

Drumnadrochit

Rowan Cottage Bed & Breakfast

Open: Mar-Nov **Map Ref: 4A9**

★★★★
BED AND BREAKFAST

10 West Lewiston, Drumnadrochit, Inverness, IV63 6UW
T/F: 01456 450944 E: rowanbandb@aol.com W: rowancottagebedandbreakfast.co.uk

Indicated Prices:

Double	from £82.00 per room	Twin	from £82.00 per room

7889

Fortrose

Hillhaven B&B

Open: All year **Map Ref: 4B8**

★★★★
BED AND BREAKAST

Hillhaven, Ordhill, Fortrose, IV10 8RA
T: 01381 620826 E: stephen.skinner@homecall.co.uk W: hillhaven.co.uk

Indicated Prices:

Single	from £35.00	Twin	from £60.00 per room
Double	from £60.00 per room	Family	from £70.00 per room

3052

 PRICES STATED ARE ESTIMATES AND MAY BE SUBJECT TO CHANGE. PRICES ARE PER PERSON PER NIGHT UNLESS OTHERWISE STATED. AWARDS CORRECT AS OF BEGINNING OF OCTOBER 2009

Fortrose

Water's Edge

Open: All year (restricted opening Nov-Mar) **Map Ref: 4B8**

★★★★★
BED AND BREAKFAST

Canonbury Terrace, Fortrose, IV10 8TT
T: 01381 621202 E: gill@watersedge.uk.com W: watersedge.uk.com

Indicated Prices:

Single	10% discount
Double	from £50.00 per person

76567

by Gairloch, Auchtercairn

Gairloch View Guest House and B&B

Open: All year **Map Ref: 3F7**

★★★★
BED AND BREAKFAST

Gairloch View, Auchtercairn, Gairloch, Ross-shire, IV21 2BN
T: 01445 712666 E: enquiries@gairlochview.com W: gairlochview.com

Indicated Prices:

Single	from £55.00 per room	Twin	from £70.00 per room
Double	from £75.00 per room		

77101

Inverness

Ballifeary Guest House

Open: All year excl 24-28 Dec **Map Ref: 4B8**

AA ★★★★ GUEST HOUSE

10 Ballifeary Road, Inverness, IV3 5PJ
T: 01463 235572 E: info@ballifearyguesthouse.co.uk W: ballifearyguesthouse.co.uk

Indicated Prices:

Single	from £40.00 per room	Twin	from £70.00 per room
Double	from £70.00 per room		

13974

Inverness

Eiland View B&B

Open: All year excl Xmas & New Year **Map Ref: 4B8**

★★★★
BED AND BREAKFAST

Woodside of Culloden, Westhill, Inverness, IV2 5BP
T: 01463 798900 E: info@eilandview.com W: eilandview.com

Indicated Prices:

Single	from £35.00 per room	Twin	from £58.00 per room
Double	from £58.00 per room		

24639

Inverness
Lorne House **Open: All year excl Xmas & New Year** **Map Ref: 4B8**

★★★★
BED AND BREAKFAST

40 Crown Drive, Inverness, IV2 3QG
T: 01463 236271

Indicated Prices:

Double	from £30.00 per person	Twin	from £30.00 per person

3639

Lairg
Park House **Open: All year excl Xmas & New Year** **Map Ref: 4A6**

★★★★
GUEST HOUSE

Station Road, Lairg, Sutherland, IV27 4AU
T: 01549 402208 E: david-walker@park-house.freeserve.co.uk W: parkhousesporting.com

Indicated Prices:

Single	from £40.00 per room	Twin	from £70.00 per room
Double	from £70.00 per room	Family	from £85.00 per room

4918

Lochinver
Davar **Open: Mar-Oct** **Map Ref: 3G5**

★★★★
BED AND BREAKFAST

Davar, Lochinver, IV27 4LJ
T: 01571 844501 E: jean@davar36.fsnet.co.uk W: davar-lochinver.co.uk

Indicated Prices:

Single	from £40.00	Twin	from £30.00 per person
Double	from £30.00 per person		

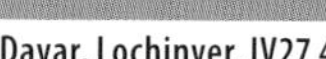

2222

Lochinver
Polcraig **Open: All year** **Map Ref: 3G5**

★★★★
GUEST HOUSE

Cruamer, Lochinver, Sutherland, IV27 4LD
T: 01571 844429 E: cathelmac@aol.com W: smoothhound.co.uk/hotels/polcraig.html

Indicated Prices:

Single	from £40.00	Twin	from £30.00 per person
Double	from £30.00 per person		

C V

50075

 PRICES STATED ARE ESTIMATES AND MAY BE SUBJECT TO CHANGE. PRICES ARE PER PERSON PER NIGHT UNLESS OTHERWISE STATED. AWARDS CORRECT AS OF BEGINNING OF OCTOBER 2009

Melvich
Bighouse Lodge

Open: All year **Map Ref: 4C3**

tunningly located at the mouth f the Halladale River, and urrounded by water on three des. A charming, warm and elcoming Scottish country house hich is very well appointed.

★★★★
GUEST ACCOMMODATION

by Melvich, Sutherland, KW14 7YJ
T: 01641 531207 E: info@bighouseestate.com W: bighouseestate.com

Indicated Prices:

Single	from £90.00 per room	Twin	from £120.00 per room
Double	from £120.00 per room		

15127

Nairn
Inveran Lodge

Open: All year **Map Ref: 4C8**

nveran Lodge offers three luxury uest bedrooms situated round a eaceful drawing room. The dining oom with antiques and crystal is our breakfast room and adjacent the Butler's Pantry where guests an help themselves to homebakes vith tea and coffee. The garden atio is an additional seating area.

★★★★
BED AND BREAKFAST

Seafield Street, Nairn, IV12 4HG
T: 01667 455666 E: info@inveranlodge.co.uk W: inveranlodge.co.uk

Indicated Prices:

Double	from £65.00 per room	Twin	from £65.00 per room

31909

Strathy Point

Sharvedda

Open: All year excl Xmas & New Year **Map Ref: 4B3**

★★★★
BED AND BREAKFAST

Strathy Point, Strathy, Thurso, Sutherland, KW14 7RY
T: 01641 541311 E: patsy@sharvedda.co.uk W: sharvedda.co.uk

Indicated Prices:

Single	from £40.00	Twin	from £30.00 per person
Double	from £30.00 per person		

5432

Thurso

Pentland Lodge House

Open: All year **Map Ref: 4D3**

★★★★
GUEST HOUSE

Granville Street, Thurso, Caithness, KW14 7JN
T: 01847 895103 E: info@pentlandlodgehouse.co.uk W: pentlandlodgehouse.co.uk

Indicated Prices:

Single	from £48.00 per room	Twin	from £84.00 per room
Double	from £80.00 per room	Family	from £90.00 per room

6829

Ullapool

Ardvreck Guest House

Open: Mar-Nov **Map Ref: 3G6**

★★★★
GUEST HOUSE

Ardvreck House, Morefield, Ullapool, Ross-shire, IV26 2TH
T: 01854 612028 E: ardvreck@btconnect.com W: smoothhound.co.uk/hotels/ardvreck

Indicated Prices:

Single	from £35.00 per room	Twin	from £70.00 per room
Double	from £70.00 per room	Family	from £85.00 per room

1271

Ullapool

Dromnan Guest House

Open: Mar-Oct **Map Ref: 3G6**

★★★★
GUEST HOUSE

Garve Road, Ullapool, Ross-shire, IV26 2SX
T: 01854 612333 E: info@dromnan.com W: dromnan.co.uk

Indicated Prices:

Single	from £40.00 per room	Twin	from £78.00 per room
Double	from £75.00 per room	Family	from £80.00 per room

23205

 PRICES STATED ARE ESTIMATES AND MAY BE SUBJECT TO CHANGE. PRICES ARE PER PERSON PER NIGHT UNLESS OTHERWISE STATED. AWARDS CORRECT AS OF BEGINNING OF OCTOBER 2009

Ullapool
Point Cottage Guest House
Open: 1 Mar-31 Oct **Map Ref: 3G6**

★★★★
GUEST HOUSE

22 West Shore Street, Ullapool, IV26 2UR
T: 01854 612494 E: macrae@pointcottage.co.uk W: pointcottage.co.uk

Indicated Prices:

Single	from £30.00 per person	Twin	from £25.00 per person
Double	from £25.00 per person		

50057

Ullapool
Westlea Guest House
Open: Mar-Nov **Map Ref: 3G6**

★★★★
GUEST HOUSE

2 Market Street, Ullapool, Ross-shire, IV26 2XE
T: 01854 612594 E: mail@westlea-ullapool.co.uk W: westlea-ullapool.co.uk

Indicated Prices:

Single	from £35.00 per room	Twin	from £65.00 per room
Double	from £65.00 per room		

75904

by Ullapool, Braemore
Braemore Square Country House
Open: All year **Map Ref: 3H7**

★★★★
BED AND BREAKFAST

Braemore, Loch Broom, Wester Ross, IV23 2RX
T: 01854 655357 E: enquiries@braemoresquare.com W: braemoresquare.com

Indicated Prices:

Double	from £32.00 per person	Twin	from £32.00 per person

16025

Northern Highlands, Inverness, Loch Ness & Nairn: Self Catering

by Applecross, Lonbain

Tigh Ruaraidh

Open: All year **Map Ref: 3F8**

★★★★
SELF CATERING

Lonbain, Applecross, Wester Ross, IV54 8XX
T: 0116 2605726 E: wales@waitrose.com W: tighruaraidh.co.uk

1 House 4 Bedrooms Sleeps 1-7

Prices – House:
£575.00-£925.00 Per Week

Short breaks available

7295

Ardross

Lower Inchlumpie

Open: All year **Map Ref: 4A7**

★★★★
SELF CATERING

Strathrusdale, Ardross, Ross-shire, IV17 0YQ
T: 01903 260334 E: margaret@lowerinchlumpie.co.uk W: lowerinchlumpie.co.uk

1 House 5 Bedrooms Sleeps 2-8

Prices – House:
£650.00-£1250.00 Per Week

8302

Beauly

Dunsmore Lodges

Open: All year **Map Ref: 4A8**

★★★★
SELF CATERING

Beauly, Inverness-shire, IV4 7EY
T: 01463 782424 E: inghammer@dunsmorelodges.co.uk W: dunsmorelodges.co.uk

3 Chalets 2 Bedrooms Sleeps 4

Prices – Chalet:
from £325.00 Per Week

Short breaks available

 **2385**

 PRICES STATED ARE ESTIMATES AND MAY BE SUBJECT TO CHANGE. PRICES ARE PER UNIT PER WEEK UNLESS OTHERWISE STATED. AWARDS CORRECT AS OF BEGINNING OF OCTOBER 2009

ettyhill
Irs Ola Todd
Open: All year **Map Ref: 4B3**

★★★★
SELF CATERING

6 Hoy Farm, Halkirk, Caithness, KW12 6UU
T: 01847 831544 E: olatodd@tiscali.co.uk W: visithighlands.com

1 House | 3 Bedrooms | Sleeps 6

Prices – House:
from £400.00 Per Week

Short breaks available

44774

:ulbokie, Dingwall
Vester Brae Highland Lodges
Open: All year **Map Ref: 4B8**

olphins at play in the waters the 'Firth'. Mountain peaks arching in ranks towards the est. Indulge your imagination om the comfort of your 4-star dges at Wester Brae. Easy access d close proximity to Scotland's atural beauty. Situated on the ack Isle. Inverness 16 miles, ingwall 9 miles.

★★★★
SELF CATERING

Wester Brae, Culbokie, Dingwall, IV7 8JU
T: 01349 877609 E: westerbrae@btconnect.com W: westerbraehighlandlodges.co.uk

4 Cottages | 2-3 Bedrooms | Sleeps 2-5

Prices – Cottage:
£280.00-£525.00 Per Week

Short breaks available

63804

Drumnadrochit

Balnalurigin

Open: Mar-Oct, Xmas & New Year **Map Ref: 4A**

Overlooking Loch Mieklie with views of the mountains beyond, this charming well equipped hillside cottage provides a comfortable base from which to explore this beautiful Highland area. Many visitor attractions and outdoor pursuits are within easy reach.

★★★★
SELF CATERING

Mrs D J Beattie, Appleton House, Errol, Perth, Perthshire, PH2 7QE
T: 01821 642412 E: idbeattie@ukonline.co.uk W: accommodationlochness.co.uk

1 Cottage | 4 Bedrooms | Sleeps 7

Prices – Cottage:
£375.00-£580.00 Per Week

6822

Glen Urquhart

Millness Croft Luxury Cottages

Open: All year **Map Ref: 4A9**

★★★★★
SELF CATERING

Millness Croft, Glen Urquhart, Inverness, IV63 6TW
T: 01456 476761 E: info@millnesscroft.co.uk W: millnesscroft.co.uk

3 Cottages | 2 Bedrooms | Sleeps 1-4

Prices – Cottage:
£550.00-£970.00 Per Week

Short breaks available

6816

ıverness
꞉lackpark Farm

Open: All year

Map Ref: 4B8

ır self catering houses are in a ꞉rfect position for touring the ghlands. Only three miles from e A9, we are easily found next the Culloden Battlefield. Skye, hn O' Groats can all be explored ithin a day's travelling.

★★★★
SELF CATERING

Westhill, Inverness, IV2 5BP
T: 01463 790620 E: l.alexander@blackpark.co.uk W: blackpark.co.uk

1 Bungalow 3 Bedrooms Sleeps 6

Prices – Bungalow:
£350.00-£800.00 Per Week

15292

.aide
꞉ndrew and Alison Gilchrist

Open: All year excl 6-27 Mar 2010

Map Ref: 3G6

★★★★
SELF CATERING

Rocklea, Little Gruinard, Laide, Ross-shire, IV22 2NG
T: 0131 441 6053 E: aandagilchrist@blueyonder.co.uk W: heimdall-scot.co.uk/laide

1 Log Cottage 3 Bedrooms Sleeps 5

Prices – Log Cottage:
£220.00-£510.00 Per Week

39436

Lochinver
Cathair Dhubh Estate
Open: All year **Map Ref: 3G**

Enjoy stunning sea and mountain views on our coastal estate overlooking the white sand beach at Achmelvich Bay near Lochinver. This is a uniquely beautiful and remote area of the north west Highlands and a scenic paradise for walking, climbing, wildlife and fly fishing.

★★★★
SELF CATERING

Lochinver, IV27 4JB
T: 01571 855277 E: cathairdhubh@btinternet.com W: cathairdhubh.co.uk

5 Cottages 2-3 Bedrooms Sleeps 4-6

Prices – Cottage:
£287.00-£896.00 Per Week

Short breaks available

185

Lochinver
Glendarroch House
Open: All year **Map Ref: 3G**

★★★★
SELF CATERING

Mr Colin Mackenzie, Braeside, Navidale Road, Helmsdale, KW8 6JS
T: 01431 821207/07771 604307 E: colin@glendarroch.net W: glendarroch.net

1 House 4 Bedrooms Sleeps 1-6

Prices – House:
£495.00-£895.00 Per Week

160

by Lochinver, Clachtoll
WWC Properties
Open: All year **Map Ref: 3G**

★★★★
SELF CATERING

Mullach, Clachtoll, Lochinver, IV27 4JD
T: 01356 626011 E: linda@wwc2.fslife.co.uk W: mullach-clachtoll.co.uk

1 House 3 Bedrooms Sleeps 6

Prices – House:
£500.00-£800.00 Per Week

8539

by Tain, Fearn

Sycamore Country Lettings

Open: All year **Map Ref: 4C7**

★★★★
SELF CATERING

Sandpiper Cottage, Fearn, Tain, Ross-shire

T: 01282 700425 E: enquiries@sycamorecountrylettings.co.uk W: sycamorecountrylettings.co.uk

1 Cottage | 3 Bedrooms | Sleeps 8

Prices – Cottage:

£500.00-£600.00 Per Week

Short breaks available

85164

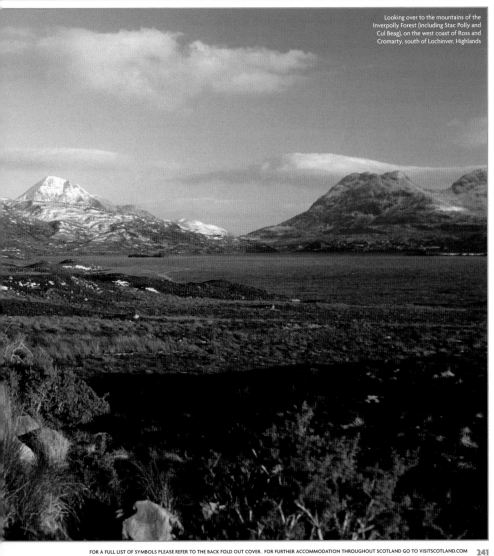

Looking over to the mountains of the Inverpolly Forest (including Stac Polly and Cul Beag), on the west coast of Ross and Cromarty, south of Lochinver, Highlands

Northern Highlands, Inverness, Loch Ness & Nairn: EatScotland Gold and Silver establishments

Lochinver
Iolaire Restaurant
SILVER

Inver Lodge Hotel,
Lolaire, Lochinver,
IV27 4LU
T: 01571 844496

Inver Lodge, with its magnificent views across to the Outer Hebrides, provides good quality fresh food cooked and served in generous portions with imagination, flair and enthusiasm.

Inverness
Rocpool Reserve Ltd.

14 Culduthel Road,
Inverness,
IV2 4AG
T: 01463 240 089

Contemporary and hip, Rocpool is a stylish place to eat and drink. Chef Davey Aspin is passionate about food and always eager to try new things.

Nairn
Sunny Brae Hotel

Marine Road,
Nairn,
IV12 4EA
T: 01667 452 309

Offering contemporary Scottish cooking using the very best seafood, game, Nairnshire Beef, pork and lamb from local suppliers, the daily changing menu reflects the commitment to seasonal produce.

Ross-shire
The Oystercatcher

Main Street, Portmahomack,
Ross-shire,
IV20 1YBT
T: 01700 821229

The Oystercatcher is a small, quality, seafood restaurant with themed decor and an intimate and quiet ambience specialising in locally caught shellfish.

Ross-shire
The Torridon

By Achnasheen,
Ross-shire,
IV22 2EY
T: 01445 791242

Fine Highland retreat offering great local Scottish produce cooked to high standard with the charm and warmth which Scotland offers best.

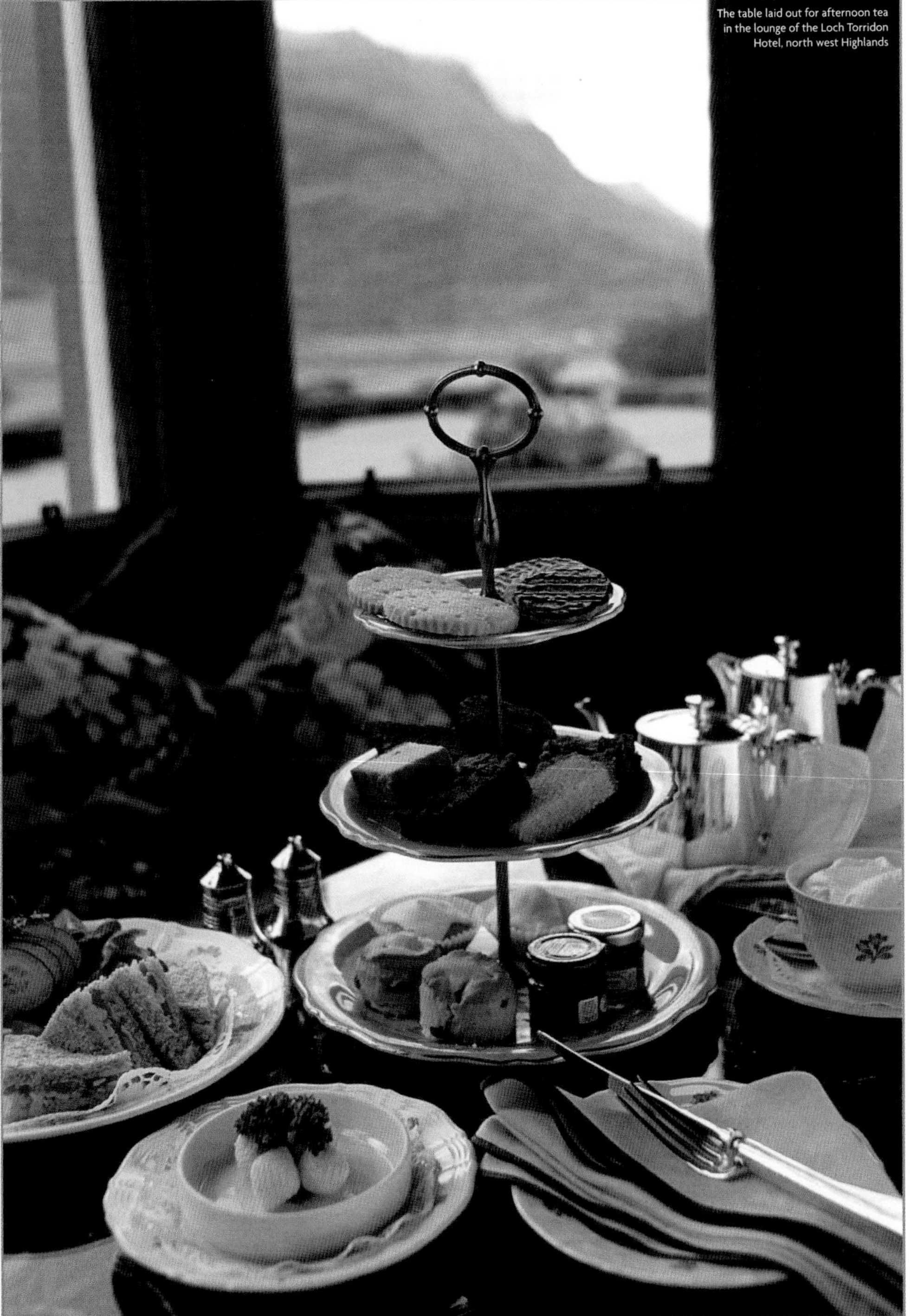

The table laid out for afternoon tea in the lounge of the Loch Torridon Hotel, north west Highlands

Fort William & Lochaber, Skye & Lochalsh: Hotels

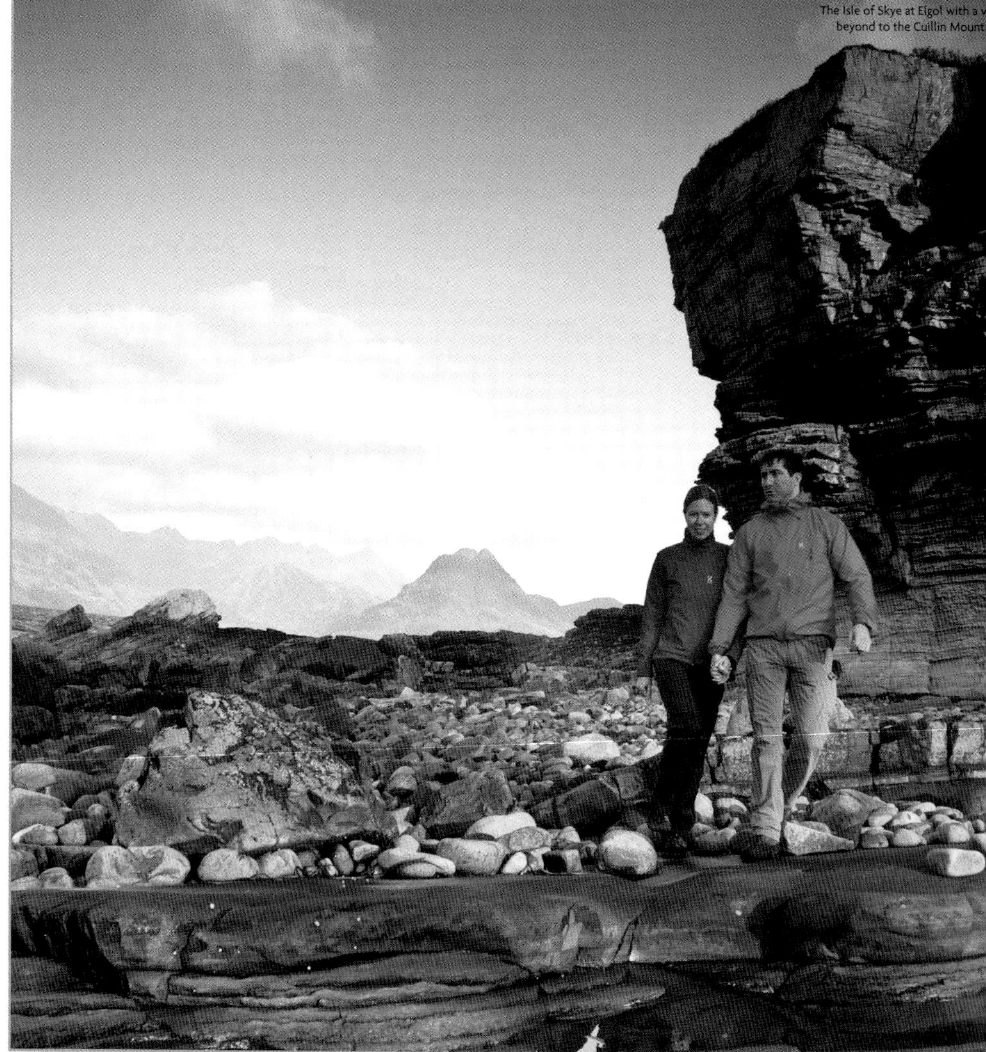

The Isle of Skye at Elgol with a v
beyond to the Cuillin Mount

ISLE OF SKYE

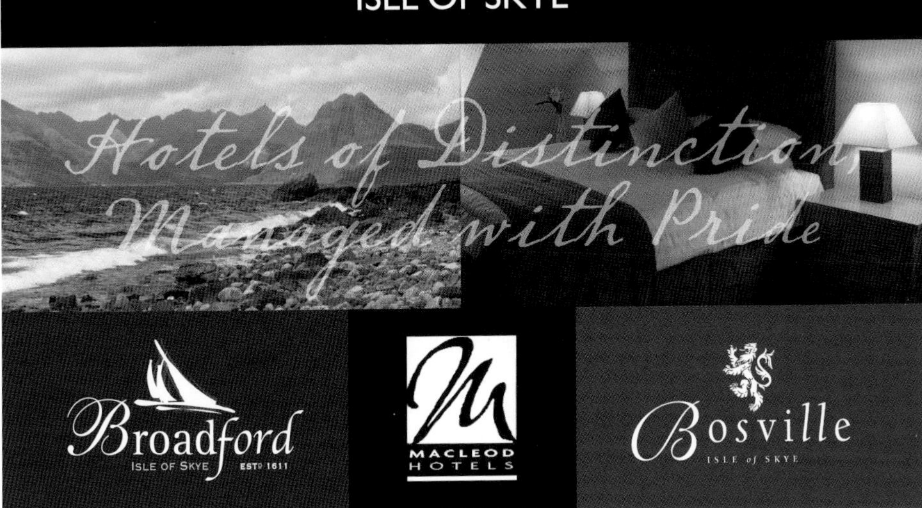

Hotels of Distinction, Managed with Pride
Broadford
ISLE OF SKYE EST 1611
MACLEOD HOTELS
Bosville
ISLE of SKYE

Established in 1611, this Hotel has been given a stunning make over to provide gorgeous accommodation and public areas looking out towards Broadford Bay.

The Broadford Hotel is the original home of Drambuie liquor, where the recipe was first made and this theme is reflected throughout in its design. This is a stylish, cosmopolitan Hotel offering good food with first class service.

Broadford Hotel, Torrin Road, Broadford, Isle of Skye, IV49 9AB
t: 01471 822204
e: broadford@macleodhotels.co.uk

A host of awards for excellence sets this Hotel apart from its competitors. Situated in the heart of Portree and overlooking Portree Harbour this is Skye's boutique Hotel. You will find fresh local produce used in the Restaurant, modern, quality accommodation and an especially warm welcome at the Bosville Hotel.

The Bosville Hotel,
9-11 Bosville Terrace, Portree,
Isle of Skye, IV51 9DG
t: 01478 612846
e: bosville@macleodhotels.co.uk

www.macleodhotels.com

Isle of Skye, Dunvegan

The Three Chimneys & The House Over-By

Open: All year excl 3 weeks in Jan & Apr **Map Ref: 3D8**

Candlelit crofter's cottage restaurant in a remote and beautiful corner of NW Skye, with six well appointed bedroom suites adjacent. Overlooking the sea, with the misty isles of the Outer Hebrides on the horizon. Renowned worldwide for fabulous local fresh food and warm, welcoming service. A 'must' on every Scottish tour. Winter deals available.

★★★★★ GOLD
RESTAURANT WITH ROOMS

Colbost, Dunvegan, Isle of Skye, IV55 8ZT
T: 01470 511258 E: eatandstay@threechimneys.co.uk W: threechimneys.co.uk

Indicated Prices:

Single	from £275.00 per room	Twin	from £275.00 per room
Double	from £275.00 per room	Family	from £370.00 per room

C £ V

 6103

Isle of Skye, Portree

Cuillin Hills Hotel

Open: All year **Map Ref: 3E9**

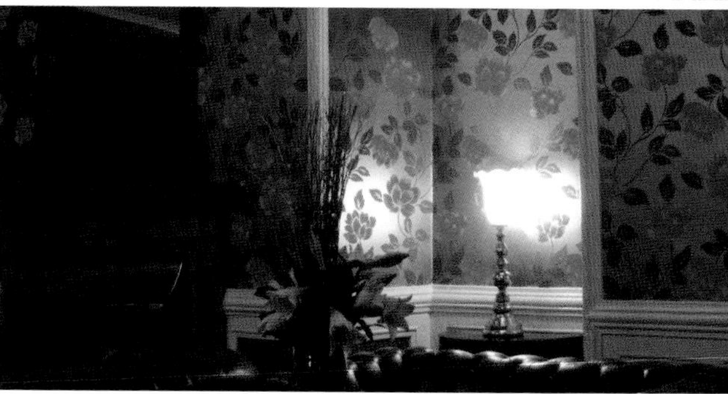

The Cuillin Hills Hotel, Portree enjoys some of the finest views in Scotland. Recently refurbished, it offers unrivalled comfort, luxury and friendliness. Award-winning food hallmarks its commitment to quality, with both fine dining and relaxed contemporary bar food. A malt embassy and great wines deliver a winning, relaxing break.

★★★★
COUNTRY HOUSE HOTEL

Portree, Isle of Skye, IV51 9QU
T: 01478 612003 E: info@cuillinhills-hotel-skye.co.uk W: cuillinhills-hotel-skye.co.uk

Indicated Prices:

Single	from £180.00 per room	Twin	from £200.00 per room
Double	from £200.00 per room	Family	from £235.00 per room
		Suite	from £300.00 per room

C £ V

 2163

 PRICES STATED ARE ESTIMATES AND MAY BE SUBJECT TO CHANGE. PRICES ARE PER PERSON PER NIGHT UNLESS OTHERWISE STATED. AWARDS CORRECT AS OF BEGINNING OF OCTOBER 2009

sle of Skye, Sleat

)uisdale House Hotel

Open: All year **Map Ref: 3F10**

uisdale House Hotel is a small, ildly romantic, luxury hotel, cated on the Isle of Skye. Totally ansformed over recent years it a perfect base for touring the land's world famous sites of terest. Our award-winning chef iowcases fresh island produce in elicious a la carte menus. Daily iling trips.

★★★★
COUNTRY HOUSE HOTEL

Sleat, Isle of Skye, IV43 8QW
T: 01471 833202 E: info@duisdale.com W: duisdale.com

Indicated Prices:

Single	from £70.00	Twin	from £65.00 per person
Double	from £65.00 per person	Suite	from £100.00 per person

SILVER **67064**

sle of Skye, Sleat

Toravaig House Hotel

Open: All year **Map Ref: 3F10**

oravaig House Hotel is an intimate, ixury hotel, located on the Isle of kye ideally located for exploring ie island and its beautiful coastline, iountains and historic castles. eautiful contemporary bedrooms ach individually designed. Award-inning fine dining showcases fresh ocal produce. Daily sailing trips on oard luxury yacht May-September.

★★★★
SMALL HOTEL

Knock Bay, Sleat, Isle of Skye, IV44 8RE
T: 01471 820200 E: info@skyehotel.co.uk W: skyehotel.co.uk

Indicated Prices:

Single	from £70.00	Twin	from £65.00 per person
Double	from £65.00 per person	Suite	from £100.00 per person

SILVER **61518**

Isle of Skye, Struan

Ullinish Country Lodge

Open: All year excl New Year/Jan **Map Ref: 3D9**

★★★★★ RESTAURANT WITH ROOMS

Struan, Isle of Skye, IV56 8FD
T: 01470 572214 E: ullinish@theisleofskye.co.uk W: theisleofskye.co.uk

Indicated Prices:

Single	from £90.00 per room	Twin	from £135.00 per room
Double	from £120.00 per room		

6831

Fort William & Lochaber, Skye & Lochalsh: Guest Houses and B&Bs

Ballachulish

Craiglinnhe House

Open: All year excl Xmas **Map Ref: 1F1**

David and Beverly Hughes welcome you to Craiglinnhe House, a loch-side Victorian villa set in a spectacular location with superb loch and mountain views. Craiglinnhe offers period charm with modern comforts, a warm, friendly atmosphere, tasty home-cooked breakfasts and evening meals. Ideal base for exploring the western Highlands.

★★★★ GUEST HOUSE

Lettermore, Ballachulish, PH49 4JD
T: 01855 811270 E: info@craiglinnhe.co.uk W: craiglinnhe.co.uk

Indicated Prices:

Double	from £56.00 per room	Twin	from £56.00 per room

73699

Ballachulish

Lyn-Leven Guest House

Open: 10 months, closed Xmas & New Year **Map Ref: 1F1**

'amily-run award winning guest ıouse with the freedom and omfort of a hotel at guest house ›rices, situated on the shores ›f Loch Leven- Glencoe one nile. Magnificent scenery with pectacular views of Glencoe and Mamore Hills. Ideal for all types ›f countryside activities. \A Selected 4 Stars.

★★★★
GUEST HOUSE

West Laroch, Ballachulish, Argyll, PH49 4JP
T: 01855 811392 W: lynleven.co.uk

Indicated Prices:

Single	from £35.00	Twin	from £64.00 per room
Double	from £64.00 per room	Family	from £80.00 per room

36649

Fort William

Carna B&B

Open: All year excl Xmas **Map Ref: 3G12**

★★★★
BED AND BREAKFAST

Carna, Achintore Road, Fort William, PH33 6RQ
T: 01397 708995 E: stay@carnabandb.co.uk W: carnabandb.co.uk

Indicated Prices:

Double	from £40.00 per person	Twin	from £40.00 per person

83178

Fort William

The Gantocks

Open: All year excl Xmas & New Year

Map Ref: 3G12

The Gantocks, overlooking Loch Linnhe, is the perfect place to have a relaxing break. With three tastefully decorated bedrooms, all with power showers, two baths, attention to detail by your Highland hosts guaranteed. The imaginative breakfast is individually prepared and based round fresh local produce and home baking.

★★★★★
BED AND BREAKFAST

Achintore Road, Fort William, PH33 6RN
T: 01397 702050 E: thegantocks@hotmail.co.uk W: fortwilliam5star.co.uk

Indicated Prices:

Double from £90.00 per room

78946

Fort William

Lawriestone Guest House

Open: All year excl Xmas & New Year

Map Ref: 3G12

A warm welcome awaits you at Lawriestone. The beautifully furnished rooms are all en-suite with TV, tea and coffee etc. At breakfast a varied selection including Scottish and vegetarian is available. Experience our hospitality and beautiful location by Loch Linnhe and the surrounding hills, only five minutes walk to town.

★★★★
BED AND BREAKFAST

Achintore Road, Fort William, PH33 6RQ
T: 01397 700777 E: susan@lawriestone.co.uk W: lawriestone.co.uk

Indicated Prices:

Double from £30.00 per person

Twin from £30.00 per person

Family from £30.00 per person

68003

 PRICES STATED ARE ESTIMATES AND MAY BE SUBJECT TO CHANGE. PRICES ARE PER PERSON PER NIGHT UNLESS OTHERWISE STATED. AWARDS CORRECT AS OF BEGINNING OF OCTOBER 2009

Fort William
Lochan Cottage Guest House
Open: Feb-Nov **Map Ref: 3H12**

★★★★
GUEST HOUSE

Lochyside, Fort William, PH33 7NX
T: 01397 702695 E: lochanco@btopenworld.com W: fortwilliam-guesthouse.co.uk

Indicated Prices:

Double	from £28.00 per person	Twin	from £28.00 per person

35986

Glencoe, Argyll
Highland View B&B
Open: All year **Map Ref: 1F1**

★★★★
BED AND BREAKFAST

Creag Dhu House, North Ballachulish, PH33 6RY
T: 01855 821555 E: highlandviewbb@btinternet.com W: highlandviewbandb.co.uk

Indicated Prices:

Double	from £32.50 per person	Twin	from £32.50 per person
		Family	from £32.50 per person

72867

Kinlochleven
Edencoille Guest House
Open: All year **Map Ref: 3H12**

★★★★
GUEST HOUSE

Edencoille, Garbhein Road, Kinlochleven, Argyll, PH50 4SE
T: 01855 831358 E: edencoille@tiscali.co.uk W: kinlochlevenbedandbreakfast.co.uk

Indicated Prices:

Single	from £50.00	Twin	from £32.00 per person
Double	from £32.00 per person	Family	from £32.00 per person

C V

24382

Plockton
Creag Liath
Open: Apr-Oct **Map Ref: 3F9**

★★★★
BED AND BREAKFAST

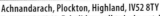

Achnandarach, Plockton, Highland, IV52 8TY
T: 01599 544341 E: holiday.well@virgin.net W: freespace.virgin.net/creag.liath

Indicated Prices:

Double	from £32.00 per person	Twin	from £32.00 per person

V

44748

Isle of Skye, Broadford

Berabhaigh B&B

Open: Mar-Oct **Map Ref: 3F10**

★★★★
BED AND BREAKFAST

3 Limepark, Broadford, Isle of Skye, IV49 9AE
T: 01471 822372 E: berabhaigh@freeuk.com W: isleofskye.net/berabhaigh/

Indicated Prices:
Double from £75.00 per room Twin from £75.00 per room

 14969

Isle of Skye, Sconser

Loch Aluinn

Open: Mar-Oct **Map Ref: 3E9**

★★★★
BED AND BREAKFAST

7 Sconser, by Kyle, Isle of Skye, IV48 8TD
T: 01478 650288 E: loch-aluinn@lineone.net W: isleofskye.net/loch-aluinn

Indicated Prices:
Double from £28.00 per person

35791

Isle of Skye, Skeabost Bridge

The Spoons

Open: All year excl 24-28 Dec **Map Ref: 3D8**

A warm welcome awaits you at The Spoons. With three individually designed ensuite bedrooms, beautiful dining room and lounge, The Spoons is the luxury base from which to explore the Isle of Skye. Delicious afternoon tea to welcome you in and gourmet breakfast to set you up for the day.

★★★★★
BED AND BREAKFAST

75 Aird Bernisdale, Skeabost Bridge, near Portree, Isle of Skye, IV51 9NU
T: 01470 532217 E: info@thespoonsonskye.com W: thespoonsonskye.com

Indicated Prices:
Double from £120.00 per room Twin from £120.00 per room

85246

 PRICES STATED ARE ESTIMATES AND MAY BE SUBJECT TO CHANGE. PRICES ARE PER PERSON PER NIGHT UNLESS OTHERWISE STATED. AWARDS CORRECT AS OF BEGINNING OF OCTOBER 2009

ʼpean Bridge

ʼaegour House

Open: All year **Map Ref: 3H12**

★★★★
BED AND BREAKFAST

Tirindrish, Roybridge Road, Spean Bridge, PH34 4EU
T: 01397 712903 E: enquiry@faegour.co.uk W: faegour.co.uk

Indicated Prices:

Double	from £32.50 per person	Double/Family	from £95.00 (for 3 people)

25454

ʼpean Bridge

ʼiverside Lodge Gardens B&B

Open: Apr-Oct **Map Ref: 3H12**

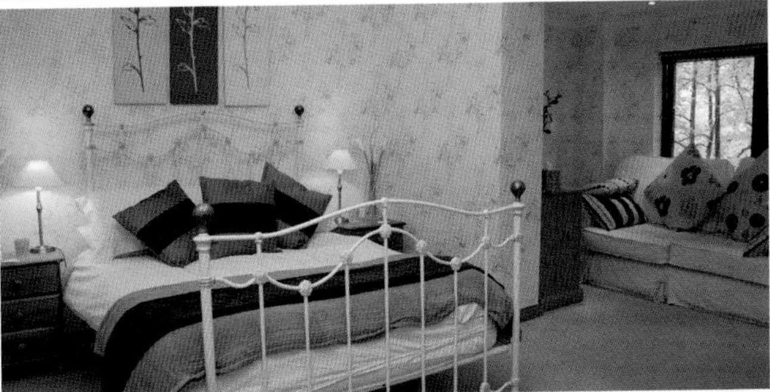

★★★★
BED AND BREAKFAST

Spean Bridge, Inverness-shire, PH34 4EN
T: 01397 712702/07789 517833 E: colincfindlay@aol.com W: visitscotland-spean.co.uk

Indicated Prices:

Single	from £45.00 per room	Twin	from £70.00 per room
Double	from £70.00 per room	Family	from £80.00 per room

et back at the end of a beautiful ee-lined cul-de-sac with the river owing past the garden. Quality, pacious accommodation awaits you ı a relaxing, friendly atmosphere. reakfast is served overlooking ıe Nevis mountain range whilst ıdulging in the wide choices vailable. Easy walking distance to xcellent eating opportunities.

67874

by Spean Bridge, Invergloy

Riverside House

Open: Mar-Nov **Map Ref: 3H11**

★★★★
BED AND BREAKFAST

Invergloy, Spean Bridge, Inverness-shire, PH34 4DY
T: 01397 712684 E: enquiries@riversidelodge.org.uk W: riversidelodge.org.uk

Indicated Prices:

Family	£35.00 per person

51706

Fort William & Lochaber, Skye & Lochalsh: Self Catering

Acharacle

Lochside Follies

Open: All year **Map Ref: 3F12**

★★★★ SELF CATERING

Greenwood, Ardslignish, Acharacle, Argyll, PH36 4JG
T: 01972 500201 E: loislivett@ardnamurchan.com W: lochsidefollies.co.uk

1 Cottage — 2 Bedrooms — Sleeps 2-4
1 Tower — 1 Bedroom — Sleeps 2

Prices – Cottage: £410.00-£500.00 Per Week
Prices – Tower: £375.00 Per Week

Short breaks available

2905

Looking across Loch Shi
a narrow loch extending 17 m
from Glenfinnan to Achara

Fort William
The Logs
Open: All year **Map Ref: 3H1**

★★★★
SELF CATERING

24 Zetland Avenue, Fort William, Inverness-shire, PH33 6LL
T: 01397 702532 E: thelogs@scotland-info.co.uk W: scotland-info.co.uk/thelogs

1 House 6 Bedrooms Sleeps 2-10

Prices – House:
£550.00-£1350.00 Per Week

Short breaks available

5955

Isle of Skye, Portree
Coolin Lodge
Open: All year **Map Ref: 3E**

Come to Skye, indulge in the comfort of Coolin Lodge, a short walk from the centre of Portree. Relax and enjoy your holiday in Coolin Lodge, designed to a high standard, providing wonderful accommodation for guests. Perfect central location for all your excursions exploring all that Skye has to offer.

★★★★★
SELF CATERING

Coolin Hills Estate, Portree, Isle of Skye, IV51 9LU
T: 01478 613240 E: info@coolinlodge.co.uk W: coolinlodge.co.uk

1 House 2 Bedrooms Sleeps 4

Prices – House:
£900.00 Per Week

8544

Isle of Skye, Portree
Gleniffer House
Open: All year **Map Ref: 3E9**

★★★★
SELF CATERING

Beaumont Crescent, Portree, Isle of Skye, IV51 9DF
T: 01478 612048 E: rohwersafaris@hotmail.com W: selfcatering-isleofskye-scotland.com

1 House 3 Bedrooms Sleeps 2-6

Prices – House:
£350.00-£750.00 Per Week

Short breaks available

28215

 PRICES STATED ARE ESTIMATES AND MAY BE SUBJECT TO CHANGE. PRICES ARE PER UNIT PER WEEK UNLESS OTHERWISE STATED. AWARDS CORRECT AS OF BEGINNING OF OCTOBER 2009

Isle of Skye, Portree

Teeny's Cottage

Open: All year **Map Ref: 3D8**

★★★★
SELF CATERING

Fasgadh, near Edinbane, Portree, Isle of Skye, IV51 9PX
T: 01470 582777 E: denis@teenyscottage.com W: teenyscottage.com

1 Cottage 2 Bedrooms Sleeps 4

Prices – Cottage:
£200.00-£450.00 Per Week

Short breaks available

68301

Isle of Skye, Sleat

Clan Donald Skye Lodges

Open: All year **Map Ref: 3E11**

ix purpose built lodges situated n the hillside above Armadale, pposite Knoydart, with utstanding views over the Sound f Sleat. We also offer the Foresters ottage that nestles in a clearing nd the tasteful Flora MacDonald uite situated within the restored table building.

★★★ UP TO ★★★★
SELF CATERING

Clan Donald Skye, Sleat, Isle of Skye, IV45 8RS
T: 01471 844305 E: office@clandonald.com W: clandonald.com

6 Cottages 2-3 Bedrooms Sleeps 4-6
1 House 2 Bedrooms Sleeps 4
1 Apartment 2 Bedrooms Sleeps 4

Prices – Cottage: £310.00-£585.00 Per Week
House: £310.00-£550.00 Per Week
Apartment: £410.00-£670.00 Per Week

Short breaks available

19449

Isle of Skye, Sleat

Mavis Bank Flat

Open: All year **Map Ref: 3F10**

★★★★
SELF CATERING

Mavis Bank, Teangue, Sleat, Isle of Skye, IV44 8RE
T: 01471 833455 E: mavisbankskye@btinternet.com W: self-catering-sleat.co.uk

1 Flat 1 Bedroom Sleeps 1-2

Prices – Flat:
£320.00-£420.00 Per Week

Short breaks available

87149

Isle of Skye, Waternish
La Bergerie

Open: All year **Map Ref: 3D8**

★★★★
SELF CATERING

32 Lochbay, Waternish, Isle of Skye, IV55 8GD
T: 01470 592282 E: enquiries@la-bergerie-skye.co.uk W: la-bergerie-skye.co.uk

1 Cottage | 4 Bedrooms | Sleeps 1-8

Prices – Cottage:
£400.00-£960.00 Per Week

Short breaks available

4270

Spean Bridge
Corrieview Lodges

Open: All year **Map Ref: 3H11**

Fully equipped lodges with two downstairs bedrooms and upstairs living area. Patio doors lead from the lounge to a small wooden balcony with panoramic views across the glen to the Nevis Mountain Range. Village shops and pubs within a few minutes walk.

★★★★
SELF CATERING

Grey Corries, Spean Bridge, Inverness-shire, PH34 4DX
T: 01397 712395 E: fantasticviews@corrieviewlodges.com W: corrieviewlodges.com

2 Lodges | 2 Bedrooms | Sleeps 2-5

Prices – Lodges:
£295.00-£550.00 Per Week

Short breaks available

2909

Spean Bridge

Gairlochy Holiday Park

Open: Dec-Oct **Map Ref: 3H11**

aravans and lodges for hire ituated south end Loch Lochy n B8004, Great Glen Way and levis Range close by. Free fishing n Loch Lochy, boat launching vailable. Linen provided, discount or two persons, laundrette, play rea. All charges inclusive.

★★★★ SELF CATERING

Spean Bridge, Inverness-shire, PH34 3EQ
T: 01397 712711 E: theghp@talk21.com W: theghp.co.uk

3 Lodges	2 Bedrooms	Sleeps 4
4 Caravans	2 Bedrooms	Sleeps 4

Prices – Lodge: £200.00-£620.00 Per Week
Caravan: £225.00-£455.00 Per Week

Short breaks available

69782

by Spean Bridge, Invergloy

Riverside Lodges

Open: All year **Map Ref: 3H11**

★★★★ SELF CATERING

Invergloy, Spean Bridge, Inverness-shire, PH34 4DY
T: 01397 712684 E: enquiries@riversidelodge.org.uk W: riversidelodge.org.uk

3 Chalets	3 Bedrooms	Sleeps 6

Prices – Chalet: £450.00-£760.00 Per Week

Short breaks available

70348

Strontian

J & Y Burton

Open: All year **Map Ref: 1E1**

★★★★ SELF CATERING

Bruadar Iain, Ariundle, Strontian, Argyll, PH36 4JB
T: 01538 385853 W: visitscotland.com

1 Bungalow	4 Bedrooms	Sleeps 2-8

Prices – Bungalow: £425.00-£925.00 Per Week

16647

Fort William & Lochaber, Skye & Lochalsh: EatScotland Gold and Silver establishments

Barcaldine

Barcaldine House Restaurant

Barcaldine House,
Barcaldine,
PA37 1SG
T: 01631 720 219

A first class restaurant offering the freshest, finest local produce. A guest dining table in the kitchen gives guests the opportunity of experiencing the 'ultimate dining experience'.

Spean Bridge

Corriegour Lodge Hotel

Loch Lochy,
Spean Bridge,
PH34 4EA
T: 01397 712 685

A view that you will never tire of, especially from the dining room with its expansive windows, this restaurant serves imaginative, award-winning cuisine, with owners who have flair, humour and a true concern for their guests.

Knoydart

Doune Stone Lodges

Doune,
Knoydart,
PH41 4PL
T: 01687 462 667

A recent Scottish Thistle award winner 2009 - Taste of Scotland, Doune provides excellent freshly prepared and cooked local foods served in a family friendly style.

Sleat, Isle of Skye

Duisdale House Hotel

Sleat,
Isle of Skye,
IV43 8QW
T: 01471 833 202

The conservatory dining room overlooks the well maintained gardens and also over the water to Knoydart. The food served here is mainly locally sourced.

Nr Fort William

Inverlochy Castle Hotel

Torlundy,
Nr Fort William,
PH33 6SN
T: 01397 702 177

The dining room at Inverlochy Castle exudes old-world charm and grace. The menu features modern British cuisine, awarded AA 3 red Rosettes and 1 Michelin Star.

Strontian

Kilcamb Lodge Hotel

Acharacle,
Strontian,
PH36 4HY
T: 01967 402 257

The restaurant at Kilcamb Lodge Hotel offers the finest food prepared from local ingredients with specialities in both fish and shellfish.

Sleat, Isle of Skye
Kinloch Lodge

Sleat,
Isle of Skye,
IV43 8QY
T: 01471 833 214

Lord and Lady Macdonald have run Kinloch Lodge for nearly 30 years. The food is excellent and a fitting testimony to the skill of Lady Macdonald, a prominent cookery writer.

Appin
The Airds Hotel Restaurant

Port Appin,
Appin,
PA38 4DF
T: 01631 730 236

This hotel restaurant provides fine dining in a beautiful setting with a modern French style, concentrating on fresh local produce, seafood and maintaining the highest quality standards.

Glenfinnan
The Prince's House Hotel

Glenfinnan,
PH37 4LT
T: 01397 722 246

Chef Proprietor Kieron Kelly provides fine quality food, sourcing fresh local produce whenever possible. Scottish cuisine with individual interpretation, and a high standard of presentation.

Dunvegan, Isle of Skye
The Three Chimneys

Colbost, Dunvegan,
Isle of Skye,
IV55 8ZT
T: 01470 511 258

The food at The Three Chimneys on the Isle of Skye truly reflects its location and this is something that has contributed to the restaurant's huge popularity over two decades.

Sleat, Isle of Skye
Toravaig House Hotel

Knock Bay, Sleat,
Isle of Skye,
IV44 8RE
T: 01471 820 200

At Toravaig House the emphasis is on peace and relaxation. Enjoy crackling open fires and home-cooking, using the very best of Scottish meat, fish and seafood, all locally produced and sourced.

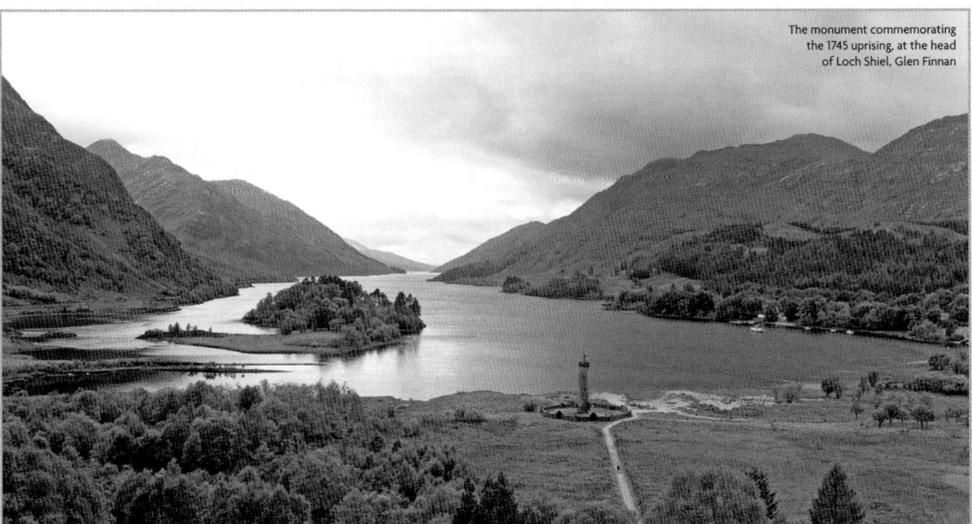

The monument commemorating the 1745 uprising, at the head of Loch Shiel, Glen Finnan

Moray, Aviemore & The Cairngorms: Hotels

Forres

Knockomie Hotel

Open: All year excl 25-26 Dec **Map Ref: 4C8**

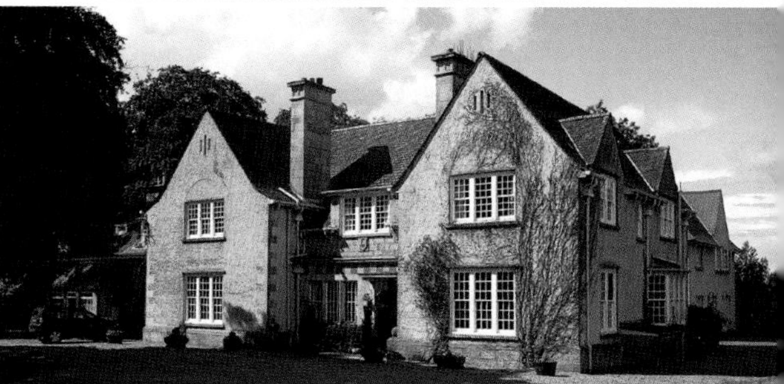

Set back in four acres of garden and woodland, Knockomie is a new generation of hotel in the country providing friendly, honest and unstuffy service. With the Grill Room offering the finest local produce and well stocked Malt Library bar, you're assured of a great time. Local attractions include Brodie Castle, Cawdor Castle, Loch Ness, Johnston's Cashmere Centre in Elgin and Benromach Distillery.

★★★★ SMALL HOTEL

Grantown Road, Forres, IV36 2SG
T: 01309 673146 E: stay@knockomie.co.uk W: knockomie.co.uk

Indicated Prices:

Single	from £120.00 per room	Twin	from £149.00 per room
Double	from £149.00 per room	Family	from £169.00 per room

 3448?

Grantown on Spey

Culdearn House

Open: All year **Map Ref: 4C9**

★★★★★ SMALL HOTEL

Woodlands Terrace, Grantown on Spey, Moray, PH26 3JU
T: 01479 872106 E: enquiries@culdearn.com W: culdearn.com

Indicated Prices:

Single	from £100.00 per room	Twin	from £130.00 per room
Double	from £130.00 per room	Luxury	from £150.00 per room

 21664

 PRICES STATED ARE ESTIMATES AND MAY BE SUBJECT TO CHANGE. PRICES ARE PER PERSON PER NIGHT UNLESS OTHERWISE STATED. AWARDS CORRECT AS OF BEGINNING OF OCTOBER 2009

Moray, Aviemore & The Cairngorms: Guest Houses and B&Bs

Aviemore

Ravenscraig Guest House

Open: All year

Map Ref: 4C10

★★★★ GUEST HOUSE

141 Grampian Road, Aviemore, Inverness-shire, PH22 1RP
T: 01479 810278 E: info@aviemoreonline.com W: aviemoreonline.com

Indicated Prices:

Single	from £35.00 per room	Twin	from £70.00 per room
Double	from £70.00 per room	Family	from £85.00 per room

51158

Elgin

The Lodge Guest House

Open: All year excl Xmas & New Year

Map Ref: 4D8

★★★★ GUEST HOUSE

20 Duff Avenue, Elgin, IV30 1QS
T: 01343 549981 E: info@thelodge-elgin.com W: thelodge-elgin.com

Indicated Prices:

Single	from £40.00 per room	Twin	from £70.00 per room
Double	from £70.00 per room	Family	from £85.00 per room

59535

Grantown on Spey

An Cala Guest House

Open: All year excl Xmas

Map Ref: 4C9

★★★★★ GUEST HOUSE

Woodlands Terrace, Grantown on Spey, PH26 3JU
T: 01479 873293 E: ancala@globalnet.co.uk W: ancala.info

Indicated Prices:

Double	from £78.00 per room	Twin	from £78.00 per room

11944

Kincraig

Braeriach Guest House

Open: All year **Map Ref: 4C10**

★★★★ GUEST HOUSE

Braeriach Road, Kincraig, by Kingussie, Inverness-shire, PH21 1QA
T: 01540 651369 E: fiona@braeriachgh.com W: braeriachgh.com

Indicated Prices:

Single	from £40.00 per room	Twin	from £70.00 per room
Double	from £75.00 per room	Family	from £90.00 per room

C V

1602

Laggan

The Rumblie Guest House

Open: end Jan-end Nov and 27 Dec-3 Jan **Map Ref: 4B11**

The Rumblie is a friendly and relaxed Highland home in a tranquil setting within the Cairngorms National Park ideally situated for exploring the area. Three spacious ensuite bedrooms each graced with fresh flowers, organic fruit, books, hospitality tray and lots of other little touches. Guest lounge and dining room.

★★★★ GUEST HOUSE

Gergask Avenue, Laggan, PH20 1AH
T: 01528 544766 E: mail@rumblie.com W: rumblie.com

Indicated Prices:

Double	from £30.00 per person	Twin	from £30.00 per person

TV P V

60279

Urquhart

B&B Parrandier

Open: All year **Map Ref: 4D8**

★★★★ BED AND BREAKFAST

The Old Church of Urquhart, Meft Road, Urquhart, IV30 8NH
T: 01343 843063 E: info@oldchurch.eu W: oldchurch.eu

Indicated Prices:

Single	from £38.00 per room	Twin	from £56.00 per room
Double	from £56.00 per room	Family	from £71.00 per room
		Suite	from £62.00 per room

C

 83612

Moray, Aviemore & The Cairngorms: Self Catering

Aviemore

Cairngorm Highland Bungalows

Open: All year

Map Ref: 4C10

★★★ UP TO ★★★★
SELF CATERING

Glen Einich, 29 Grampian View, Aviemore, PH22 1TF
T: 01479 810653 E: linda.murray@virgin.net W: cairngorm-bungalows.co.uk

3 Bungalows 2-4 Bedrooms Sleeps 2-8

Prices – Bungalow:
£195.00-£850.00 Per Week

Short breaks available

27905

Aviemore

Culduthel

Open: All year

Map Ref: 4C10

★★★★
SELF CATERING

48 Davieland Road, Giffnock, Glasgow, G46 7LX
T: 0141 638 1258/07815 290169 E: g.c.mcwiggan@btinternet.com

1 House 2/3 Bedrooms Sleeps 4/6

Prices – House:
£370.00-£490.00 Per Week (excl New Year)

Short breaks available

69557

Glencoe

Invercoe Highland Holidays

Open: All year

Map Ref: 1F1

Surrounded by the most spectacular scenery of mountains, forest and loch, our cosy cottages and luxury lodges offer the best for your comfort. All are fitted out to a very high standard to make your stay a relaxing one. Super base to explore Fort William, Oban, Skye and Mull. Wi-fi available (chargeable). Local leisure facilities included.

★★★★ SELF CATERING

Invercoe, Glencoe, PH49 4HP
T: 01855 811210 E: holidays@invercoe.co.uk W: invercoe.co.uk

3 Cottages | 2 Bedrooms | Sleeps 2-4
3 Lodges | 3 Bedrooms | Sleeps 2-6

Prices – Cottages: £380.00-£580.00 Per Week
Lodges: £425.00-£820.00 Per Week

Short breaks available

31965

Lossiemouth

Beachview Holiday Flat

Open: May-Sept

Map Ref: 4D7

★★★★ SELF CATERING

62 Fernlea, Bearsden, Glasgow, G61 1NB
T: 0141 942 4135 E: info@beachviewholidayflats.co.uk W: beachviewholidayflats.co.uk

1 Apartment | 3 Bedrooms | Sleeps 8

Prices – Apartment:
£510.00-£550.00 Per Week

14546

 PRICES STATED ARE ESTIMATES AND MAY BE SUBJECT TO CHANGE. PRICES ARE PER UNIT PER WEEK UNLESS OTHERWISE STATED. AWARDS CORRECT AS OF BEGINNING OF OCTOBER 2009

Nethy Bridge

Osprey House and Red Kite House

Open: All year **Map Ref: 4C10**

Two excellent houses providing superb quality accommodation for your holiday. Every aspect is maintained to five star standard and with meticulous attention to customer care, we won a Scottish Thistle Award, the highest accolade in Scottish tourism. Choose Osprey House or Red Kite House and you will be highly delighted.

★★★★★
SELF CATERING

Funach View, Crossroads, Durris, Banchory, AB31 6BX
T: 01330 844344 E: info@cairngorm-executive.com W: cairngorm-executive.com

2 Houses 7 Bedrooms Sleeps 1-16

Prices – House:
£525.00-£895.00 Per Week

Short breaks available

17431

Newtonmore

Gaskbeg Holidays

Open: All year **Map Ref: 4B11**

★★★★
SELF CATERING

Gaskbeg Farm, Laggan, by Newtonmore, Inverness-shire
T: 01528 544336 E: gaskbeg@btinternet.com W: gaskbeg.co.uk

2 Cottages 4 Bedrooms Sleeps 1-4

Prices – Cottage:
£260.00-£500.00 Per Week

Short breaks available

27369

Moray, Aviemore & The Cairngorms: Food & Drink

Kingussie

Duke of Gordon Hotel

Open: All year

Map Ref: 4B11

Cullinary Type:
SCOTTISH

Newtonmore Road,
Kingussie, PH21 1HE
T: 01540 661302
E: reception@dukeofgordonhotel.co.uk
W: dukeofgordonhotel.co.uk

Best For:
- Breakfast
- Business and Bar Meals
- A la carte, Weddings and Functions

Prices:

Starter from:	£3.50
Main Course from:	£8.50
Dessert from:	£4.50

Opening Times:
0700-2100

Situated in the heart of the Cairngorms National Park, the hotel is renowned for its seasonal local menus, serving good food All Day Every Day. A la carte, bar meals, children's menus, weddings and functions. Providing Scottish entertainment every evening throughout the year.

17444

Moray, Aviemore & The Cairngorms: EatScotland Gold and Silver establishments

Forres

Brodie Countryfare

Brodie,
By Forres
IV36 2TD
T: 01309 641 555

As part of a specialist department store the Restaurant at Brodie Countryfare offer a mixture of the informal and traditional focusing on locally grown produce.

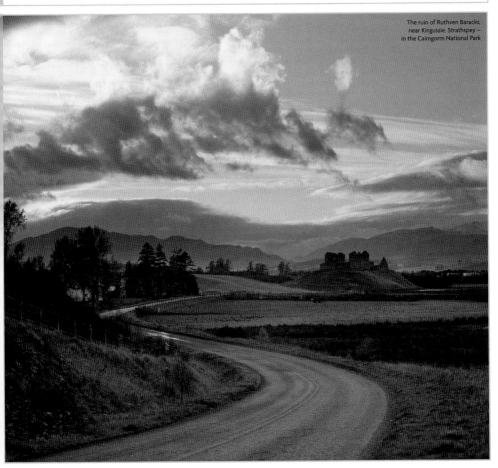

The ruin of Ruthven Baracks, near Kingussie, Strathspey – in the Cairngorm National Park

Outer Hebrides: Guest Houses and B&Bs

Isle of Lewis, Stornoway

Broad Bay House

Open: All year **Map Ref: 3E4**

Stay in style at our luxury beachside guest house. Four spacious en-suite bedrooms with flat screen TV, DVD system, leather armchairs, personal decking areas and luxury bathrooms with Molton Brown goodies. Enjoy the freshest local produce in the dining room overlooking the bay and sample our interesting wine and whisky list.

★★★★★ GOLD
GUEST HOUSE

Back, nr Stornoway, Isle of Lewis, HS2 0LQ
T: 01851 820990 E: stay@broadbayhouse.co.uk W: broadbayhouse.co.uk

Indicated Prices:

Single	from £109.00 per room	Twin	from £149.00 per room
Double	from £149.00 per room		

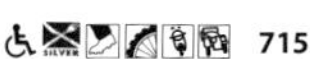

7153

Outer Hebrides: Self Catering

sle of Harris, Leverburgh

;halom Cottage

Open: All year **Map Ref: 3C7**

★★★★★
SELF CATERING

12 Strond, Leverburgh, Isle of Harris
T: 01859 520259 E: info@shalomcottage.co.uk W: shalomcottage.co.uk

1 Cottage 3 Bedrooms Sleeps 2-6

Prices – Cottage:
£750.00-£900.00 Per Week

Short breaks available

73719

sle of Harris, Seilebost

Beul Na Mara

Open: All year **Map Ref: 3C6**

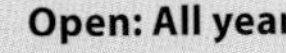

wo well-equipped cottages tuated on the west coast of Harris verlooking sandy beaches for hich Harris is renowned. Seilebost rovides an excellent base from hich to explore the magical Isle f Harris.

★★★★
SELF CATERING

12 Seilebost, Isle of Harris, HS3 3HP
T: 01859 550205 E: morrison.catherine@virgin.net
W: beulnamara.co.uk and harris-holidaycottage.co.uk

3 Cottages 6 Bedrooms Sleeps 5-7

Prices – Cottage:
£350.00-£950.00 Per Week

Short breaks available

15046

Isle of North Uist, Claddach Kirkibost

An Airigh

Open: All year **Map Ref: 3B**

★★★★★
SELF CATERING

John MacIsaac, Corunna Road, Aberdeen, AB23 8DU
T: 01224 825509/07990 975566 E: john@qestuk.com

1 House 4 Bedrooms Sleeps 7

Prices – House:
£700.00-£1200.00 Per Week

7775

South Harris

Harris White Cottage

Open: All year **Map Ref: 3C**

★★★★
SELF CATERING

8 Rodel, South Harris, Hebrides, HS5 3TW
T: 07787 851155 E: wkoller14@aol.com W: harriswhitecottage.com

1 Cottage 2 Bedrooms Sleeps 4

Prices – Cottage:
£200.00-£625.00 Per Week

Short breaks available

2963

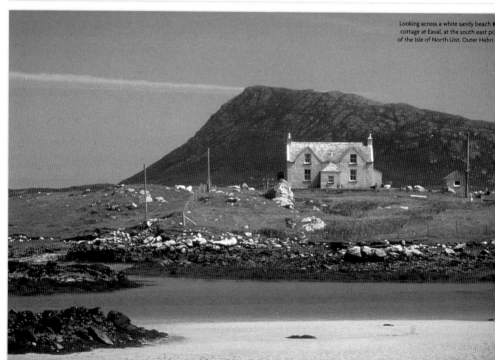

Looking across a white sandy beach to a cottage at Eaval, at the south east point of the Isle of North Uist, Outer Hebrides

Outer Hebrides: EatScotland Gold and Silver establishments

Back, Outer Hebrides

Broad Bay House

SILVER

Back, Nr Stornoway,
Outer Hebrides,
HS2 0LQ
T: 01851 820 990

The restaurant forms part of this luxury purpose built guesthouse. Dinner consists of 4 courses plus coffee served in the dining room with views overlooking the bay.

Stornoway, Outer Hebrides

Park Guest House and Restaurant

SILVER

30 James Street,
Stornoway, Outer Hebrides,
HS1 2QN
T: 01851 702 485

Relax and enjoy flavoursome and creative dishes skilfully prepared and presented by chef Roddy Afrin. Menus feature lamb, game and seafood from the finest of local and Scottish produce.

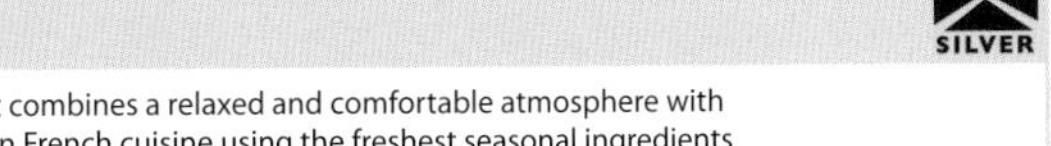

Port of Ness, Outer Hebrides

Sulair Restaurant

SILVER

Port of Ness,
Outer Hebrides,
HS2 0XA
T: 01851 810 222

The restaurant combines a relaxed and comfortable atmosphere with superb modern French cuisine using the freshest seasonal ingredients sourced from throughout the Island and across Scotland.

The harbour at Stornoway, the Isle of Lewis

TRAVEL TO SCOTLAND

BY AIR

Flying to Scotland couldn't be simpler with flight times from London, Dublin and Belfast only around one hour. There are airports at Edinburgh, Glasgow, Glasgow Prestwick, Aberdeen, Dundee and Inverness. The following airlines operate flights to Scotland (although not all airports) from within the UK and Ireland:

bmi
Tel: 0870 60 70 555
From Ireland: 1332 64 8181
flybmi.com

bmi baby
Tel: 09058 28 28 28
From Ireland: 1890 340 122
bmibaby.com

British Airways
Tel: 0844 493 0787
From Ireland: 1890 626 747
ba.com

Eastern Airways
Tel: 08703 669 100
easternairways.com

easyJet
Tel: 0905 821 0905
From Ireland: 1890 923 922
easyjet.com

Flybe
Tel: 0871 700 2000
From Ireland: 1392 268513
flybe.com

Ryanair
0871 246 000
From Ireland: 0818 30 30 30
ryanair.com

Air France
Tel: 0871 66 33 777
airfrance.co.uk

Aer Arann
Tel: 0870 876 76 76
From Ireland: 0818 210 210
aerarann.com

Jet2
Tel: 0044 203 031 8103
jet2.com

Air Berlin
Tel: 0871 5000 737
airberlin.com

Aer Lingus
Tel: 0871 718 5000
From Ireland: 0818 365 000
aerlingus.com

BY RAIL

Scotland has major rail stations in Aberdeen, Edinburgh Waverley and Edinburgh Haymarket, Glasgow Queen Street and Glasgow Central, Perth, Stirling, Dundee and Inverness. There are regular cross border railway services from England and Wales, and good city links. You could even travel on the First ScotRail Caledonian Sleeper overnight train service from London and wake up to the sights and sounds of Scotland.

First ScotRail
Tel: 0845 601 5929
scotrail.co.uk

Virgin Trains
Tel: 08457 222 333
virgintrains.co.uk

National Express
East Coast
Tel: 08457 225 225
nationalexpresseastcoast.com

National Rail
Tel: 08457 484950
nationalrail.co.uk

BY ROAD

Scotland has an excellent road network from motorways and dual carriageways linking cities and major towns, to remote single-track roads with passing places to let others by. Whether you are coming in your own car from home or hiring a car once you get here, getting away from traffic jams and out onto Scotland's quiet roads can really put the fun back into driving. Branches of the following companies can be found throughout Scotland:

Arnold Clark
Tel: 0844 576 5425
arnoldclarkrental.com

Avis Rent A Car
Tel: 0844 581 0147
avis.co.uk

Budget
Tel: 0877 544 3407
budget.co.uk

easyCar
Tel: 08710 500444
easycar.com

Enterprise Rent-A-Car
Tel: 0800 800 227
enterprise.co.uk

Europcar
Tel: 0870 607 5000
europcarscotland.co.uk

Hertz
Tel: 08708 44 88 44
hertz.co.uk

National Car Rental
Tel: 0871 384 11 40
nationalcar.co.uk

Sixt Rent A Car
Tel: 0844 248 6620
sixt.co.uk

Alamo Rent A Car
Tel: 0871 384 1086
alamo.co.uk

It's really easy to get to Scotland whether you choose to travel by car, train, plane, coach or ferry. Once you get here travel is easy as Scotland is a compact country.

BY FERRY

Scotland has over 130 inhabited islands so ferries are important. And whether you are coming from Ireland or trying to get to the outer islands, you might be in need of a ferry crossing. Ferries to and around the islands are regular and reliable and most carry vehicles. These companies all operate ferry services around Scotland:

Stena Line
Tel: 08447 70 70 70
From Ireland: 01 204 77 77
stenaline.co.uk

P&O Irish Sea
Tel: 0871 66 44 999
From Ireland: 01 407 34 34
poirishsea.com

Caledonian MacBrayne
Tel: 0800 066 5000
calmac.co.uk

Western Ferries
Tel: 01369 704 452
western-ferries.co.uk

Northlink Ferries
Tel: 08456 000 449
northlinkferries.co.uk

John O'Groats Ferries
Tel: 01955 611 353
jogferry.co.uk

Pentland Ferries
Tel: 01856 831226
pentlandferries.co.uk

BY COACH

Coach connections include express services to Scotland from all over the UK, and there is a good network of coach services once you get here too. You could even travel on the Postbus – a special feature of the Scottish mail service which carries fare-paying passengers along with the mail in rural areas where there is no other form of transport, bringing a new dimension to travel.

National Express
Tel: 08717 818 177
nationalexpress.com

City Link
Tel: 08705 50 50 50
citylink.co.uk

Postbus
Tel: 08457 740 740
royalmail.com/postbus

DRIVING DISTANCES

	ABERDEEN	BIRMINGHAM	CARDIFF	DOVER	DUMFRIES	DUNDEE	EDINBURGH	FORT WILLIAM	GLASGOW	HARWICH	HAWICK	HULL	INVERNESS	KYLE OF LOCHALSH	LONDON	MANCHESTER	NEWCASTLE	OBAN	PERTH	PRESTWICK	ROSYTH	STIRLING	STRANRAER	THURSO	TROON	ULLAPOOL
BIRMINGHAM	421 687																									
CARDIFF	529 851	113 182																								
DOVER	617 993	200 322	224 361																							
DUMFRIES	214 344	234 376	335 539	436 700																						
DUNDEE	71 114	357 575	465 749	553 890	149 240																					
EDINBURGH	131 210	290 467	398 641	486 782	80 128	62 99																				
FORT WILLIAM	161 258	396 637	504 811	592 952	179 288	123 197	138 221																			
GLASGOW	152 243	286 461	394 634	482 776	76 122	84 134	45 72	108 173																		
HARWICH	604 972	187 300	242 390	130 210	370 595	540 869	473 761	578 931	469 754																	
HAWICK	178 287	243 391	344 554	417 671	53 86	113 182	50 81	185 298	85 137	370 596																
HULL	387 619	137 221	251 405	255 411	205 330	318 509	255 408	384 614	275 440	214 346	206 331															
INVERNESS	118 189	446 717	553 890	641 1032	239 385	134 214	162 259	69 110	178 285	628 1011	209 337	444 710														
KYLE OF LOCHALSH	200 320	469 755	577 929	665 1070	253 407	179 286	207 331	76 122	184 294	652 1049	254 408	459 734	82 131													
LONDON	549 878	118 190	150 242	75 122	349 561	481 770	412 659	514 822	406 650	78 126	358 576	216 346	573 917	590 944												
MANCHESTER	345 556	93 150	201 324	281 453	157 252	281 453	214 345	320 515	210 338	268 431	166 267	95 154	370 595	393 633	201 322											
NEWCASTLE	244 390	208 336	323 519	350 563	91 147	175 280	112 179	267 427	159 254	309 498	64 102	148 237	274 438	343 549	288 461	147 237										
OBAN	190 304	385 620	493 794	581 935	168 270	121 194	125 200	50 80	96 154	568 914	175 281	371 594	112 180	125 200	502 803	309 498	310 496									
PERTH	86 139	348 560	449 723	550 884	128 205	21 34	43 69	104 166	64 104	484 778	96 155	319 513	114 183	158 254	463 744	271 436	152 245	94 151								
PRESTWICK	177 285	304 489	411 662	500 804	61 98	113 182	79 127	131 210	32 52	486 783	105 168	279 449	201 324	204 329	418 673	228 366	168 271	120 193	96 155							
ROSYTH	115 185	324 522	425 684	477 768	104 170	48 77	14 23	124 200	47 76	430 692	67 108	265 426	145 233	189 304	437 703	247 398	123 198	114 183	31 49	79 127						
STIRLING	120 193	313 503	414 666	514 823	92 149	55 89	38 61	97 157	29 47	448 722	87 141	284 456	145 234	172 277	427 688	236 379	143 231	87 140	37 60	61 99	26 42					
STRANRAER	241 386	297 478	404 651	489 787	71 115	172 275	133 213	196 314	89 142	475 765	125 202	284 454	265 424	272 435	415 664	224 358	161 259	172 277	149 240	54 87	131 211	114 611				
THURSO	234 374	555 893	663 1066	750 1208	348 560	250 400	278 445	183 293	293 469	737 1186	319 513	559 894	112 180	177 283	690 1104	499 798	391 626	233 373	221 311	355 500	254 409	252 406	382 183			
TROON	183 295	314 505	415 668	516 830	64 104	119 191	82 132	126 203	35 56	450 724	106 171	285 459	209 336	200 322	429 690	237 381	171 276	116 186	101 162	5 8	80 129	63 101	60 96	316 508		
ULLAPOOL	179 286	499 803	607 976	695 1118	293 472	194 310	222 355	119 190	238 381	681 1097	263 424	504 806	63 101	91 146	635 1016	444 710	335 536	169 270	168 270	255 411	199 320	199 320	128 205	327 523	263 423	
YORK	343 552	132 212	246 396	273 439	151 243	279 449	191 308	318 511	208 335	233 374	152 245	41 65	367 591	391 630	208 335	70 113	90 146	307 495	237 382	226 363	212 341	230 370	477 767	218 352	231 372	421 678

M KM

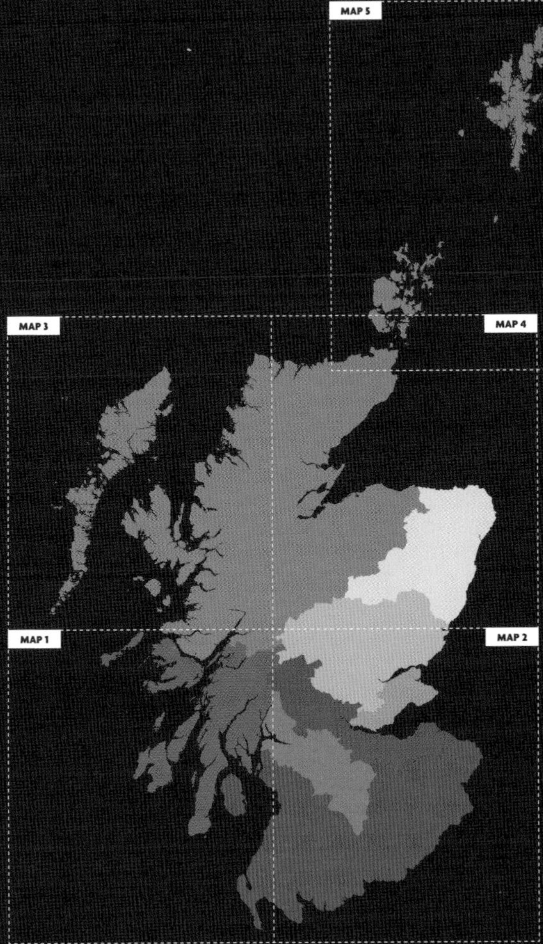
MAP 5
MAP 3
MAP 4
MAP 1
MAP 2

AREA MAPS

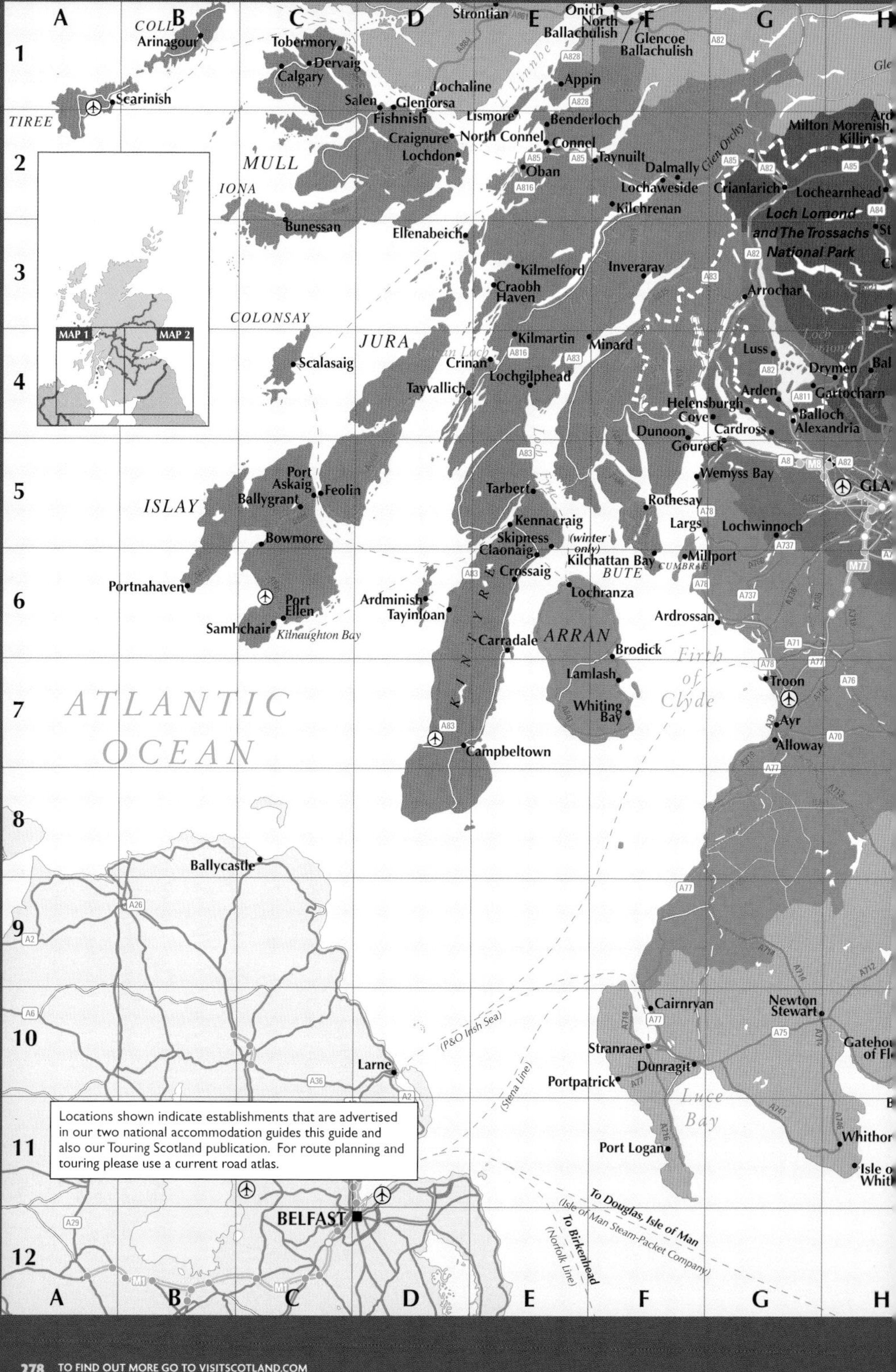
A
B
C
D
E
F
G
H
1
2
3
4
5
6
7
8
9
10
11
12
COLL
Arinagour
TIREE
Scarinish
Tobermory
Dervaig
Calgary
Salen
Glenforsa
Fishnish
Lochaline
Craignure
Lochdon
MULL
IONA
Bunessan
MAP 1
MAP 2
Strontian
Onich
North Ballachulish
Glencoe
Ballachulish
L. Linnhe
Appin
Lismore
Benderloch
North Connel
Connel
Oban
Taynuilt
Dalmally
Glen Orchy
Lochaweside
Kilchrenan
Ellenabeich
Kilmelford
Craobh Haven
Inveraray
Milton Morenish
Killin
Crianlarich
Lochearnhead
Loch Lomond and The Trossachs National Park
Arrochar
COLONSAY
Scalasaig
JURA
Kilmartin
Minard
Crinan
Lochgilphead
Tayvallich
Luss
Drymen
Arden
Gartocharn
Balloch
Alexandria
Helensburgh
Cove
Cardross
Dunoon
Gourock
Wemyss Bay
Loch Fyne
ISLAY
Port Askaig
Feolin
Ballygrant
Bowmore
Portnahaven
Port Ellen
Samhchair
Kilnaughton Bay
Tarbert
Kennacraig
Skipness
Claonaig
(winter only)
Kilchattan Bay
BUTE
CUMBRAE
Millport
Rothesay
Largs
Lochwinnoch
Crossaig
Lochranza
Ardminish
Tayinloan
KINTYRE
Carradale
ARRAN
Brodick
Lamlash
Whiting Bay
Ardrossan
Firth of Clyde
Troon
Ayr
Alloway
ATLANTIC OCEAN
Campbeltown
Ballycastle
Cairnryan
Newton Stewart
Stranraer
Dunragit
Portpatrick
Luce Bay
Port Logan
Whithorn
Gatehouse of Fleet
(P&O Irish Sea)
(Stena Line)
Larne
BELFAST
To Douglas, Isle of Man
(Isle of Man Steam-Packet Company)
To Birkenhead
(Norfolk Line)
A82
A828
A85
A816
A83
A84
A811
A8
M8
A78
A737
M77
A71
A77
A76
A70
A79
A75
A714
A712
A747
A746
A716
A718
A26
A2
A6
A36
A29
M1
Locations shown indicate establishments that are advertised in our two national accommodation guides this guide and also our Touring Scotland publication. For route planning and touring please use a current road atlas.

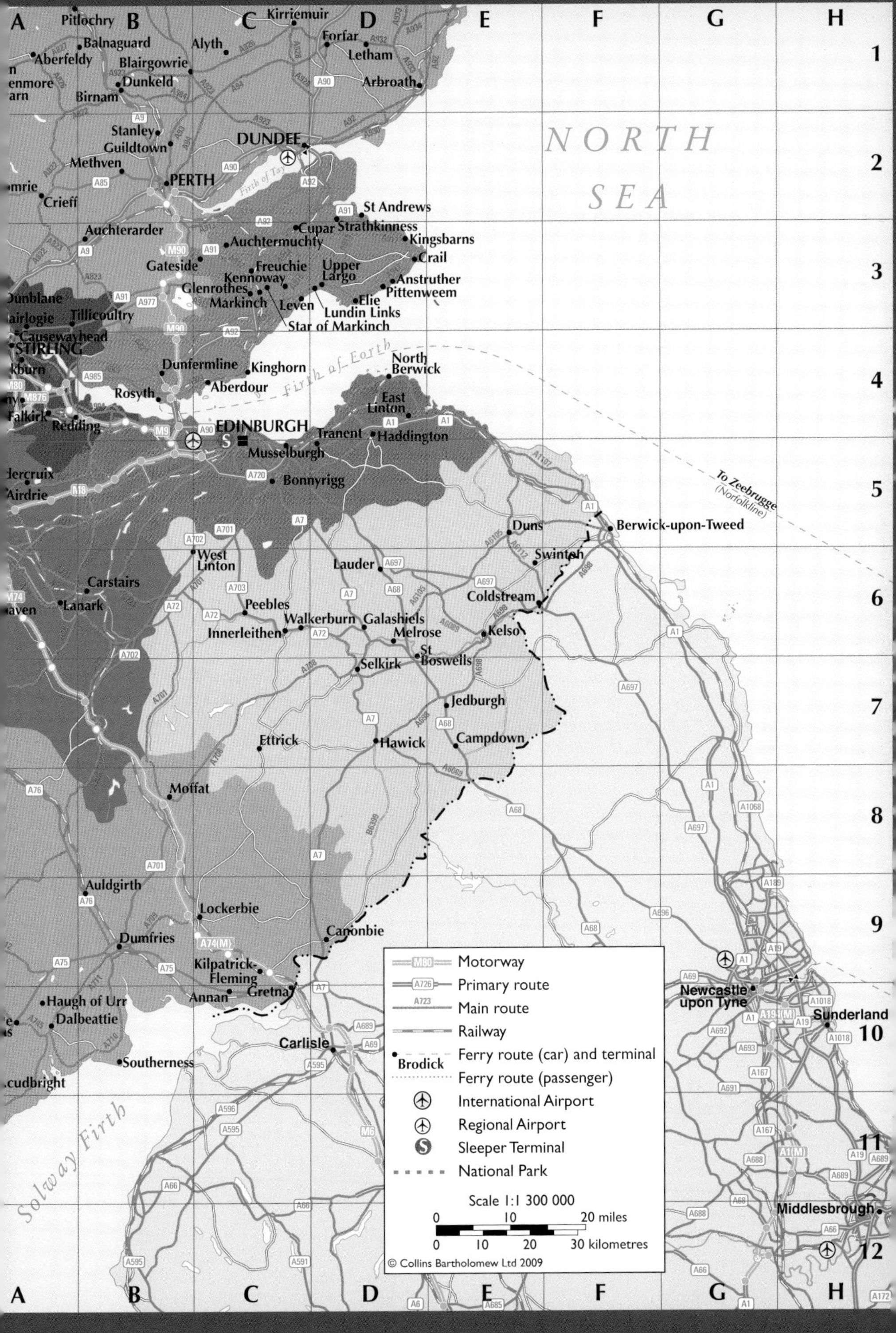
NORTH SEA
DUNDEE
PERTH
EDINBURGH
STIRLING
Firth of Tay
Firth of Forth
Solway Firth
To Zeebrugge (Norfolkline)
Berwick-upon-Tweed
Newcastle upon Tyne
Sunderland
Middlesbrough
Carlisle
Motorway
Primary route
Main route
Railway
Ferry route (car) and terminal
Brodick
Ferry route (passenger)
International Airport
Regional Airport
Sleeper Terminal
National Park
Scale 1:1 300 000
0 10 20 miles
0 10 20 30 kilometres
© Collins Bartholomew Ltd 2009

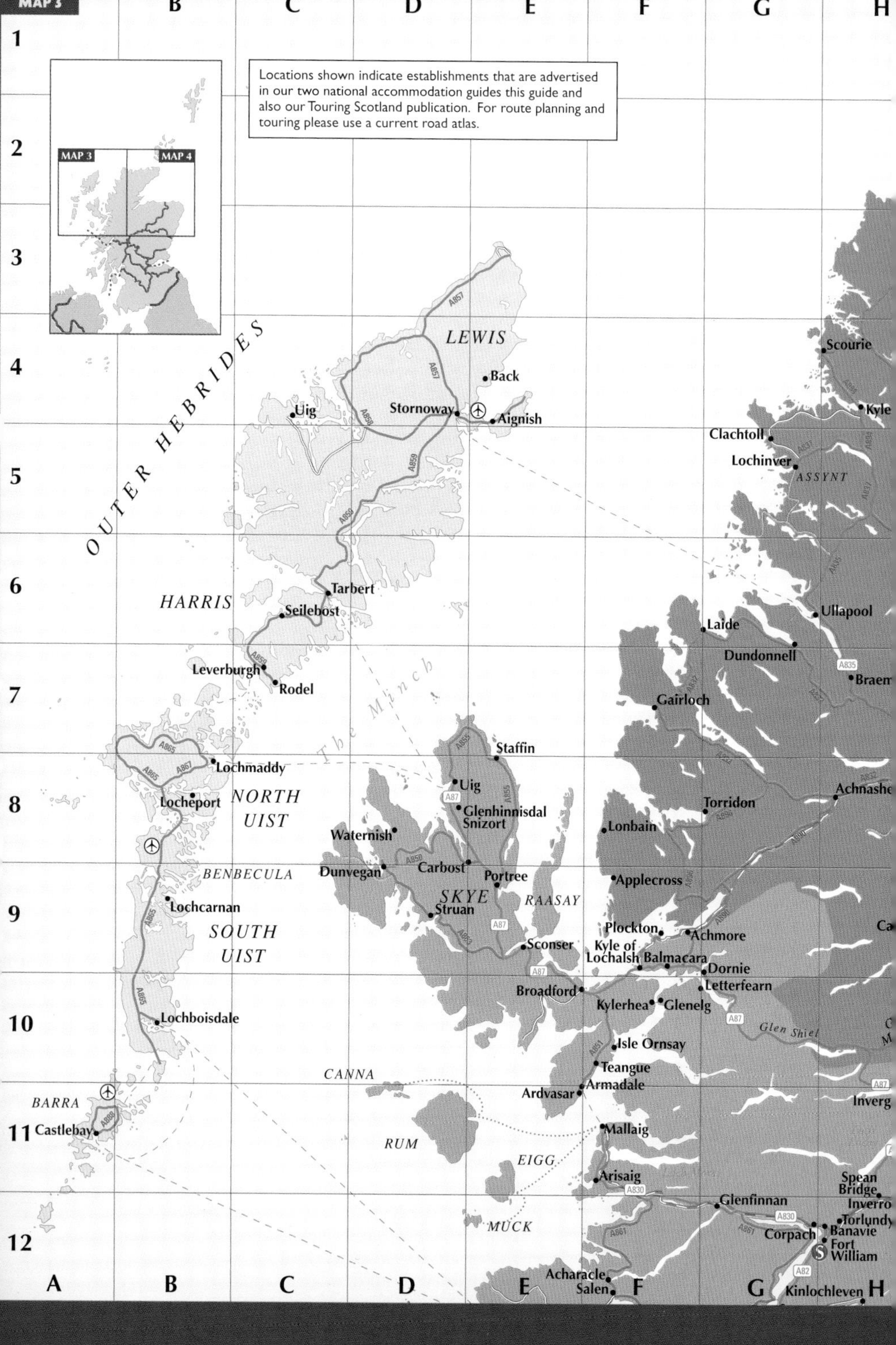
MAP 3
Locations shown indicate establishments that are advertised in our two national accommodation guides this guide and also our Touring Scotland publication. For route planning and touring please use a current road atlas.
MAP 3
MAP 4
OUTER HEBRIDES
LEWIS
Back
Uig
Stornoway
Aignish
HARRIS
Tarbert
Seilebost
Leverburgh
Rodel
The Minch
Lochmaddy
NORTH UIST
Locheport
BENBECULA
Lochcarnan
SOUTH UIST
Lochboisdale
BARRA
Castlebay
Scourie
Kyle
Clachtoll
Lochinver
ASSYNT
Ullapool
Laide
Dundonnell
Braem
Gairloch
Staffin
Uig
Glenhinnisdal
Snizort
Waternish
Dunvegan
Carbost
Portree
SKYE
Struan
RAASAY
Torridon
Achnashe
Lonbain
Applecross
Plockton
Achmore
Sconser
Kyle of Lochalsh
Balmacara
Dornie
Letterfearn
Broadford
Kylerhea
Glenelg
Glen Shiel
Isle Ornsay
Teangue
Armadale
Ardvasar
CANNA
RUM
EIGG
MUCK
Mallaig
Arisaig
Glenfinnan
Spean Bridge
Inverro
Torlundy
Banavie
Corpach
Fort William
Acharacle
Salen
Kinlochleven
Inverg

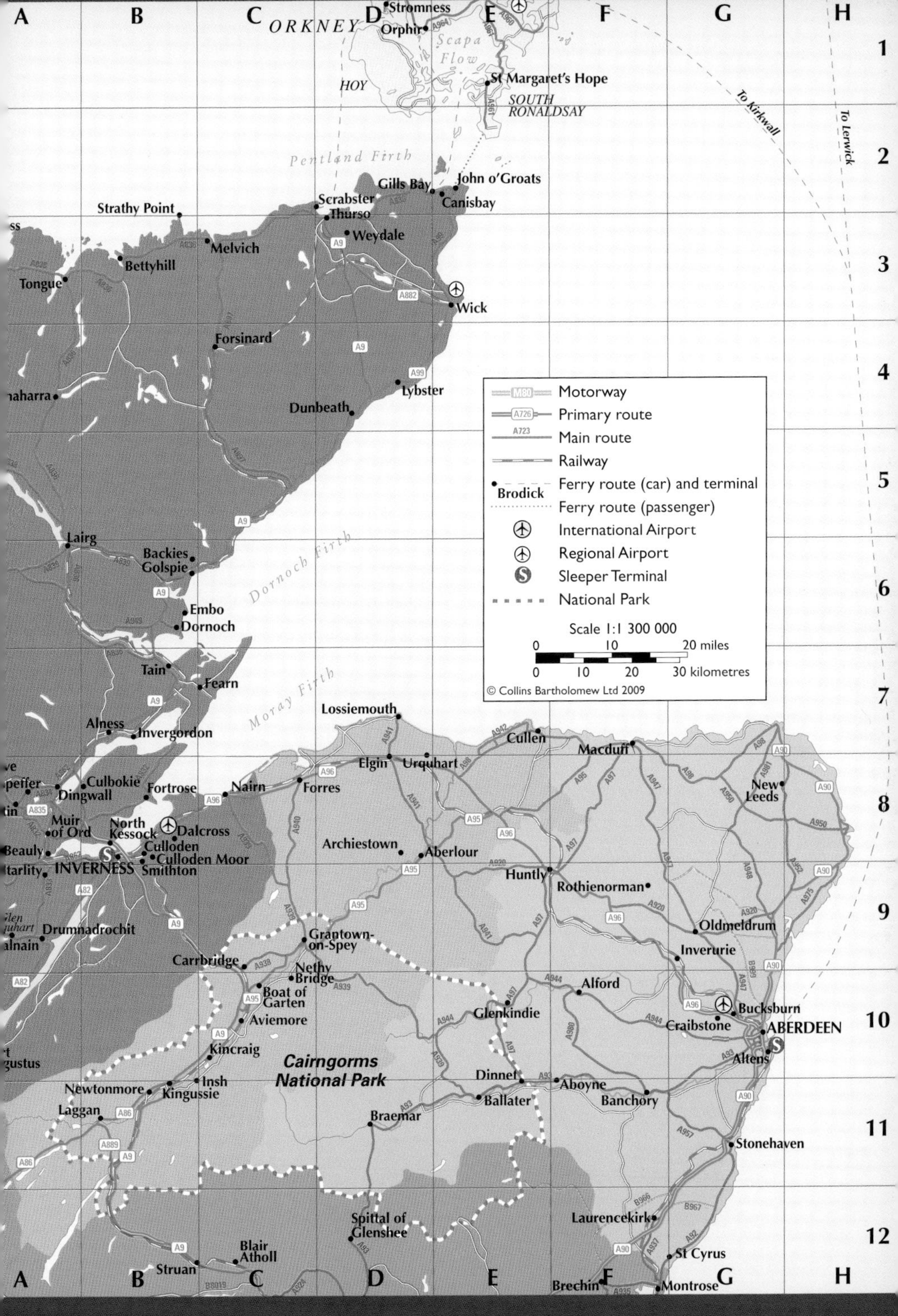
ORKNEY
Stromness
Orphir
Scapa Flow
HOY
St Margaret's Hope
SOUTH RONALDSAY
To Kirkwall
To Lerwick
Pentland Firth
Gills Bay
John o'Groats
Canisbay
Scrabster
Thurso
Weydale
Strathy Point
Melvich
Bettyhill
Tongue
Wick
Forsinard
Lybster
Dunbeath
Lairg
Backies
Golspie
Dornoch Firth
Embo
Dornoch
Tain
Fearn
Moray Firth
Alness
Invergordon
Lossiemouth
Cullen
Macduff
Elgin
Urquhart
Culbokie
Dingwall
Fortrose
Nairn
Forres
New Leeds
Muir of Ord
North Kessock
Dalcross
Culloden
Culloden Moor
Smithton
INVERNESS
Beauly
Archiestown
Aberlour
Huntly
Rothienorman
Drumnadrochit
Grantown-on-Spey
Oldmeldrum
Inverurie
Carrbridge
Nethy Bridge
Boat of Garten
Aviemore
Alford
Glenkindie
Bucksburn
Craibstone
ABERDEEN
Altens
Kincraig
Cairngorms National Park
Newtonmore
Insh
Kingussie
Dinnet
Aboyne
Ballater
Banchory
Laggan
Braemar
Stonehaven
Spittal of Glenshee
Laurencekirk
Blair Atholl
Struan
St Cyrus
Brechin
Montrose
Motorway
Primary route
Main route
Railway
Brodick
Ferry route (car) and terminal
Ferry route (passenger)
International Airport
Regional Airport
Sleeper Terminal
National Park
Scale 1:1 300 000
0 10 20 miles
0 10 20 30 kilometres
© Collins Bartholomew Ltd 2009

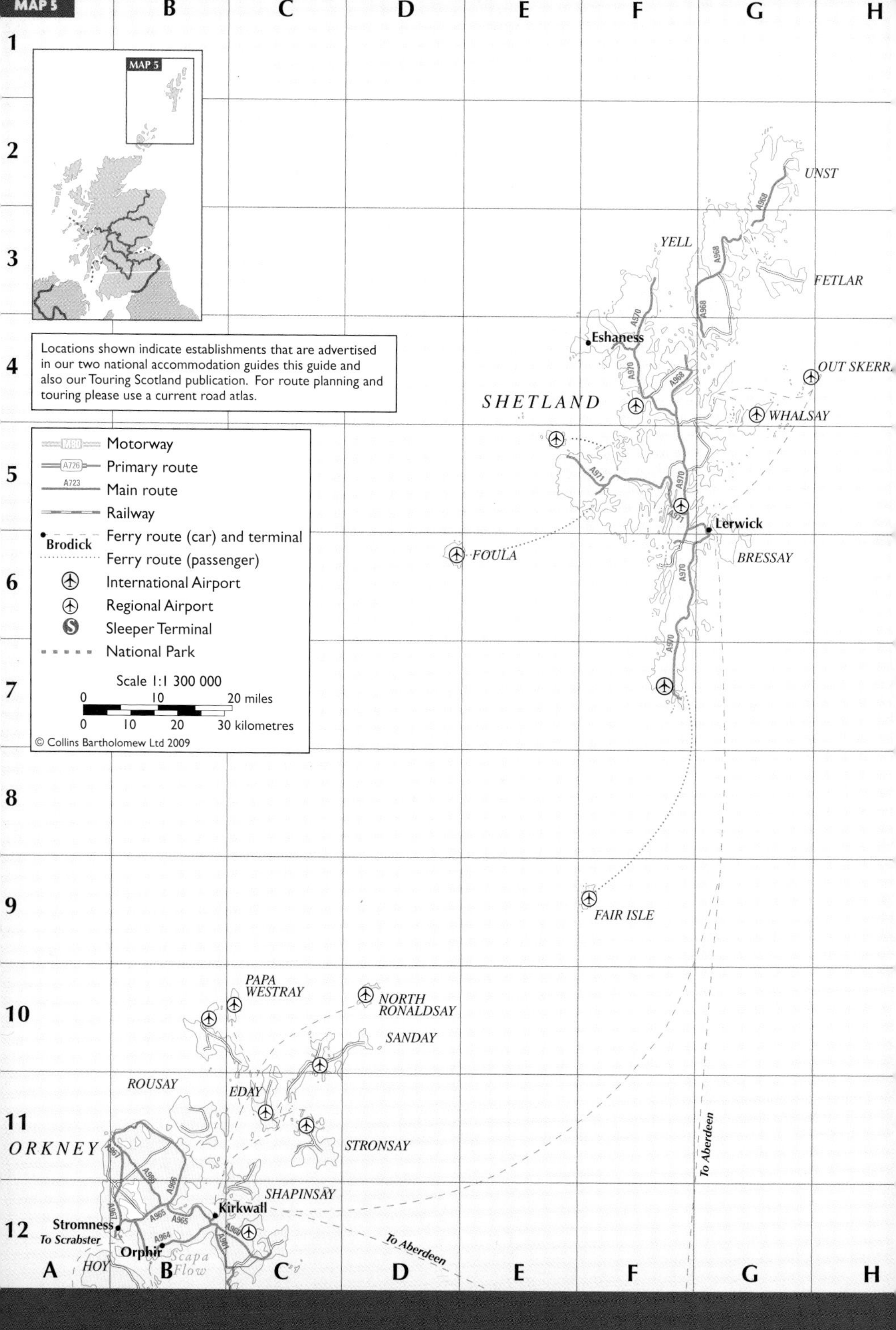
MAP 5
A
B
C
D
E
F
G
H
1
2
3
4
5
6
7
8
9
10
11
12
MAP 5
Locations shown indicate establishments that are advertised in our two national accommodation guides this guide and also our Touring Scotland publication. For route planning and touring please use a current road atlas.
M80 Motorway
A726 Primary route
A723 Main route
Railway
Brodick Ferry route (car) and terminal
Ferry route (passenger)
International Airport
Regional Airport
Sleeper Terminal
National Park
Scale 1:1 300 000
0 10 20 miles
0 10 20 30 kilometres
© Collins Bartholomew Ltd 2009
UNST
YELL
FETLAR
Eshaness
OUT SKERR
SHETLAND
WHALSAY
Lerwick
FOULA
BRESSAY
A968
A970
A971
FAIR ISLE
PAPA WESTRAY
NORTH RONALDSAY
SANDAY
ROUSAY
EDAY
ORKNEY
STRONSAY
SHAPINSAY
Kirkwall
Stromness
To Scrabster
Orphir
HOY
Scapa Flow
A965
A964
A966
A967
A961
A960
To Aberdeen
To Aberdeen

Loch Scavaig and the Black Cuillin, Elgol, Isle of Skye

PLAN YOUR STAY